DEMYSTIFYING TABOOS …
AND SEX - THE MOTHER OF ALL HUMANITY

By Joyce Jenje-Makwenda

Joyce Jenje-Makwenda
Collection Archives

ACKNOWLEDGEMENTS

I would like to thank all who walked with me in this journey. *The Herald Newspaper, Zimbabwe* for giving me the platform to express myself. It was a wonderful experience. I would like to thank my brother William Chikoto for the support and encouragement and giving me space to express myself in the Herald Newspaper and all those I walked with.

I would like to thank my parents who deposited the genes in me which make me to think the way I do. *Ndinotenda Mrewa* (my father) – David Jenje, *Ngiyabonga MaDube* (my mother) – Canaan MaDube Jenje. Your genes wired my brain to be what it is. To be free to talk about Sex and Sexuality. I would like to thank where you also got the genes from - your parents and those who came before them - my Ancestors. *Ngiyabonga kakhulu, Ndinotenda zvikuru.*

I want to thank my children and my grandchildren for the support in many ways. *Ndinotenda vana vangu, vazukuru vangu, Ngiyabonga bantwa bami, abazukulu bami.* My sisters and brothers, relatives, friends, and colleagues thank you for everything. All the institutions which gave me support in many ways. Thank you.

Let me take this opportunity to mention those who were directly involved in the project in different ways. Nomsa Mwamuka my sister for your encouragement and editing, you were so generous. Louis Mhlanga my friend thank you for your support always and more so on this project. Yolanda Birivadi thank you for being there and for the layout. Jeff Milanzi many thanks for availing yourself on a number of my projects and on this one. Alex Murombo thank you for always bringing life to some words from our Shona to English. My friend Sarudzayi Chifamba thank you for being there since the articles in the newspaper and to seeing the articles being shaped into a book, *ndinotenda MaSibanda.* My sisters for following the journey since the articles - Juliet, Joseline and Josephine, thank you. Tandiwe and Mya, my daughter and grand daughter for those long distance conversations we had on the Red Woman- thank you. Oh Mya I still remember what you asked me to do to be a cover girl, you are something else, you are such an inspirational being my granddaughter!!! My daughter Sasani Naome what can I say, thank you so much for all the positive energies which have seen me through working on the project - *ndaonga aNyaMpande muje kutali ndimotu.* Pat Brickhill thank you so much for all your encouragement and advice you have always been supportive in my projects and on this one I do not have words and Amy Brickhill the cover oh dear – thank you Amy! Tafadzwa Madzimbamuto you have followed this journey since the articles – thank you. My sister in love (sister in law) Amai Diva- Memory Hombasha Jenje for proofreading this book and also the encouragement, I know my brother Alexio was around encouraging, thank you. Thank you Margaret Dongo muroora you have seen the book evolve since the articles and now the book and also for always providing your Mhondoro home as a residence for resting. Mary Ann for the encouragement when I was writing the stories for the newspaper - thank you so much for the support VaNdai. Pathisa Nyathi my brother for translating some of the words from Ndebele to English. Charity Hodzi Sibanda my daughter for making me feel I was doing the right thing since the newspaper articles. Sekuru Farai (Fatso) Mashinini, thank you for everything, for the guidance always, you have always wished me well in everything I do. *EMashinini lakusasa.* TC, oh *Sahwira* thank you for the encouragement since the newspaper articles. Dana Whabira lets continue the converstaions on sex and sexuality. Thank you for the encouragement. Hope Chigudu my sister thank you so much for supporting my work, for preaching women's healing and sex and sexuality which I talk and write about is part of and recently you made it possible for me to have the platform to talk about this important topic. Thank you! Thanks to my sister Ndana Bofu - Tawamba, for inviting me to the Feminist Republic Festival. Talking about Women and sex and sexuality was an empowering experience where the pre- colonial kitchen played an important role. Discussing about these issues will help to demystifying sex and empower women to understand their bodies, sex and sexuality. Rudo Chitiga my sister, thank you so much for allowing me the freedom of speech to see what I do as normal, you listen and you say these are the conversations we need to have. You have baptised me sexologist!

To The Almighty Creator and The Universe thank you for shining your light on me. *Ngazvirambe zvakadaro, Makuhlale kunjalo.*

FOREWORD

Joyce Jenje-Makwenda has a passion for cultural and music ignited by her parents interest in music in Mbare. Both her parents encouraged her interest in urban culture and music. She has created an archive which includes unique collection of township music and musical and cultural memorabilia. In 2005 Joyce wrote the book *Zimbabwe Township Music* followed by *Gupuro* or *Divorce Token* and many other books. She has also written many articles. In this latest book 48 articles written over several years are brought together under one cover. Using euphemisms and avoiding sensationalism the author unpicks a wide range of taboo subjects. She uses an extensive expertise of culture and traditional wisdom to provide the reader with innovative insights and solutions to a myriad of problems present in modern life.

The patriarchy, the colonial legacy, Christianity and an increasingly urbanised society have led to a widespread loss of tradition. The breakdown of African rural communities and loss of oral culture have undermined the role of extended family members who once played signifi ant roles in everyday living. This has resulted in taboos to control behaviour and a mystifi ation of relationships, sex and sexual problems which are often considered embarrassing and distorted unmentionable.

Each chapter interrogates a different topic: arising along the journey from childhood to adulthood: learning about the male and female body, menstruation, sex, giving sexual pleasure, sexual problems, lobola, childbirth, marriage, in-laws, motherhood, gender based violence, communication in relationships, infid lity, sex in older women and more!

The use of language and comparisons is both entertaining and informative. For example Menstruation – the 'red woman' and her monthly visits – is discussed without being unmentionable and out of bounds. The 'mamba style' examines the need for giving and receiving pleasure in the bedroom and the importance of sex. The chapter on men's 'cooking stick' and issues of 'malnourishment' is a wonderfully humorous but sensitive portrayal of a common relationship problem. Describing the adaptation of traditional aspects of the past: once geographical *matongo - same roots* can now be interest-based, work-based, religion-based or politically based; the author gives tradition its fi m place in today's world. Joyce does not shy away from controversy. The chapter on **ribbons** (labia) originally created a storm of interest: Young men see their penises every day so know *their ancestor*. The preparation of *ribbons* - pulling of the labia – and encouragement to explore and prepare their *ribbons* gave young women the same opportunity to know *their ancestor* and take full control of their bodies.

Using euphemisms and avoiding sensationalism the author unpicks a wide range of taboo subjects. She uses her extensive expertise of traditional wisdom to provide the reader with innovative insights and solutions to a myriad of life problems. Once opened this innovative, ground-breaking book is impossible to put down. Handled sensitively it will not embarrass or offend even the conservative or unadventurous reader and should be rites of passage reading.

Pat Brickhill
October 2022

PRELUDE

This book is a compilation of the articles that I wrote on sex, sexuality, and taboo issues mostly in *The Herald* newspaper between 2009 - 2011 and 2015 - 2016. The language which I used in these articles was very thoughtful as the Herald is a family newspaper. To cater for this, I decided to coin new words in order not to avoid being too explicit, and yet ensure that mature people would understand what I was talking about. Th s creation of suggestive terms in the sex and sexuality arena became fun for the readers!

Writing for *The Herald* column was such a joy, an enriching experience but unfortunately, I had to stop contributing to the column because of other pressing issues. Among other things, I started working on the book: *Women Musicians of Zimbabwe - A Celebration of Women's Struggle for Voice and Artistic Expression* which took most of my time. When that book was published, I returned to the column but again, did not stay long because of situations beyond my control.

The Herald newspaper column had started under the title *Women's Histories* but ended by labelled *Inside Out* as issues of sex, sexuality and taboos came to the fore. Th s was sparked after I wrote an article in which I mentioned how women used music to air their grievances, grievances such as how their husbands 'performed badly' in the *main room* - the bedroom. Th s triggered something in my brain. I even surprised myself, by writing about sexuality issues. Aah, I thought, this is how my brain is wired. Th s wiring, I accepted, had been influenced by several factors - my genes, my socialisation, and my view of the structure of society.

As a result of the interest that the articles generated, I started to receive invitations to give talks at different organisations - women's groups, youth groups, Couples Associations, and even conferences. I even won an inaugural award for the special category, *Triple T - Tackling Taboo Topics* at the *Fourth Gender and Media Summit Awards* convened by *Gender Links, Gender, and Media Southern Africa* (GEMSA) and the *Media Institute of Southern Africa* (MISA) in Johannesburg.

I have decided to compile these articles into a book so that they can be in one place and more accessible for you.

I hope you enjoy the stories!

CONTENT

I have always seen the need to demystify sex and sexuality. The mystification of sex, sexuality has caused us serious problems which I cannot even start to recount. The ignorance which is brought about by not wanting to understand our 'mother of all humanity' called sex who is *our ancestor* has contributed to unhappiness and the confusion that we sometimes find ourselves in. From the youth to adults this failure to acknowledge our *ancestor* - for reasons known or unknown to us has been a serious problem. For people to say - *kozibani kuzelwe umntwana oyintombi or umfana* in Ndebele/Zulu; or *kwanhingi kwazvarwa mwana mukomana kana musikana* in Shona; or to say *so and so's family has been blessed with a daughter or a son* in English is because our *ancestor* that we carry between our legs, has come to life. It is this *ancestor* that defines us. This failure to recognize the power of our *ancestor* has led to the demise of human beings, we are suffering some form of amnesia, pretending to be what we are not, and who we are not. However, our *ancestor* always reminds us that **'I am the one that defines you and you will have to acknowledge and embrace me.'** As long as we do not lay bare issues of sex and sexuality from a young age, we will not be able to live full lives and we will forever be mystified by this *ancestor* and fail to handle her/him and find ourselves in serious problems.

I will share a story with you of the myth which surrounds our *ancestors* which I think will help you understand how important it is for us to demystify the way we look at sex and sexuality. There was once a young man who used to peep at girls at school just to catch a glimpse of their *ancestor*. Although now, that he is grown up, he does not have to peep, it is said he has changed woman, after woman, after woman. That excitement that he felt when he peeped saying: *"Ndazozviwona, sengikubonile, I have seen it,'* has unfortunately stayed with him. He keeps changing women thinking that one day he will find something that is out of this world and yet there is nothing like that. He is aroused for a moment but keeps looking for something new as he did when he was young. He has not embraced the *ancestor*. If he had been initiated into manhood, like how it was done in the olden, pre-colonial days, then he might have been grounded in his own *ancestor* and live with it in harmony. My desire in my *Herald* column which I wrote from 2009-2011 and again from 2015 - 2016 was to demystify sex and sexuality so that we could all exist in peace with that which in essence defines us. My writing was not limited to just sexuality but addressed traditions, taboos, and various social issues as a whole.

The article which initiated me into writing about sex, sexuality and taboo issues was titled - ***Women use Music as Communication Tool*** (14 October 2009: The Herald), and discussed how women used music and song to express their feelings about non-performing husbands in the bedroom. In the article I wrote about a mother who intervened when her daughter-in-law complained that her husband was refusing her, her conjugal rights and sleeping in his overalls. The angry mother-in law threatened her son that she would kill herself if he continued in his ways of not satisfying his wife. To show that she was not joking, she spent the night repeating her threats outside her son and daughter-in-law's bedroom door. That night, so the story has it, the woman conceived twins! Although, it is important to protect oneself from sexual transmitted diseases, it is encouraged to use protective measures. The mother-in-law knew the importance of sex in a marriage. In traditional Shona culture, not honouring sexual obligations towards your wife is known for bringing about *ngozi - an avenging spirit in the family*. This story generated a lot of interest amongst readers.

The story - **Girl You Will Be a Woman Soon** - (23 December 2009: The Herald) educated girls on how to be better prepared and to embrace the *red woman* - menstruation - when she visited, was about celebrating menstruation as an initiation into womanhood. In the past, the visit of the *red woman* was welcomed as crossing the bridge from being a girl to being a woman and accepting that the *red woman* would control the greater part of one's life, so young girls were advised on how to co-exist with her to make life enjoyable and much easier. After the publication of the article a Zimbabwean father of two girls who was/is based in Namibia wrote to me and said he had not known how to discuss the issue of menstruation with his daughters, but the story had helped him navigate this. He was very grateful that I had written it.

Learn to be A Chef and Win (13 January 2010 - The Herald) - discussed the issue of 'broken sticks' - erectile dysfunction - and how in some homes there was 'malnourishment' which was written on the woman's face. In the story, to hide his affl tion, the husband was playing hide-and-seek with his wife crawling into bed in the early hours of the morning because he was hiding his *cooking stick* that had long been broken down. It was only when the elders took charge and helped to correct the situation that things went back to normal. The story was to encourage men to seek help and not be shy when their *cooking sticks* got broken and to stop playing hide-and-seek with their wives as this brought about unrest in the home.

The Bewitching - Communication - Key Tool in Thriving Unions (29 December 2010: The Herald) and **Happy Eating: DIY Should Not Be an Option** (8 June 2011: The Herald) were received with mixed feelings as some readers had never heard of oral sex and some women thought men who were into *happy eating* were hiding their incompetence, of either *broken sticks* or *weak backs*. Those familiar with this form of *playing* found it a fulfilling way of showing each other love to the fullest. When I gave a talk at a women's church union, and I mentioned this way of *playing* an older woman protested and left because to her this was unimaginable, and she said this is what brings HIV/Aids. The young women in the room had no kind words for her and said:

Endai zvenyu tinyatsonzwa zvinhu zvinyowani tinoda variety - *Please go, we want to hear of new things, we want variety.*

The story on **ribbons** - labia - (26 April 2011: The Herald) was one of the most talked about and is a topic I have continued to research as part of a thesis or a stand-alone book. In pre-colonial times, African culture was more liberal, and a woman was encouraged to understand her body from an early age, to prepare herself for womanhood and understand that one day her *ribbons* would be used for many things. When the time came, a young girl was encouraged to enjoy *'playing'* without any inhibitions. There were mixed feelings to this story, some thought the preparation of *ribbons* was done to please men; when in fact *'the preparation'* was to empower a woman to understand her own body. I asked: How many times do women touch their vaginas? I realised women hardly do except maybe when they are having a period and must wash it or after urinating or having a bath. Girls rarely had the opportunity of seeing their vaginas, whereas in comparison boys saw their penises every day while urinating, touched themselves and even said some words to it. From a young age, boys were in touch with their *ancestor.* When girls touched themselves when preparing their *ribbons,* it gave them the right to understand themselves, to be in tune with their sexuality, to love themselves and not to be scared of their *ancestor.* Many women expressed how it drove them wild when a man would touch them there and take full control of their bodies. I wrote with self-touch a women could become better in tune with her own sexuality and own the power over their own womanhood. The preparation of *ribbons* - pulling of the labia - was meant to empower women from a young age.

I believe as sexual beings we have to understand sex and our sexuality and demystify it. It is only when we understand sex and our sexuality that we can be able to control it, or it will control us. Sex has for many years controlled us; hence many have psychological, emotional, mental, social, and economic problems that we cannot face. Sex and sexuality play a central role in our lives that we might not be able to see until things start to go very wrong in our lives!

ARTICLE 1

Music: Communication Tool for Women
14 October 2009

Music has been part of the lives of African women from time immemorial. African women have used music for various reasons and on particular occasions. Women used music to cope with the day-to-day challenges of life so as to manage their daily chores, to deal with their emotions, to air their grievances, to challenge all forms of oppression, and to celebrate womanhood. Women were major players in the life cycle of their communities in which music played a central role. Women were free to express themselves and, it was easy for them to use music as a communication tool.

Protest music was used to complain about certain injustices in the society. It could be complaining about a situation or sending a message in riddle form to someone who had aggrieved them. They conveyed these messages to each other at various gathering places, for instance, or in the fi lds where they took turns to help each other work. The process would start with a provocative song to create an atmosphere to express their grievances.

These pre-colonial and rural traditions were carried over into the townships where black people lived communally.

Th s way of conveying grievances through song and riddles helped to create a generally peaceful atmosphere amongst women. Confli ts or misunderstandings communicated through music, were used as a way to alert friends to come to their rescue and play peacemaker. Th s ensured that the antagonists remained courteous.

Women also used music to air their grievances to their husbands. For instance, while grinding or pounding a woman might sing a song to her husband's family informing them that her husband was not treating her well or was not performing well in bed. Th s resulted in, in some case the husband's relatives administering some 'herbs' to the man in order to help him to function properly.

In an interview that I had with ethnomusicologist Mwesa Mapoma he confi med that a woman might sing to alert her husband's relatives of her discontent, and this would avoid confli t between the two as the relatives became the peace makers. Francisca Muchena an all-round woman traditional music instrumentalist agrees with Mapoma, explaining that if a woman confronted her husband directly the couple would end up fi hting. For this reason, she used music to communicate her grievances to the relatives, in order that they might rescue the situation. Th s shows that in the past pleasurable sexual intercourse was taken as one of the most important aspects of a successful marriage, as opposed to today where singing such a song would probably result in the woman singer being perceived as someone of loose morals. When a husband was good in bed a woman sang a song to thank and encourage him. In the song she chanted his totem in what is known in Shona as *kudeketera mutupo - to recite the clan praise poetry*. Music would be composed spontaneously as the woman recited her husband's totem.

In recent years, a friend of mine had problems with her husband who was going to bed in his overalls. She informed the relatives and apparently the mother of the husband threatened her son that she would kill herself if the son continued in his ways. To show the son that she was not joking she went and repeated her threat at the door of their bedroom. That night my friend conceived twins! Although, it is important to protect oneself from sexual transmitted diseases, it is encouraged to use protective measures. The mother-in-law knew the importance of sex in a marriage. In traditional Shona custom not honouring sexual obligations towards your wife is known for bringing about *ngozi - avenging spirits* in the family. May the soul of this wonderful mother-in-law rest in peace. It is unfortunate I did not get to interview her.

Music was also used as a form of romance and warning especially when a husband was coming from beer drinking or had been away from home for a long time. According to Amai Muchena the husband would sing to soften his wife as the wife would be unhappy with the husband's absence. The husband would start singing when he was approaching his home and by the time he got home the wife would be happy, and this would prepare her for pleasurable sex. Although some refer to this era as primitive, one wonders what was primitive about it if men were this romantic.

Some of today's musicians have continued with this kind of music. A song such as *Chitekete* by musician Leonard Dembo can be sung by those men who cannot compose spontaneously. No wonder it is an all-time romantic classic. In *Chitekete* it also goes on to say *Bvunzai Muroora waamai - Ask My Mother's Daughter-in-Law*, it was because a mother-in-law had some stake in her *muroora*, her *daughter-in-law*. That is why my friend's mother-in-law wanted her *muroora* to be happy. There are many songs like *Gwava Jelly* by Jonny Nash, *Lindi - Lindi urimwana wakanakisisa - Lindi you are a beautiful woman* by the City Quads and *Wake - Iwe une Wako - You also have yours* by Tanga wekwa Sando.

To convey messages of discontent between a mother-in-law and a daughter-in-law, a relationship widely acknowledged as very complicated, music would be used as a communication tool. A daughter-in-law could challenge her mother-in-law in a song, using language that was metaphorical. She would do this where there was a gathering of people that included the mother-in-law and other important members of the family. As a result, relatives would come together and solve the problem between the two. In such instances music makes it possible for the less powerful to communicate with the more powerful. In some instances, a daughter-in-law would reverse the roles by addressing her mother-in-law as her daughter-in-law. This swapping of places made it easier for the younger woman to say what she wanted to say to her mother-in-law. The naming of children by a daughter-in-law was also used as a communication tool, to register her concern to her in-laws, names like *Sarudzayi* - Discrimination, *Tambudzayi* - Making me suffer, *Netsai* -Troubling me *Muchaneta* - You will get tired, or *Godknows* as examples.

Today women cannot challenge their husbands and remind them of their duties because of the so-called civilisation. This questions what we mean by civilisation and the so-called primitive cultures which, allowed women a voice. 'Civilised cultures' thrive on sweeping things under the carpet by wanting to paint a good picture to make people think things are okay whilst so-called primitive cultures thrived on recognising the basics of life.

Women should celebrate their womanhood. That is what this column encourages them to do.

ARTICLE 2

Women Must Celebrate Their Bodies
18 November 2009

My fi st production in the arts was a dress that I made when I was around 8 years old. My father worked for an imports and exports company and would buy rolls of material for my mother and my grandmother. I was attracted to the material that my father brought home. The material was white and shiny and had a nice borderline and the colours I still remember on the borderline were yellow and red. I took the material and made myself a "bottom" or "pull" dress, which was white, with a yellow and red borderline. It had frills around the shoulder and the neck. Because I had taken the material without permission, I made sure that no one saw me until I fin shed sewing it. When I had fin shed sewing the dress, I showed off the dress to my parents and waited for their reaction. They looked at me and did not know what to say. Realising that they were tongue-tied I told them I had made the dress. They were shocked. Although I could see that they were not happy that I had helped myself to the fabric, they did not want to disturb the artist in me by punishing me. Th s also confi med my love for fashion, I was very much aware of the new fashion trends in town. In the 1970's I wore the *mini*, the *guvhu out - 'navel out' a crop top* which leaves the navel showing, platform shoes - or *buruka mumango* - literally meaning '*get down the mango tree' shoes* and I spotted an afro. Yes, fashion has always fascinated me, and I have always wanted to know how it was like with women who came before us.

While I was researching on how women dressed in the past, I came across a photo titled *The Shona Girls* which was taken around 1880. In an earlier article, I featured the photo of Gogo Lozikeyi, Lobengula's fi st wife. Readers who e-mailed me said Lozikeyi's photo was stunning, although the breasts were blacked-out by the editors. When you look at the Shona girls carrying fi ewood, clay pots of water, what comes to mind is the expression: *Nhai vasikana kuhuni nekumvura kwega kwamunga bva machena mukadayi: Girls were you only going to fetch fired wood and water to be dressed to kill like that*? The girls wanted to feel good. Dressing up makes one feel good and confide t. Girls had to dress up even if there were going to fetch fi ewood because that was where they met boys whom they would later marry.

The necklaces, the bracelets, and anklets - *ndarira;* it is through this jewellery - *zvishongedzo* that the community knew how hard a young woman worked to get extra money from *Marikicho* or *working in other people's fields to get paid* or any other kind of work to buy herself the jewellery. Th s was also a way to measure how she valued herself as a woman. The girl would also get herself *chuma* or *ubugqogqo* - beads. Dressing up and decorating the waistline is not done for other people to see that *wakashonga* - that you are dressed but for yourself as a woman to feel good and knowing that the waistline is an important part of your body. Because when you feel good about the waistline it means you understand its many purposes that include sexuality and reproduction. When a girl got married the aunties and the grandmothers would add on the *zvishongedzo* and buy *chuma* or *ubugqogqo* for the waistline. The beads were also artefacts to provide music during romance.

Women in recent years have taken the collecting of beads for the waistline very seriously. In 7th Avenue, the street where I grew up in Mbare Township, there was a house where women gathered to play *chiware - gambling of waistline beads by women*, in order to have a big collection of these beads. Some prominent women frequented this house, and some lost a lot of money because you won the beads through gambling. The more beads one won, the better one felt. There were also songs composed about *chiware*. One song was by the *Limpopo Jazz Band*, a popular group in the 1960's, it was called *Akapisa Nyama Nokuda Chiware – Anopenga, Anewaya - She Burnt Meat Because Of The Love of Chiware - She Is Mad, She Is Nuts.* So *chiware* - beads gambling - was big business, such that it became part of one of the most recognised vehicles of popular culture - music.

When women bathed at the river, they showed-off who had more *chuma/ubugqogqo* - beads than the others. The beads were as a status symbol and by discussing how one got her *chuma/ubugqogqo* it was possible to tell one's love life. Th s practice was carried over into the townships were black people lived communally and used communal toilets and bathing facilities, women continued to show off what they were worth through waistline beads.

Girls were allowed to show off their breasts and to be proud of them. But more importantly this helped the young women to be in touch with their bodies and understand them. Because today's women do not understand their bodies, they have become mere sex objects and they don't enjoy the trip in the main room, it is the men who enjoy the trip because they know what they want.

The Victorian era kind of dressing made women in Zimbabwe and Africa strangers to their own bodies. These long dresses were designed for the cold weather in the United Kingdom and other countries to the north, there was no need for women in the Zimbabwean climate to put on those long dresses. Th s was done in the name of civilization. It was also done deliberately in order to destroy women's confide ce. The influence of some powerful institutions deliberately destroyed women's confide ce by confusing the way she understood her sexuality. Not understanding her sexuality caused a lot of problems for the African woman as she over covered herself and she felt inhibited.

Today's young women are being harassed and even raped for wearing miniskirts. And yet a long time ago, this was how young girls used to dress. When women on the streets of Harare were beaten for wearing miniskirts in town in 1992, ethnomusicologist Mwesa Mapoma asked me whether the girls had shown off their 'tattoos'. When I told him that I was not sure, he said if they had not shown their tattoos then they had done nothing wrong. According to Mwesa Mapoma, tattoos made by *chisvo - blade incisions* that were on the thighs under the mini skirt were strong symbols of sexuality. A man would only have access to a woman's body after she had allowed him to see and touch those *tattoos* under the skirt.

There will be illustrations and diagrams of things that have been discussed in this article in the book *Women's Histories of Zimbabwe* that I am writing, in the section: *Fashion and Sexuality*. Watch this space for details.

In closing I say: *My daughter, thrust out that chest and everything else will fall in its place. Walk tall and celebrate your body. Women let's continue to celebrate our bodies.*

ARTICLE 3

Lobola fuels gender-based violence
9 December 2009

As we commemorate the *16 Days of Activism Against Gender Based Violence*, we should remember that the payment of bride-price has lately been completely misunderstood. It was intended to help to bring the marrying families together. A token fee was usually paid in the form of a hoe or the *mukwasha/mukwenyana- the Son-in-law* would spend time at his in-laws to work for bride-price – which was called *kutema hugariri*. Traditionalist Alex Murombo explains what *kutema hugariri* is: "It is pegging your stay at the in-laws to work in lieu of your lobola/bridal price. Thus, living in with your in laws for a specifi d period in which you will perform given tasks the equivalent of the bridal price. It means fi stly you agree on what the bridal price is before you set out to do that. To put it in more palatable English as work in lieu of lobola."

Sarudzayi Chifamba-Barnes, a gender activist and Publisher had this to say about *kutema hugariri*; she explained the symbolism behind the giving of hoe and other tools to till the land and farm by the son-in-law was a way of showing that he would produce food and provide for the family: "The hoe symbolised life, it was through it that the couple would be able to feed themselves and their family. The hoe was also given to a woman when the marriage broke down as *gupuro - a divorce token*. She explains: "In the past our forebears used *badza* (hoe) to pay *lobola* (bride price) or *gupuro* (divorce token) because in both cases the hoe symbolised new life: it is a tool that is used by a person to start a new life to till the land and to sow plants that bring new life and nourishment. Axes, *tsvimbo* (knobkerries) or any other implements such as spears, were not given as *gupuro* because they symbolise warfare."

When the son-in-law went to his in-laws to work for his bride-price, it was a way of proving to them that even though he was poor, he was capable of working and providing for their daughter. Th s was done in good faith, and it was a way to bring the two families together.

Unfortunately, the concept of paying bride price has changed so dramatically over the years. It has become commercialised and transforms a woman into a commodity that is owned by the husband. The commercialisation has seen families charging not only alarming figu es but adding new items to the bride price list. Everyone in the family wants something out of this poor wife-to-be who has suddenly been turned into a commodity.

Recently, friends of mine returned from paying bride-price on behalf of their cousin who is in the United Kingdom. Th s was their first time to undertake such a big responsibility. Before going, they had made inquiries on what other people were paying. They made a list of items required: groceries were number one on the list, followed by other things they needed to buy which included: *vhura muromo* (to open the mouth), *zvibinge* (smaller items like a wooden plate, *ndiro* (plate), *makandinzwa ani* (who told you about me fee), *matekenya ndebvu* (for the time the wife-to be used to play with the father's bead), *kutsengera miti* (herbs which were chewed for the daughter being married when she was a baby), *mapfukudza dumbu* (a payment for their wife-to-be kicking the womb of her mother before she was born), *gusvi raambuya* (a fee greeting the grandmother), *mauchiro* (a fee for greeting the family), *kupinda mumusha* (a fee to enter the family homestead), *kunonga – musikana* (a fee that the wife-to-be collects from the money in the plate), *vatete* (a fee for the auntie – the father's sister) *varamu* (a fee for the wife-to-be and sisters), *Danga - dzinotsika* (cows for the kraal), *mombe yaamai* (mother's cow), *dzemari* (cows to be translated into money), *hwiradanga* (fee to father of the bride-to-be for climbing wall of the cattle enclosure where the *roora* cattle are kept), *shamu* (a sjambok which would be used to drive the cattle from the man's home to their in-laws), *kukumbira muchato* (a fee for permission to be officially married), *majazi ababa* (father's jackets), *zvipfeko zvaamai* (mother's clothing). The items came to a staggering 17!   My friend wanted to know what each item meant, and it was explained.The budget for all these items came to an estimated US$10 000! Fortunately, they had enough money with them.

When my friends returned from the *lobola/roora* ceremony, they were not as happy as they had left. Besides the exorbitant prices they were charged, they could not believe some of the things they were asked to pay. Yes, the money issue was something they were not happy about but at least one could spend years working to pay *lobola/roora* which was not an issue. Something else had really upset them. He exclaimed: "Can you believe it; we were asked to pay *mbariro* (a roof fee)? We were told that when our wife was conceived the mother was facing *mbariro* - the roof."

If those who were conceived while their mothers were facing the ceiling, the charge would transform to 'money for the ceiling,' then those who were conceived in the bush, their parents might as well charge money for the sky! Talking to some women on how they feel about this, they said *mbariro* was their turn to maximise their benefit from *lobola/roora* because men have been the ones benefiting most. Can one blame them? After all, their fee is only a drop in the ocean compared to what men charge and get.

When is the greed surrounding *lobola/roora* going to stop? What else are we going to hear after *mbariro*? Do parents ever stop to think how this affects the woman at the centre of all this?

While we commemorate the *16 Days of Gender Activism*, parents should bear in mind that by turning the pride price into a commercial venture they are promoting gender-based violence. We have heard so many times men saying to their wives that they bought them and that they are their property. This is evident when the woman is divorced, most wives have left the home without anything as they are reminded that there were bought. Most women leave their homes with just a paltry $2.00 note as *Gupuro* - a divorce token and yet they will have contributed so much to the home. Because they were supposedly 'bought', they cannot claim anything in the home. This is happening although they will have married in a civil court, which is proof that tradition dies hard. Even having married in a civil ceremony, men conveniently revert to tradition and paying the bride-price gives them the leeway to abuse women under the guise of owning them.

A wife cannot refuse to have unprotected sex with her husband even when she knows that he has a *small-house - a mistress* somewhere because sex is assumed as his right; a package that comes with bride-price. Even the roles of *madzitete - the aunts* in matters like this tend to oppress the woman who is aggrieved. She will be reminded that: *"Ari semakumbo ndeake anoita zvaanoda nawo - the legs belong to him, the husband, and he can do whatever he wants with them."*

When women are beaten up by their husbands and they try to seek sanctuary at their parent's home, they are told that *kugara mumba kushingirira - marriage requires resolve on the woman's part.* In the end, they go back to the abusive husbands until some of them are maimed or killed.

We have heard of women who could not divorce their husbands because the parents could not afford to repay the pride-price since they had charged exorbitant prices.

Parents and society should make this world a better place to live for women by not promoting gender-based violence using culture as a shield, particularly the bride price which has seen women suffering quietly because they were bought.

Families, it is your duty to protect women in your families and treat them as human beings. As we commemorate the *16 Days of Gender Activism Against Gender Based Violence*, let's look back and see how we have treated the women in our midst. Bride price should only be paid as a gesture for kinship, and not a commercial activity.

Girl, You'll Be a Woman Soon
23 December 2009

"Girl. ta ra, you will be a woman, and soon and soon..." a classic by singer Neil Diamond. You can fin sh off the words or add new ones. I can hear this song playing in my head. While this song was playing one would feel like they were already a woman, even if they were nowhere near that. It is amazing how when you are a young girl, you want to be a woman and, when you are a woman, you wish to turn back the hands of time. Sometimes whilst playing this song, a girl would take her mother's bras, fill them with paper or tennis balls and pretend they had well-developed breasts. She'd put on her mother's stilettos and stagger around as if they are learning to walk - because the high heels did not make it easy. They would also take their mother's handbag and swing it around like a grown woman or a model. Being a woman was something that many girls looked forward to. One would get closer to being a woman by playing *the amandlwane, mahumbwe* or *playing house* where they would play 'mother' and get themselves a 'husband' and 'children,' the children usually being dolls, depending on how good one was at assembling her cast. But, my dear, that was *emadlwanen, kumahumbwe, playing house.* You want to be a woman? Welcome to the real world of womanhood. The real fi st port of call is when that *red woman* visits you, she heralds you into womanhood and she will visit you every month from then. That is called going on a period, having menses or menstruation.

The visit by this *red woman* was celebrated long time ago because that is how one crossed the bridge from being a girl to being a woman. Th s *red woman* would control the greater part of a girl's life, hence she had to be embraced and as a girl you were advised on how to co-exist with her, to make your life enjoyable and much easier.

Today when this woman visits it is not talked about, it is a secret. Th s *red woman* is said to be dirty. The way this *red woman* is treated today has caused anxiety for many young women and they do not know how to deal with her. When that day comes most don't even know what it means.

My daughter told me that she is preparing my granddaughter Mya for her periods as some of her age mates had already started having their periods. I could not believe it. I exclaimed: "Do you mean at 9 years of age my grandbaby is going to be a woman?" I phoned Mya to hear it for myself. I asked her what she knew about periods. Mya replied: "We are being taught that at school. We have to be careful about some stuff that travels to the egg and creates a baby."

"How does the stuff et there?" I asked.

"If you sleep with a man." She replied.

"Oh, I see." I said softly.

"What are you going to do when the *red woman* visits?" I went on.

"Gogo, you mean period?"

"Yes, Mya," I answered.

"If that happens while I am at school, I will let my teacher know."

"Are you looking forward to your fi st period, Mya?"

"Yes, Gogo Jenje." She *'laughed'*.

"Why, Mya?" I asked.

"Because I will have grown up," she replied.

I was so touched by the fact that my girl is looking forward to being a woman, and I said to her: "Sweetheart, welcome to womanhood and when that day comes turn the house red and Gogo, grandmother, will design user friendly pads for you just like the ones your great grandmothers used and they will be in red." She laughed and she said: "Thank you Gogo Jenje."

In the olden days when a girl got a visit from this woman it would be celebrated by their family, relatives, and friends. The girls would be taken away to a secluded place to be taught what to do. This was their first stage of initiation into womanhood. Girls were taught how to look after themselves, how to exercise, and the *snake dance* was one of those exercises they were taught during initiation. The snake dance relaxes the mind and the body and makes the periods bearable. This was practiced amongst some Zimbabwean people', and it is still being practiced by the Venda who came from Zimbabwe and are now settled in the northern part of South Africa and southern part of Zimbabwe. There are many ways girls were taught how to manage the time and certain herbs were administered and particular foods were served to the girl.

The Tonga tribe in Malawi in Nkatha Bay bordering Tanzania would celebrate the coming of the fi st period of a girl by taking the girl to the homes of friends and relatives with a plate and the friends and relatives would acknowledge she was now a woman by putting beans or money in the plate and wish her all the best. Th s made it easier for the young woman to know that what she was going through was acceptable and appreciated by the greater community and she felt confide t about what she was going through, knowing that she was being supported and encouraged to be a wom-an and understand everything that makes her a woman. Today there are no support systems to help a girl go through this rite of passage, as the whole thing has become mystified and associated with being dirty, which makes it difficult for girls and makes them feel confused when this *red woman* visits them every month. Some girls/women suffer from severe period pains and, until recently, there were no adverts on medication for period pains as all this was shrouded in secrecy.

However, there are some people who are there for their daughters to help the girls go through this passage with ease. My brother Farayi, realising that his daughter was about to be a woman, bought her pads as a present. The *red woman* took some time to arrive but, when she fi ally arrived, his daughter informed him. He explained: "It was an emotional moment, my daughter cried, she was overwhelmed. I was there for her, and I said to myself more fathers should be there for their girls during this important time." He continued: "I wonder about those fathers who are not there for their girls at this important time?" While he was saying this, I could see his eyes welling up with tears. Yes, it is a great and emotional time going through the passage from being a girl to being a woman.

For TC, a single father - the inevitable like-it-or-not time for the *red woman* came. The visit came without prior notice. In the given circumstances, the daughter had no one to turn to but her dad - and TC had to go through a crash course - immediately! As the *red woman* manifested her paintworks - poor panicking dad, was faced with no alternative, he just had to bite the bullet and headed for the welcoming kit at the local Pharmacy, by himself. Th s was best helped by the fact that TC had always been there for his daughter - and this made welcoming the *red woman* and setting up a monthly trust fund for the same a much easier task.

Sometimes when the *red woman* is visiting, she can be harsh, she wants attention. It is known that some women get mood swings during this time, they lose emotional balance, or get what is called Pre-Menstrual Syndrome and Postmenstrual Stress (PMS). PMS is characterised by anxiety, irritability, and mood swings.

American singer Mary J Blige sang a song about the *red woman* and in her lyrics mentioned how difficult menses can be. The 5th stanza goes like this:

Goin' through somethin' tonight, some in the day
Y'all need to understand where I'm comin'
See I'm PMS-ing
Yeah, y'all ladies, told you you would be able to relate tonight
My lower back is aching
PMS
And I don't know what I'm gonna do next
I'm full of stress
I want y'all, I want y'all to hear what I'm sayin'
Won't you hear what I'm sayin'?
Yeah PM, PMS, PMS, PMS

Sharon (not her real name) had serious problems when her time arrived, but her husband would help her to get through the pain. Unfortunately, problems started when she wanted to go out of the country to further her education and the husband could not let her go. When her aunt was called to try and understand from the husband why he was not letting her go, he said, "Who will hold her when she is about to have her period?" The aunt thought it was a joke, but he was very serious, and he said he would not want anyone hold his wife when that time comes. Sharon said she boycotted the holding in order to blackmail her husband so that he could let her go to further her studies. Seeing that the marriage was about to go into problems the husband also decided to go and further his studies at the same university where his wife had been offered a place. Sharon confesses that the time she was on boycott was not an easy one at all.

The second stage of initiation would be to educate the girl to understand her body. In some cultures, this is where a woman can be thrown into confusion as the understanding of the body is not encouraged, some cultures encourage genital mutilation but in some Zimbabwean cultures a girl is instead encouraged to "*create ribbons*" to enhance their sexuality.

At the initiation, the young women would also be taught how to look after the home and their husbands. The husband-to-be would also have received similar education from his uncles and grandfathers. Th s wonderful practice of initiating a girl into womanhood disappeared because of influences from other cultures and religions that convinced us, and mocked us, saying that what we were doing was wrong and yet we were quite ahead of our times in terms of understanding sex and sexuality.

When a girl reached puberty, women leaders in the community organised a ceremony to celebrate and to welcome a young girl into their club of women. Before a girl was accepted as a full, mature woman she would have to go through initiation. Female initiation rites were concerned with the regeneration and continuity of life. All over Africa, these rites were enacted as a symbolic rebirth into adulthood, a process through which the community passes on knowledge and symbolic metaphors and practices.

In contemporary, particularly urban life, 'kitchen tea parties' serve as surrogate initiation ceremonies to prepare women for marriage. Like 'baby showers' and 'baby welcomes,' at a kitchen tea party the woman's friends, relatives and connoisseurs are invited to give advice to the young woman on how to look after her home and her husband. Music is played at these parties, and the dancing is usually sexually evocative. Th s creates the mood of the subject being discussed, which helps to explain some of the issues regarding motherhood and womanhood - though they are a little bit different from the olden days, the concept is more or less the same.

These parties are strictly for women-only. Although males are sent away, they sometimes become curious and fi d ways to see what is going on. There are some men who even dress up like women to secretly gain access to these parties.

In the past, when the initiation process was over, social gatherings were organised for girls and boys to meet and chose their life partners.

Ceremonies called *Jenaguru* in Shona, or *Ukugcwala Kwenyanga* in Ndebele were organised where girls and boys would sing and dance the whole night. These ceremonies were organised when there was a full moon as it was believed that certain positions of the moon determined the ideal time to look for one's life partner. *Jena* meaning 'light' and *guru* meaning a 'big' (a big event), *ukugcwala* meaning 'full', *kwenyanga* meaning 'moon' is still being practiced particularly in the rural areas although it is no longer purely traditional and some of the songs played are now in modern *jiti* music style.

To conclude: My granddaughter, when that *red woman* visits you for the first time, please embrace her and throw a party; turn the house red; the sweets - red; cake - red; balloons -red; the dresses - red; perfume - red; for gogo… red wine, and we will celebrate womanhood!!!!

We wish you all a Merry Christmas and a Prosperous 2010

ARTICLE 5

Do Women have choices and space?
30 December 2009

My friend phoned me and he was sounding very unsettled, I tried to ask him over the phone what it was that was troubling him and what he wanted to see me about. He would not disclose until he got to my place. He looked very disturbed, and when I offered him a drink he drank it all in one go. He stood up, removed his jacket - he was sweating. He asked us to go and sit outside where he would feel more comfortable with the fresh air. I waited for him to settle down and he said; "You know" he scratched his head; I was now feeling unsettled, a lot of things were now playing in my mind. What could it be? He said, "You know I respect women, and I know how you feel about that." I was now getting nervous.

Then he gave me the laptop to read what he had pasted from the email. It went like this; "I have never loved anyone the way I love you" I looked at him and I was not amused, thinking that it was directed to me. "You are not serious......." I said. He asked me to fin sh the letter fi st. I composed myself and I read the letter, and when I fin shed it, it was signed K. "Who is K?" I asked. Th s is a woman who has been on my case, she sends me emails, she sends me text messages, and as you can see, she phones everyday just to hear my voice, she says. Th s woman has a psychological problem. I could not understand why he thought the woman has a psychological problem. "I respect women, but for a woman who proposes to men, she is sick!" He paced around the veranda, scared and confused. I said to him, "Now I know what to do if I want to scare you, I will send you K". It was strange to him how a woman could propose to a man - a woman, being a hunter, instead of being the hunted.

Do women have choices and space to express their feelings? The way our society is structured does not allow women to have such choices and space. But in the olden days women were allowed to have choices, and space was created for them to choose the man they loved. One way of doing this was to be close to the mother of the man that you wanted to propose. A woman would do this by fetching water or wood for the mother of the man that she wanted, and other gestures just to bring to her attention that she would want to be her son's wife. The mother would alert her son about the girl and say good things about her. – My aunt (*umamaoncane*) Spiwe Ncube Mushonga confirmed that young women had space during *endulo/ pasichigare* by approaching the mother of the man they wanted and the mother of the son seeing the efforts of this young woman she would say to her son, "*ubodlalela kozibani phela mtanami kulamankazana amahle. Umtwana uyabe esekuzwile ebesesenza njengakhonokho.* (you need to pay frequent visits to so and so's homestead there are beautiful/good girls there." Another way was to be friends with the sisters and they would take word to their brother. Although the mother-in-law and sister-in-law relationship can be a complicated one, it is said if it is introduced in such a way that you start as friends it can be healthy as you will be told the family's secrets.

According to Beauty Mahlahlane another way of proposing to a man in the olden days was to make *ubuhlalo* (bead necklace) for the man that you were eyeing and ask friends to accompany you to his homestead and when the girl gets to the kraal she and her friends would start singing and the single men from the family would come to the kraal, the girl would put the necklace on the man that she wanted and if he accepted the necklace then it means that he is also interested in the girl. The friends would be witnesses to the event that would eventually turn into a marriage.

Another way was at *Jenaguru* or *Ukugcwala Kwenyanga* were young girls and boys met. *Jena* meaning 'light' and *guru* meaning a 'big' (a big event), *ukugcwala* meaning 'full,' *kwenyanga* meaning 'of the moon' *Jenaguru/Ukugcwala Kwenyanga* was organized when the moon was set/full moon as it was believed that certain positions of the moon determined the ideal time to look for one's life partner. At *Jenaguru* if a girl saw the man that she loved she would sing a song like "*sarura wako kadeya deya nendoro chena, wangu mutema/mutsvuku kadeya, deya nendoro chena....*" pointing to the guy that she is interested in and if the guy was interested he would join in the circle and the rest would be history. The same also applied to the man.

Women then had space and choices, but how can the sister who is after my friend be able to do what she is doing without being seen as mad or having a psychological problem? How many women have been brave enough to go for the man they want in life? Maybe as Tanga wekwa Sando said "*Iwe une wako*" (you have the one you love) and for the sister, *ndiye wake waakawona* (and for the sister that is the one she loves), and also Sando's latest song *Nguye; Nguye engim' thandayo, Nguye engam'khethayo, Nguye, nguye inhliziyo yami.* – (is the one, is the one that I love, is the one I love, Is the one my heart has chosen)

If today's women decide to use the old ways of proposing to a man or drawing attention from his circles, it could be seen as stalking. Charity Rumbidzai Hodzi a Law Graduate and Gender Activist has this to say, "It is unfortunate that in this so called modern day and age, if a woman shows interest in a man and emails him, calls him or tries to relate her feelings to him, she is regarded as a 'stalker'. She cannot take up the traditional way of getting close to the man through his family since she will be viewed as a psychopath and desperate woman. Isn't it funny how a man proposes? He will follow you, wait at the corner of your road every day, and speak to your friends, family, anyone and everyone. Is he ever looked at as a psychopath? NO."

When I spoke to some women they said they do not see anything wrong with what our sister did (proposing to a man). One woman said that a large percentage of women in our country may be living with men that they do not love because they were waiting to be picked by any man who comes along and when they are now living together they will just have to make do with what they have. If the woman is not picked then she withers. Some women have 'psychological' problems and stress related problems because they 'were not picked'.

Another woman said I proposed to a man, but I will never do it again - because when we broke up the man said after all *ndakangokuda nokuti ndakakunzwira tsitsi pawakandinyenga* (After all I only fell in love with you because I felt sorry for you because you proposed). This became known by the community and I was abusively mimicked and mocked that *ndakanyenga murume* (I proposed to a man). I asked, "So what are you going to do if you find a man that you want and he does not approach." She said *"Ndinongo actor"* (I will just act). "What if he does not see It?." I asked, and she answered, *"Ah inenge yafa yakarodha"*, (the story will end just like a gun that is loaded and is not fired).

A man who also does not believe that a woman is supposed to propose to a man said, "Even if I am not able to propose to a woman I would not want a woman to propose to me. I prefer that if a woman wants to propose to me, should do it in a covert manner".

There is an old couple that I have known for years - and it is the woman who proposed to the husband. The woman said, proudly, "I approached him, I love him and that nothing could have stopped me from showing him the way I felt about him." The couple has children and grandchildren, and they are happy. The man always jokes and says if she had not approached him he might not have married up to now because she is the one he was waiting for.

What worried me though about the email that nearly turned my friend into a wreck is that the woman said, "You are the only man that I will ever love, and I will never love again." My sister, remove that from your vocabulary, if he is not the one, be able to move on with life. By then you will be a lot wiser. As Don Williams said, "Learn to let go when love lets you down, so that you don't miss the one who is waiting to be found …only love is gonna bring you around."

Susan Mapfumo composed a song in the 80's called *'Mukoma Ticha Ndinokudayi'*. ('Brother' Ticha I love you) This song gives confidence to women that if you see a man whom you love 'go for him' or don't be scared to approach him. For a woman to find happiness it is important for her to get what she wants in life, but not many women have husbands they really wanted to have, as it is not encouraged for women to propose love to men. They have to wait for a man to propose love to them and sometimes the man they want does not come forth. In the end this compromises a lot of marriages, as they just have to make do with the man who will be 'willing' to approach them.

But my sister your approach should be genuine and out of love, and also bear in mind that you are dealing with a human being who has grown up in certain structures and views that are already set.

Hey my sister you are one brave woman! After all life is a gamble.
To my friend; have an open mind.
Women continue to celebrate your womanhood by getting what you want, have choices and create your own space.

Learn to be a Good Chef & Win
13 January 2010

A woman whose husband started acting strange did not know what else to do but to inform the elders to help her solve the issue. When she went to inform the elders what was happening in her home, she carried with her some evidence and one of them was the food that her husband had not eaten for a week. He had gone for almost six months getting home late, when everyone else was asleep and he would crawl into bed. One week's food was enough evidence to show the problems that her marriage was going through which were also written all over her face. The elders registered her concerns and assured her that they were going to deal with the issue. They advised her not to leave any food for him anymore whilst they sorted out the problem. Somehow, the husband started coming home early but the wife was no longer leaving any food for him. It worried him. He decided to go to the elders to register his concern. They looked at each other knowingly. He complained about his wife not cooking for him. They in turn asked him whether he was cooking for her.

He was surprised. He said he had never heard of men cooking as it was the duty of women to cook. The elders descended on him as if they were chastising a young boy. There were disappointed that he did not understand what they meant. He was told very clearly that if he did not carry out his duties, the wife was also not obliged to honour hers. He was confused but they were serious. They said it was only when he had fulfilled his duties that they would talk to him. He accused them of following practices that advocated for men to cook, and he declared that he would not allow it to happen with him. But the elders stuck to their guns. Realising that they were not going to be intimidated *nemwana wavakabereka - their own child, the child they gave birth to*; he decided to comply and asked how he was going to learn how to cook at his age. They sat him down and revealed to him that his wife had registered her concern about his behaviour, that he was getting home late and that he had stopped eating the food the wife cooked and that was why the wife had stopped cooking for him. It was only when he had done his part of cooking and presented a report that the elders would take it up from there. They said they expected a report from a top-class chef that certainly included a three-course meal and not a paltry sandwich.

They said a three-course meal would mean a starter, the main dish, a desert and if the meal was as good as they expected, it would be followed by a siesta. A good chef will also see that he serves his food in a good environment, the room where the food is served should just make one salivate, the table, the tablecloth, the lights, the music, and everything. A good chef would follow up to see whether the food has been good. If the food was good, those eating would acknowledge by nodding their heads as a sign of satisfaction but at the same time not wanting to be disturbed. It was only then that the chef would know they had done a good job.

Realising he was cornered the man broke down and explained that his cooking stick had broken a long time ago! That was why he was playing hide-and-seek with his wife. The elders gave him some herbs to drink and in addition advised him to see a medical doctor. Soon after, his engine was roaring again, back on track. He went on to prepare one of the best three-course meals that was followed by a siesta.

Some women that I have talked to say this woman is a lucky woman, one in a million because her husband came out and asked for help. He was man enough. There are women who cannot stand the food that their husbands serve, the room where it's served, the table, the chef himself, everything. One woman said her husband would first beat her up before going on to demand what he claimed was rightfully his. The husband would often say that even if they fought, it was not with Thombi/Ntombi that he was fighting with (Thombi/Ntombi is a girl's name that is sometimes used to mean the private part of woman). Him and Ntombi could still be friends and play. For him Ntombi was removed from the whole body. She was an island; no starter, no desert, nothing.

Th s is the okwe qudhe lensikazi - hwejongwe netseketsa, cock and hen play - which some women complain about when they say men are selfish. But some men are too timid to admit they have a medical problem and need to seek professional help. Chef-fing is in the mind and the mind has to be trained to be patient enough to cook a three-course meal. Some tribes teach their sons that they have to wait for the woman to fin sh eating and then remove the plates. But there are some chefs who, while the woman is still in the middle of enjoying the food, hurry to clear the table and as a result, it spoils the meal.

There are tribes which are known for initiating young men into manhood in style and one of the lessons and training they are taught is to never practice the cock and hen play as it frustrates women. They are trained in such a way that the cuisine can go for a long time, a full three course meal indeed.

While the man was looking for recipes, he realised that to enhance the cuisine he had to start with the usual kitchen, healthy food, which would eventually add up to a three-course meal to boost the bedroom play. He became an all-round chef. The wife also became an all-round chef looking for her recipes too. In the end, recipes and cuisines were fl wing around the home and it showed on their faces.

When elders visited to check on the progress, they did not need to ask any questions. It was written all over, there was no trace of malnourishment in the house. Women celebrate life and womanhood. Let the cuisines roll!

Treat the Goose & Gander Equally
3 February 2010

Women who decide to have relationships after being widowed, divorced or their husbands being absent for a long time have not had it easy within society, from the highest echelons to the grassroots.

Some cultures prefer that a widowed woman choose a man from the family, usually from the brothers of the deceased. A woman who is not forthcoming choosing a man from her husband's family is threatened and punished in different ways.

A young woman who lost her husband in a car accident was asked to choose a husband from her husband's family but refused. The in-laws asked her that since she was young, and her blood was at its boiling peak how was she going to cool it down. To the amazement of all who were there she said: *ndinonotsvaga musango - I will look in the bush or elsewhere* for a man. I asked her why she was so blunt, she said, that she had her reasons and one of the reasons was that all the brothers of her husband were married, and she was not going to be a home breaker. She explained how some *amaigurus* and *amaininis - her sisters-in-law* did not want to speak to her during the days leading to choosing a husband. The other reason was that she did not want a husband anymore, but maybe someone to share life with - a companion. Because she refused to choose a husband from her husband's family, they monitored her movements, but later they got tired and gave up.

There are women who prefer to follow so-called traditions and choose a husband from the family of their deceased husband, and it does not matter whom they hurt. A friend of mine who was naïve of her husband's family ways of doing things was invited to a traditional ceremony where her younger brother's wife was choosing a husband. The *amainini – the sister-in-law to the young brother of her husband*, gave her $10.00 and she received it. The sister-in-law and the *vatetes* - sisters to the husband who can be called aunties - and the husband went into a room, she remained seated outside and in no time the *vatetes* came out of the room leaving the *amainini* and her husband in the room. In a short while the *amainini* and her husband came out of the room and the *vatetes* and other relatives ululated. It was then that she felt that something was not right. One of the sisters-in-law who was against what was happening, told her that her husband and the *amainini* had just had a 'two-minute honeymoon,' they were now husband and wife and that it was going to be announced later. She was angry and confronted the *tetes* and the husband, but she was told that she had consented by accepting the $10.00. She tried to fi ht it in the court of law but then decided that it was not worth it and instead left the husband. She made a good decision because her husband and *amainini* died. The *babamudiki* - her husband's younger brother - had apparently died of Aids. She remarried, and in her own words she said: "I went on a real honeymoon, not a two-minute romp."

Women just like their male counterparts also want to have a relationship when they are widowed or divorced. They still need that intimacy with someone, but they are denied it by society because their sexuality is highly controlled by almost everyone around them - the husband's family, institutions and sometimes by their own children.

Yet men are facilitated by society to have relationships after divorce or after the death of their wives or if their wives are absent for a long time.

A man whose wife died and did not seem to have a love relationship got her relatives worried until one of the aunts told the family: "*Do not, worry anako kwaanoenda kunosukurudza ropa rake - do not worry he goes somewhere to purify his blood.*" Th uncle could not hide his relief by saying: "At least I know he is normal." It is because he knew the importance of purifying blood. Women also need to purify their blood.

It is said the lack of purifi ation of blood can cause a lot of problems for women, like lack of self-confide ce, being moody, and bad tempered.

Some of the benefits of "purifying the blood" according to Kathleen Doheny in WebMD Feature are that 'sex relieves stress - lowers blood pressure, boosts immunity by giving higher levels of an antibody called immunoglobulin A or IgA, which can protect one from getting colds and other infections, burns calories - i.e., that 30 minutes of 'play' burns 85 calories or more. It may not sound like much, but it adds up: 42 half-hour sessions will burn 3,570 calories, more than enough to lose a pound! Sex also improves cardiovascular health, boosts self-esteem, and helps one sleep better, amongst other things'.

The lack of purifi ation of blood has caused untold problems for women.

One day we were driving with a friend in Johannesburg and a woman driver cut in, in front of us, despite the fact that she was wrong she started swearing at us. My friend had no kind words for her either, she said: "Th s one must be starving I tell you, that is why she is acting like that." Maybe she had not had her blood purifi d for a long time.

The purifi ation of blood is not taken seriously as far as women are concerned and its after-effects are dire, leading to serious health problems mostly stress related.

There are women whose husbands go away for a long time either because of work or various other reasons. A colleague in Cape Town made me laugh when she told me about her father who worked on a cruise ship and would only come home once a year or after two years. They, she, and her siblings, knew that every time her father visited, her mother would fall pregnant. Several women whose husbands did the same job as her father's failed to wait for their spouses for a variety of reasons.

A woman who broke an all-time record of being separated from her husband was Winnie Mandela, her husband Nelson Mandela spent 27 years in prison. When Mandela came out of prison, unfortunately Winnie did not enjoy the fruits of her waiting, as all sorts of confusion rocked the marriage. Mandela went on to marry Graça Machel, and there were mixed feelings about the marriage but one thing that Graça did, is that she demystified the notion that a widowed woman cannot remarry.

When Jacqueline Kennedy decided to remarry when her husband John F. Kennedy was assassinated, her marriage to Greek shipping tycoon Aristotle Onassis, was not received well, but she went on and did what she wanted to do.

While it is difficult for widowed women to remarry it is even more challenging for divorced women to do the same.

Family and friends advise most divorced women that they should pray all their lives for the estranged husband to change his mind and come back. This makes the lives of women unbearable; it becomes difficult for a woman to deal with pressures that are made easier by having someone to share life with.

As human beings we need company, we need to be loved, we need to love, it is normal to have company in life, otherwise it could be lonely.

Women choose what you want in life, live a healthy and fulfilled one and avoid stress. Continue to celebrate life and womanhood.

ARTICLE 8

Get out of your Box, Celebrate Womanhood
10 February 2010

At a funeral, an old woman gathered the *Umanyano/ Ruwadzano* women - the *Mothers' Union Members* in order to express her concern about the way they had attended a funeral, by not sleeping over at the funeral as it ended up being her and other old women. She was furious with the younger women who decided to spend the nights at their homes with their husbands. The old woman was unhappy with the way the young women were not doing their duty as the *Mothers' Union Members*. The other old woman decided to cool her down and she said, *"Nhai iwe unozvinetsereiko. Ava vachirikuchovha bhasikoro. Rega isu tisisagone kuchovha bhasikoro tirare zvedu. - Why are you so angry with these young women? They are still able to cycle, and we can no longer cycle let us sleep over at the funeral, let them go and cycle."*

When some women get to a certain age, they want to take it easy on *cycling* - or stop completely. Some move to another room in the house so that they are not tempted with what the gym or *leisure centre* has to offer. I used to wonder about this set up. One day I asked one of my grandmothers to explain to me. She said: "Some are afraid to cycle because the *red woman* has stopped visiting them as it is believed that, when the *red woman* visits you, she takes away with her the month's 'dirt'". However, she said, she did not subscribe to this notion as one of her aunts introduced her to a herb which could take care of the same work the *red woman* did. This herb is called *mukutura*. So, for her, it was going to be until death does them apart with her husband. Looking at this herb, now - it is more of a detoxifier, and detoxifying is good for the body - and one can be active in whatever they do, including *cycling*.

Some old couples have other ways they use to exercise, to get to their destination, and relax, that are not as tiring as *cycling*. A colleague of mine said: *'unongowona chembere dzikatarisana dzotobuda misodzi, votorara...zvinenge zvatopera - Geriatrics just look at each other and you see tears coming down - and they go to sleep, and relax, they will have taken each other to that world and back."*

Th s demonstrates that when one wants to exercise, to get to their destination, fi d pleasure, and relax it is not only by *cycling* but there are many other ways of doing it. Th *leisure centre* provides all sorts of exercises, some intense, others calm - like yoga, massage, and reiki. Several women I have spoken to, prefer reiki, massaging more than just *cycling* and press-ups.

It is sometimes a challenge for couples to introduce new ways of doing things. One man regretted why he ever introduced a new style. The wife was shocked when she was introduced to other alternatives that the *leisure centre* offers, that she informed her husband's brothers. An entourage of her husband's brothers, and their wives paid the couple a visit in order to resolve the problem.

They asked him what had got over him to start eating people, as that is how the wife had reported it to them. The brothers asked him to explain how he had become a wizard, and to give details where he got the bewitching spirit. He did not know what to say, but hot tears just came down rolling on his face. They then asked their sister-in-law to explain, and she said: *"Kuda kundidya inini anofunga kuti ndiri vaye vehusi-ku here? - How can he want to eat me does he think I am like those ladies of the night?"*

It was then that the brothers understood. They did not know how to solve this one. The sisters-in-law who had accompanied their husbands asked the wife in private to discuss this bewitching. They could not believe how their sister-in-law was so naive. They told her that they had heard about this bewitching business from books and DVDs and wished they could try it. Sometimes the monotony of *cycling* did not provide them with the relaxation and the pleasure that they wanted.

When the men were left alone, the husband explained to his brothers how he had tried many things, and even cooked lentils to fi e up his woman. He regretted why he had even started it, as all the efforts had gone to waste. One of the brothers was very sarcastic about the whole thing and he said: *"Ndiko kunonzi kudyiswa chaiko uku - this is what I call a real love portion...,"* but he sympathised with his brother.

Another woman whose husband became a wizard and started 'bewitching' her was worried at fi st, but said to herself, "let me see where it is going." She said before she got used to it, she wondered how she was helping her husband to relax and to get to his destination with such kind of exercise. But the husband asked her to take it easy, and relax - and relax, she did. When she explains how she was eventually taken to a different destination than the usual, then one understands why she also decided to become a witch. When she became a witch, she discovered that it is in the bewitching that she also found joy and seeing how her husband was showing signs of relaxation; they cruised to an unknown world together and when they came back, they were relaxed.

Some couples have fought while trying to introduce new ways of relaxing as the one partner starts to suspect might have learnt it from someone else, when in reality the partner might have read a book or seen it on DVD or just heard about it from friends. A couple had a misunderstanding when the husband wanted to introduce the via satellite way, as the husband was far away, and he wanted to connect and make the two relax and get to their destination over the phone. The wife said: *"Unofunga kuti ndinopenga? Penga wega - Do you think I am mad don't include me in your madness"*, but all he wanted was to bring pleasure into their life and to connect spiritually and emotionally.

My musician friend Sando is going to hold a sterling show on Valentine's Day, and I know when you come from dancing to township romantic songs such as *Paida Mwoyo* or *Bohera*, you will be too tired to go through *cycling*. Why don't you relax and let the wizard bewitch you, while you play *Take Me* by Louis Mhlanga.

Women get out of that box and celebrate womanhood to the fullest! The *leisure centre* has a lot to offer.

Continue to use protection. Whatever you choose from the *leisure centre* enjoy yourself to the maximum and celebrate life.

Happy Valentine's Day!

Women Must Get Out of The Box
17 February 2010

I had set aside the last two weeks of March to reply to emails that I had received regarding some issues discussed in this column. My last week's article especially was not understood by many people, and I have decided to explain it in this week's column, together with other letters on other issues.

Of the emails and phone calls that I received on last week's issue, 60% did not understand the story and 40% did. What surprised me is that I have been receiving emails mostly from men of late, which is a bit worrying. But with this article I also got emails from women, who were part of the 40% who understood the article.

Some said they did not understand about the *cycling*. I thought it was obvious as this is how sex is sometimes referred to, metaphorically. *Cycling* is one of the common words used generally by older women. I try not to be too open when talking about some of these issues. Th s is the time when I wish I was like my grandmothers, who used to say things as they are. Sex can sometimes be a complex subject to handle. That is why the old woman at the funeral also decided to use metaphorical language - *cycling*.

Maybe to go back to the funeral where it all started with last week's article, I would like to quote a *"jiti"* song which is very popular at funerals, called *"Pabhasikoro - On the bicycle"*. It goes: *"Pabhasikoro, bata mwana wadonha, bata, bata, bata, bata, bata, mwana wadonha - On the bicycle hold the child is falling, hold, hold, hold, hold, hold the child is falling."* The dance to this song is called *"hota kota"* which is danced in a sexual way. Th s song is sung at almost every funeral that I have attended which shows how sex controls almost all aspects of our lives since it is our greatest ancestor. Th s song is about sex. Thi gs will be heating up in bed, and someone is saying, "Hold me baby, and don't let me fall." The bicycle has been used figur tively in reference to sex. I started with *cycling* - a way of fi ding pleasure between a man and woman and helping them to get to their destination – an orgasm and relax. For clarity, *cycling* is sexual intercourse.

Th *"Leisure Centre"* was also not understood. Since the bicycle is for exercising, I put it in a gym - and the gym is the *leisure centre*. I looked at sex being performed in the *leisure centre*. It is a venue used to provide that pleasure for adults which, can be the bedroom, the bush, on top of the roof and so on.

The two old people who look at each other and feel some sensation, is another way of having sex, communicating using body language; just looking at each other did the trick. Over a period of time the couple would have gotten so used to each other in their love life that they can tell which way the other is going emotionally. *Cycling* for old people can be tedious and sometimes with breaks along the way and may even fail to reach their destination, save for a heart attack. Other milder ways of getting pleasure and relaxing are massaging, touching, and hugging. Th s also helps keep lovers connected.

What do you mean by exercise? Someone asked. Sex is itself exercise, in my article: *Treat Goose and Gander Equally* (Herald of 03 March 2010), I explained how having sex is the *purification of blood* and how sex is exercise. Statistics show that half an hour of sex can burn around 85 calories. That is the equivalent of running three minutes up and down the stairs, six minutes of tennis or seven minutes on an exercise bike.

The *via satellite* is also a way of breaking the monotony associated with *cycling.* This usually works well for couples who are generally *'well-synchronised'* and spiritually connected but for one reason or the other are separated by distance. To compensate for the emotional feelings, they can use the telephone or email. The lovers can be so intimate over the phone or on email that they get to their *destination* or feel the sensation and relax together.

During those good old years, before phones and emails became a common phenomenon, lovers used to write each other creative letters to deal with distance, on creatively designed writing pads, and even the envelopes! The letters would also be creatively crafted with love drawings of hearts and words like I love you, a man and woman holding hands, red fl wers, and cupid among other romantic images. Songs and poems would also be included.

Young lovers would also write each other letters as a way of dealing with distance, which can be a result of school or work commitments. Th s would help them maintain their love and keep them connected. The relationship could go on for a long time without *cycling* as this also provided that sexual ecstasy which was not physical.

Witches and wizards are people involved in witchcraft - *kudya vanhu - to eat people* - which, in this context is a metaphor to explain the alternative way of having sex - oral sex that the man was trying to introduce to his wife. The wife reported this as: *"Munin'ina wenyu arikuda kundidya - Your brother wants to eat me."* The brothers thought their young brother had become a wizard, practising witchcraft - eating people. They did not understand that this had to do with sex, which is why they asked the brother where he had got the bewitching spirit. So, *bewitching* is a term I used to explain another way of fi ding pleasure in the leisure centre, outside of *cycling*.

There are those who did not have any problem understanding this article because they practice the bewitching style.

Women who emailed me said they enjoyed this more since it was directed at one of the places where the greater part of their pleasure is stimulated. Women who prefer this kind of sex say that they feel being loved completely and unreservedly.

The purpose of the article was to try to highlight the fact that there are various ways of enjoying sex and being innovative in the *leisure centre*, so as to avoid the monotony of *cycling*. If couples have the necessary variety in the *leisure centre*, it helps to curb sexual transmitted diseases as they will not look somewhere else for satisfaction.

Some of the topics that generated a lot of interest and debate are *Women Must Celebrate Their Bodies, Learn to Be a Chef, Win, Girl You'll Be a Woman, Soon,* and *Do Women Have Choices, Space, Women Proposing to Men.* Some of the comments I got:

- *"I was really thrilled to read your newspaper article 'Women Must Celebrate Their Bodies.' It was a really interesting article in this day and age where women think they are sexier if they are thin as opposed to a curvaceous body. It is important that women should love their bodies whether 'slim' or 'fat'. I am on the 'fat' side and used to be self-conscious and tried dieting several times until I realised that that's who I am. Being sexy is all in the mind. I have learnt to dress well, and it boosts my confidence. I get comments such as 'nice body', 'ende mune zvinhu zvenyu - and you have your things' from both males and females. It would be important if you could do columns on how women with different body structures should dress in order to highlight their best features for a more confident woman."*

- *"Your article came to me at the right time, being a father of two daughters and the first born is going into Grade Seven and from her outlook it seems she might be welcoming her red woman soon or later and your tips on how to handle it have really strengthened my ammunition. The contemporary girl child who gets her first visit from the "red woman" is more often than not, will find herself in total emotional disarray. Therefore, it is very timely that you brought this issue up. I trust that the Ministry of education through school teachers could play as important conduit to routinely address this important life event that girls must experience."*

- *"As a father of only boys, your piece particularly the part about how African cultures welcomed this life event has touched me. Being a doctor, I can perhaps recount some relevant facts about the difficulty of the red woman. Incidentally, pre-menstrual tension (PMT) which bothers many women in their prime of life, is far less overt when the society is cognisant of this condition than when it is not. Many girls who suffer from PMT may perform less well at exams and tasks that require enormous concentration should the latter coincide with it. Many women may have difficulties in the workplaces because of lack of understanding among fellow workers when mood swings overwhelm some during these "feminine visits". Many violent acts have been committed by women in state of PMT."*

- *"The recent article, "Girl You'll Be a Woman, Soon," reminded me of my pastor at a men's fellowship braai when he said that a woman needs to be huddled by her husband during her red period. The paragraph on Sharon and her husband, vexed my mind. My question is, "is it important for a husband to comfort his wife during her "red", and if so, what does it contribute psychologically to both parties. The reason why I ask is that it seems I am not comfortable to hold my wife during her red. Ndinotosema! - I am disgusted - holding a woman while she is having a period. At one point in time, she raised the issue, and I could not provide a satisfactory answer. I only managed to apologise."*

- *"Well! well! As much as we may want to evolve culturally and also embrace modernity, there should be somewhere where we draw the line. As much as I am a modern man and one who supports equal opportunities, I feel women should end at "acting" and not further. Honestly, sis, just imagine what will happen if the society Okays the whole idea and all of sudden women are free to walk to any men and propose. It will be almost like 'a ngoda in Chiadzwa rush - diamond rush in Chiadzwa experience.' There will be chaos everywhere and I do not want to imagine how it will be like. Anyway, thanks sis for a refreshing view - it takes away the mid-week hangover."*

- In closing, I say, women celebrate your bodies, celebrate the *red woman*, have choices, and create your own space, continue to celebrate life and womanhood!

Does Motherhood Have a Shelf Life?
10 March 2010

It is assumed that when a woman reaches a certain age or social standing, she is not supposed to have children. There are many assumptions about what the right age is to have babies, and medically speaking, having children in your mid 30s and 40s is believed to be unsafe.

Apart from these perceived medical problems, there are also some social and cultural issues/implications that can determine whether a woman can have or not have children above a certain age. Despite these medical warnings and social and cultural red tape, an Indian woman, at the age of 70, became the oldest mother when she mothered twins on 5 July 2008. In 2006, a 66-year-old Spanish woman, Maria del Carmen Bousada de Lara, gave birth to twin boys on 29 December of that year. However, she died less than three years on. Both women conceived through fertility treatment. When she conceived, Maria del Carmen Bousada de Lara said: "I have always wanted to be a mother all my life, but I have never had the opportunity or met the right man." A woman is sometimes left with no choice but to have children late in her life. Should a woman be deprived of motherhood simply because of her age?

While reasons for late motherhood vary, socially and culturally in Zimbabwe and other African countries, for a woman with grandchildren and grown children is not deemed right to be making babies. It is a cultural taboo. If a woman with a son or daughter-in-law decides to have children, it raises society's eyebrows. The general perception is that she has 'retired' from having children or engaging in acts that lead to conception. She is supposed to retire from lovemaking and leave it to young poeple.

The concern is that a grandmother who is still having babies will not have time to look after her grandchildren, as she will pay more attention to her own babies.

Is it fair for a 35-year-old woman to be deprived of conceiving or sexual fulfilment because of societal expectations?

When a friend of mine fell pregnant when she was a grandmother, one of our friends was very unhappy about it. Her concern was about the social and cultural implications it would have on the expectant mother. She asked her; "So when you have the baby what is your *mukwasha - son-in-law* going to think about you?" The pregnant friend replied: "He will congratulate me and say *makorokoto - congratulations.*" But the concerned friend was not satisfi d.

"*Makorokoto kuti maiiteyi? - Congratulating you for what? What were you doing in order to have that baby or to be pregnant?"* We all laughed but she took it very seriously and asked: "How could you an old woman want to compete with your daughter showing your son in-law that *'ndichirikuzvinzwa - you are still fit.* Instead of looking after your grandchildren here you are, competing with your daughter so that everyone knows what you are doing behind closed doors." She was naturally a humorous person, and we all thought it was one of her jokes, but deep down we could see that this had really affected her.

When we organised the baby shower for our friend, the mother-to-be, our concerned friend said she was going to be in charge of invitations. On the invitation cards she wrote, 'bring used clothes, no new clothes, anyone who will bring new clothes for the baby will be penalised.' I asked her why she was doing that, and she said: "We need to send a message to this grandmother, that she should not repeat what she has done. She should not embarrass us again!"

When I told this story to an elderly woman to seek her opinion, she said that in the olden days it was taboo for a woman who had a son-in-law, a daughter-in-law, or grandchildren to become pregnant. If she told family and friends that she had missed her period, they would perform what is called *ukuqunywa - to cut,* and she would go back to her normal cycle. I asked her if that was not abortion. She replied: "*Angizange ngitsho ukuthi wayekhipha isisu, ngithe waye qunywa - I never said she had an abortion, but she was just taken back to her normal cycle and a process called 'to cut' was performed"* She gave me the look of don't put words into my mouth.

Nevertheless, the old woman continued to explain that in case the woman did not inform family and friends soon after she missed her period and leave it until it was too late, some powerful women in the community would descend on her and ask her what she thought she was doing. She would be told as a matter of fact that people did not want to know what she did in her bedroom at her age to become pregnant, now everyone knew. From the way the elderly woman was talking, I was persuaded to think that she would be one of those women who would descend on pregnant grandmothers.

There are however many reasons why women are having children in late ages. Pursuing careers is one of the reasons. Due to economic empowerment, women now have the option to defi e for themselves when they should have families, rather than sticking to a schedule dictated by society. Climbing the corporate ladder in the workplace is also one other reason why a woman would leave having babies until later life. Employers are not always happy to hire women employees who will take time off to go on maternity leave when men do not.

Education and a stable job are great tools for women's economic empowerment. Women who are not fi ancially stable have not been able to provide for themselves and their children adequately. In some instances when the man is the only breadwinner in the home, he dictates what the wife and children should have. Not many people understand that a full-time mother is as good as working in fulltime employment. Due to this misconception, many women now decide to work outside the home so that they can provide for themselves and their children. When a woman fi ally decides to have children, it might be too late, and she will sometimes experience complications, or she might not be able to conceive.

Sarudzayi Chifamba Barnes, an author/publisher based in the UK and a mother of four children, had her fi st child when she was very young and not working. She had her other three children when she had a stable job. She says both experiences have advantages and disadvantages: "For me to have one child at the age of 17 and three children at the ages of 31, 35 and 37; I found that the experiences of motherhood were very different. At 17 I was young, career-less, insecure and relying on other people for survival. It was an emotional thing to have a baby when most of my friends were fin shing their O Levels and going to A Levels or tertiary education. However, apart from the obvious economic disadvantages and an oblique future, I found early motherhood rewarding in a way because I am very close to my son. It meant we 'grew up' together. I was also not in a relationship when I had my fi st child, so the experience is incomparable with the ones I had when I was married." She continues:

"With the kids I had in later life, I was fi ancially stable, which had a positive impact on my parenting skills and providing for them. I was not worried about a career anymore as whatever form of education I ventured into was kind of optional and not a necessity."

When I asked Sarudzayi what it means to her to have children, she replied: "Having children to me is a good thing as it fulfils my role as a woman. As you know, gender is a social construct; and one of the social expectations for a woman is to have children. Culturally too, this is expected as well. Biologically, I would like to think that the human life cycle is complete if we are able to reproduce. Th s is optional though. I think the most important thing is not how old one is when they have children, but are they able to provide for them? Unfortunately, in a capitalist economy, the convenient time is when one has fin shed education and becomes economically productive to provide for the children." she said.

Many women feel the same as Sarudzayi. Sandra, not her real name, was approaching her late 30's and had no children, she got her mother worried, because all her young sisters had children and her mother had seen how she was yearning to have her own children, but her problem was that she was not married. Her mother was a very conservative person, but Sandra was surprised that her mother indirectly encouraged her to have children if she wanted to. She was in a steady relationship with her boyfriend and decided to have two children with him as she felt the clock was ticking away. They married because of the children but the marriage did not last. Th s did not bother Sandra because all she really wanted was to have children.

Some women have not been that lucky when trying to conceive, several of them give up when they reach a certain age, but some do not. According to a report in the *Daily Mail* by Richard Shears - 8 December 2008, A 70-year-old Indian mother Rajo Devi, gave birth to her first child a girl after she had been trying for 50 years to get pregnant with her 72-year-old husband, who had failed to become a father in two prior marriages. It was undetermined whose egg and sperm were used in the treatment, the newspaper reported. Rajo became pregnant through in vitro fertilisation at a clinic in the northern Indian state of Haryana after doctors determined that she was healthy enough to survive a high-risk pregnancy. The mother and her infant daughter were reportedly both doing well.

While I was in the UK a few years ago, I met a Zimbabwean young woman who told a story of how her elder sister was having problems conceiving and how she was prepared to have her sister's egg planted in her womb and carry the baby for her. I also had some discussion with another young woman who she wanted to have her eggs frozen since she wanted to concentrate on her education and career and when she is ready to have a baby, she would retrieve her eggs from the bank! This was all new to me, but these are all alternatives to the traditional ways of having babies. Reproductive health, science and technology give opportunities for women to plan.

It seems there is no best time/age for a woman to have children, *E-How.com* reports: "Every age comes with distinct advantages and disadvantages for having a baby, meaning there is no one best age for everyone. Parents who have experienced having a baby in their teens, twenties, thirties, forties or beyond might all have their own opinion on what age is best. In determining the best age to have a baby, potential parents should consider many factors, including medical, financial, career and relationship issues."

For some women it might not be possible for them to have their own biological children, but still feel that they want to be mothers. Adoption is another option for one to be able to become a mother. Women, if motherhood makes you happy, there are many options to choose from. Continue to celebrate life, motherhood, and womanhood.

Mating Game: Go On, Play Your Part
24 March 2010

Last year while I was in South Africa I went into the bank, and I did not notice that my petticoat was showing. The woman at the enquiries desk asked: "Cecilia (my other name), is there any man whom you are trying to draw attention to?" I was surprised about what she was saying, and I said: 'What do you mean?" She replied: "Your petticoat is showing…" I laughed and said: "Okay, but what has that to do with drawing attention to some man?" She looked at me like, "You don't know?" And then I remembered… We both laughed and some young women who were there could not understand, the petticoat story.

Yes, back in the day a woman would leave her petticoat showing as a way to draw attention to the man whom she was interested in. It is amazing that this was a universal trend, which prompted fashion designers in the 70's to design skirts and dresses with petticoats permanently showing.

But my problem with using a petticoat to draw attention to a man whom one is interested in, is that one might end up drawing attention to the wrong man and the real target may not see it.

Th s is the problem that one reader Tinashe is having: he does not understand this acting business. Here is the letter he wrote in response to the article: *Do Women Have Choices, Space?*

"*Thanks for such a juicy article, very informative and touches everybody's life and I want to believe it touches all ages. I wish it had part one and two with part two focusing on how the cultural perception could be changed to allow women to play a part. Or, to advise women on how best they can "act" according to changing time. Joyce, you highlighted a very touching problem with women, especially well-to-do women, I mean women who sit in high positions at a tender age making them difficult to mingle with and talk to. I am a 35-year professional man and should admit, men do not rush to say something before they note some "chemistry" and so it is important that women should act to show the presence of some prospects. Obviously, there is a pair out there who does not know what to do. One is not sure how the other will react whilst the latter is confused and does not know how to act. People are the only creatures who have confusion, I have seen animals doing it from both sides a female proposing to male and vice versa. Go on write the second part of this article and finish off the suspense. How should women "act". How do we as men know that this is "action?" You are a researcher, get into the field. For your own information, the article will be more beneficial to men than women. Because I know men who have married the wrong spouses because their intended target's "actions" were not clear enough to be approached. I heard guys saying: "I wanted the friend of my wife but ended up marrying the wrong person". We have seen ladies' friendships ending because the friend intercepted an approaching gentleman and married him. Joyce, I think you have unfinished business here."*

A scientific journal peer-review study had hidden cameras in the ceiling of a large singles event with about 200 men and 200 women. They filmed the entire party, including who approached whom, who danced with whom, and who left with whom. Then the researchers replayed the tape and analysed it. They found most of the time when a guy came over to talk to a girl, she had subliminally "lured" him over with one "subtle signal" or another. Other researchers have come to similar conclusions where they found most of the time when a man asks a woman on a date, the woman had already sent off certain types of body language signals beforehand. Most of the time when a man gets rejected by a woman, the woman didn't actually send him these body language signals. Although men do the asking, there is supposed to be a type of fli ting traffi signal system going on:

1. Women select a potential;
2. The woman gives the man a green light (regardless of whether she is consciously or subconsciously aware);
3. The man has to take action or else she'll send signals to someone else;
4. If a woman is not interested, she will give a red light. (Physics Forums)

I interviewed some men to explain what they understood about acting, but there were going round in circles not because they did not want to come with a solution, but it is because of the complexities surrounding "acting." One man T.C, said: "It is important to know who you are and who you would want to be, it is only then that you can look for a partner - someone who compliments your vision, and it will be easy to understand who is acting for you. He also said there are men who also 'act', it is not just women, although men have other alternatives." He continued: "Why people do not make their intentions clear is that they fear rejection, but in the acting you must make sure you are portraying who you are."

Some young women that I spoke to feel this acting business is draining as one has to scheme, strategize, and the planning can be tedious. One said: "Th s takes a lot of time, and it can be draining. Especially if the acting is stretched it can be traumatic." She said she wishes the olden day's structures could be replicated where the intentions of the other part were very clear.

However, elder women and men I spoke to agree on one thing that, it did not matter which channels are used to propose and who proposes but the most important thing is to know each other well before becoming a couple.

Here are some more emails that I received concerning the subject:

- *"I have been following your articles in the Herald. I was so touched by the one about women proposing to men. I really see no logic in why men are against the idea of women taking the initiative. The world is changing, and I am sure ladies have choices.*
- *"I have just read your article in the paper about a woman who proposed love to a man. It really touched me, especially the way the man has responded. You have stated the ways, norms and the beliefs of the Shona and Ndebele people's culture of proposing love that was done long ago. It was the woman who proposed to the man that she loved. Culture is passed from generation to generation, which means those norms of proposing love to a man are still recognised in our culture although it is now being regarded as madness."*
- *"I have a question here Joyce. What is going to happen bearing in mind that Zimbabwe has more women than men? Of which the same women are looking forward to getting married by these men who have suddenly become pompous and very arrogant to us unmarried women. Who is going to marry those that do not get husbands? If these Zimbabwean men are too smart for Zimbabwean women, then let other men from other countries come to collect us and fall in love with all of us so that no one remains unloved. Everybody needs to be loved."*
- *"People do not want to face reality and do what had to be done simply because they are afraid of other people's opinions. They just fall in love because of chance especially for women and with the guys they are double minded about whereas the one they are looking for is there, simply because they don't exercise their freedom of choice. Love is all about choices both to men and women."*

Another article which created some debate, was *Get Out of Your Box, Celebrate Womanhood*. I wrote about *cycling*, but some people did not understand it and I had to do some explanation and rewrite the article. But they are those who understood what I meant the fi st time.

- *"Thank you for your issue. I understood it the first time and I must say it is really food for thought. Keep up the good work, however most women do not want to explore much in bed in fear of being called names by their husbands or being interrogated about where they learn new stuff. I am a young independent woman and I always communicate with my husband and tell him what I want, how I want it and when I want it. We have to be in charge of our bodies, be confident and celebrate our womanhood."*
- *You go girl. I truly enjoyed your article – I really did. It left me in stitches what with the Leisure Centre and the bewitching.*
- *I had such a laugh reading "Get Out of Your Box, Celebrate Womanhood." It was such a light-hearted easy read that rand as true of our lives as African women. I remember at one funeral vanatete - the husband's sisters - were*

questioning why I wouldn't sleep over at a funeral and that zvinoshoresa - it does not give a good picture - but my husband wouldn't hear any of that. He insisted we go home and come back early in the morning.

- *"The way you wrote your story "Get Out of Your Box, Celebrate Womanhood" - It is just about time that we demystify the anathema associated with sex. If we talk openly about sex, we might be able to reduce the AIDS prevalence rate by a certain percentage due to awareness. There are so many forms of enjoying sex that we can engage on. If we are to celebrate women and still think sex is something that can only be discussed behind closed doors, then we are not going anywhere. From your story there is a woman whom you said she later enjoyed what her husband had introduced to her, this actually liberates women. It gives them a sense of domination and that's where it should start from, and later to the open public where we treat women as equals not merely as sex objects and machine to produce children for us. I am a married men and a Christian."*

- *"The article on education inspired women not to give up on their dreams: I'm a 22-year-old lady who feels greatly inspired by your writings. Through them I've realised the immense value I possess as a woman especially the one you wrote on women as key educators in society. In 2008, when I started Mass Communication National Diploma everyone in my family was against the idea of a woman pursuing journalism as they argued that it's a male dominated field and it's engulfed by so much controversy. My father even insisted that I should take up nursing if I were to nurture enough womanly characteristics. Despite that I managed to successfully complete my studies and it is not until recently that I've gained more confidence in myself and the strength to carry on. I believe there is a hidden power behind your writings. Please do continue to revive the down-trodden spirits of our sisters."*

- *"I read your article "Women: Zim's Unsung Educators" in The Herald of 20/01/10 and what an inspiration it was. I was grappling with the idea of whether or not I should go back to school and when I read the article, I got my answer. Having thought about this I voiced my wishes to friends and colleagues and guess what some comments were quite discouraging, and I quote from your article, "It is important for women to associate themselves with people who will support them in order to achieve their goals..." This is so true, and I really got the momentum to actually embark on a course or two this year. I hope many women will read the article and also get inspired by people like Littah. I personally believe education is power and if invested in a woman even more so. Thank you."*

I am happy that some parents emailed me asking where they could enrol their girls to study musical instruments, it is important for women to know how to play instruments. They are places like - *The Zimbabwe College of Music*, Music Crossroads and Zimbabwe Academy of Music in Harare and Amakosi in Bulawayo.

There are also individuals like Mono Mukundu who provides lessons on his podcast and Lincholn Muchinga who also gives private lessons.

Of all the articles that I have written - *Learn to Be a Chef, Win,* generated a lot of interest. The response was overwhelming. One man wrote: "After reading your story, I am now motivated to amending my resolutions so that there is not going to be 'any malnutrition' in my house."

Thank you for the emails, which makes me laugh and sometimes cry. They help me learn and grow in my research and writing. The *Women in History* page was six months last Wednesday, this is my 29th article since 16th September last year. It is a month of celebrations - today at 8pm, I turn 52, and I feel blessed. I am wiser than last year. I will make sure I tighten the elastic of my petticoat so that it does not end up showing, sending wrong messages.

Women continue to have choices and create your own space and express yourself honestly; celebrate life and womanhood.

ARTICLE 12

The Dos, Don'ts, and Mysteries of Childbirth
7 April 2010

The birth of a child is something to celebrate in many families. But before and after the baby's arrival, there are many rituals to be observed by the parents-to-be, especially the mother.

Many factors have influenced change in many traditional customs in Zimbabwe and in other African countries. But many women still take seriously the rituals dealing with pregnancy, labour, and childcare. Even today, many still believe that herbs extracted from a certain thorny bush/tree that will have been pre-chewed by the mother and then spit into the baby's mouth are the best cure for infant stomach problems. Th s is known as *kutsengera*. Women who want to continue with this practice should take necessary precautions, since they may end up transmitting diseases to the child instead of curing it.

The future mother's family teaches many such customs. Women, particularly those pregnant for the fi st time, often return to their parents' home during the last three months of pregnancy, usually without their husbands. It is only the wife's blood relatives who are allowed to care for the pregnant women. For some women, pre-natal care means having a female relative checking to see if the path for the baby is opening, from the eighth month of pregnancy to the ninth month.

Many women consume herbs during the pre-natal and postpartum period. The herbs, taken from the barks and leaves of indigenous trees and from other plants, are pounded and consumed with either water or porridge. Some tribes cover the pregnant woman with a blanket to inhale the smoke from herbs over burning coals. The blanket is only removed when the woman is sweating, a sign that the 'cleansing' is fin shed. Th s 'cleansing' is believed to be particularly effective on those women who are likely to have been bewitched or have unfaithful husbands and conditions which are said to complicate a pregnancy.

When a fi st-time expectant mother is six months pregnant, she goes back to her parents so that they can administer some herbs, which will make it easy for her when giving birth. In the Shona culture this is called *Kusungirwa*. Th s is symbolised by a goat, which is brought by the husband's family to their in-law's home, and it is tied to a tree. The goat is then slaughtered on the *Kusungirwa* day. The ceremony is held as an agreement between the two families that the expectant mother will be left in the care of her parents and relatives of both families, and the community are witnesses to the formal ceremony.

The mother of the pregnant woman and other female members of the family, like the grandmother or an aunt, see to it that the expectant mother gets the necessary herbs that will make it easy for her when giving birth.

It is important for the expectant mother to go back to their parents in the third trimester of their pregnancy so that she can be looked after well, and the herbs can be administered properly. It is believed that if the herbs are administered while the pregnant woman is with her husband, they may not be that effective. It is assumed that some husbands may be secretly seeing other women, and this may cause the herbs not to work. While the woman is at her parent's home, she is not allowed to have sex with her husband, when he visits her, in case the husband "is not clean" as this may bring problems or complications for her or the baby.

While the expectant mother is at her parent's home, she also fi ds time to rest, as she is not under pressure to do work like a *muroora - daughter-in-law*, as she would at her in-law's home. Th s is also the time that the mother of the pregnant woman and some female relatives of the family teach the mother-to-be how she is going to look after herself and the baby, and other challenges that come with motherhood.

A story is told of an expectant woman who was not taken to her parent's home when she was due for *kusungirwa*. She had problems giving birth. Instead of the in-laws taking her to hospital, they asked her to confess all her infid lities, which she did not know of. They insisted that, if she did not confess, then she was not going to make it. The pain became more unbearable, she was in labour for longer than her body could handle. It was too much for her and she died. It was later discovered that she needed a caesarean or a C-section operation to be performed which is when an incision is made just below the bikini line. Her path was very small, and she could not have normal childbirth.

When a woman gives birth, she is still required to be at her parent's home for the next three months and for these three months she is not allowed to be near her husband or to be intimate with him. Elderly women say that this weakens the mother's breast milk, and it will not be that nutritious to the baby, resulting in the baby becoming *mwana anongoperezeka - a weakling*.

When the umbilical cord falls off both families are informed and discuss how it will be buried. The umbilical cord is very important in many African cultures. It has to be handled properly, depending on the family's traditions. Some tribes bury the umbilical cord at the entrance of their home; others bury it in the fi eplace. Most tribes whose totem has to do with water throw the cord in the river since their totem identifies with fish and throwing the cord in the water is a sign of respect for the spirits that will help ensure the child's health.

The fi al resting-place of the umbilical cord is taken very seriously amongst African people. Winnie Madikizela-Mandela, former wife of former South African president Nelson Mandela, was even using the custom as a reason not to hand over her house as a national historic monument. The house, where Mandela started his liberation struggle, is also where their children's umbilical cords are buried.

A mother who would have had the baby far from the parents or home must keep the umbilical cord and hand it over to her parents or in-laws to bury it properly.

The first day that a new mother shares the bed with her husband after a good six months - three months before giving birth and three months after giving birth - a ritual is again performed; this is called *kuyisa mwana pakati - putting the child in the middle* or *kuvhura mwana nzeve - opening the baby's ears*. What is said to happen is that the mother and father switch places, jumping the baby, and informing the baby that mom and dad will be doing grown up things. Then after jumping the baby, they finally do whatever mom and dad do in that room; that is opening the baby's ears. The ritual is to show respect to the baby by informing it what father and mother are about to do, as they share the room with the baby. Today most babies sleep in a baby crib but sometimes they share the bed with their parents. Sharing the bedroom with the baby is said to bring the parents close to the baby but it is also said to have its problems. We have heard stories of fi hts between the baby and the father. Some fathers have been pulled by the hair from the mothers' breasts, because the baby becomes jealous of the father using mom's breasts - their food as a pillow. Fathers who cannot take this challenge humorously, move out of the house and sometimes to 'small houses,' as they cannot handle the competition. As a result, they deprive themselves of the chance to see their baby grow.

A young woman that I interviewed who was taken to her parents for *kusungirwa* when she was six months pregnant and was to stay at the parents' house for another three months after the birth of her fi st child, says that six months is a long-time separation for couples. She said that when she had her second child, she was with her husband until the time she went into labour. She said that her child was as healthy as the fi st one. After six weeks they decided to open the baby's ears. There were no problems about the breast milk becoming weak and the baby losing weight as was traditionally believed.

The young woman did not understand why she was separated from her husband during her third trimester of pregnancy and the fi st three months after the birth of her child. She said that this is the time that she needed to be with her husband more than ever. But an elderly woman said it is important for fi st time mothers to be initiated into motherhood properly, whatever they will decide to do after that period will be up to them as the mothers, grandmothers and aunties will have shown them the way.

Besides administering herbs by chewing them and spitting them into the baby's mouth, the mother is supposed to do a ritual, which, supposedly, controls the sexual appetites of her baby later in life when they are grown up. The mother would express her milk on to the private part of her baby, this is known as *ukusengelwa*. It is assumed that if one becomes a sex addict, it is blamed on the mother not having expressed milk on to the private part of her son/daughter at a young age. The elderly will say: *akasengelwanga - milk was not expressed on to her/his private part.* Different tribes and African nationalities have different ways of doing this ritual.

There are some tribes who do not allow a woman to cook during the first three months of giving birth. There are many reasons why a woman is not allowed to cook during the first three months after having a baby. Whatever the reasons are, this allows the woman to rest and recover.

Mothering can be fun if everyone involved plays their part.

Women continue to celebrate life, motherhood, and womanhood

ARTICLE 13

When Geographical Location Defines Marriage
28 April 2010

Some years ago, I met a friend of mine in the bank, she was organising some traveller's cheques as she was about to travel overseas to her son's wedding. She said to me: "Th s is all your fault that I am now going to attend my son's wedding with a woman I hardly know." I said, "Why is it my fault?"

She said: "You did not encourage your daughter enough to marry my son." I laughed as I thought she was joking, but she continued.

"I don't know the background of this woman my son is marrying, culturally we are miles apart, the woman is not one of us ..." I interrupted her before she went far and I said: "I think you need to be open minded and accept your *muroora - daughter-in-law*, as long as your son is happy with her, that is what is important." As if she did not hear what I had said, and she replied: "I don't think I will be close to her as I would have been with your daughter. I am just going there because I have to give my son my blessings." People who were in the bank laughed, and she continued. "Can't your daughter do something, so that these two don't wed?" She was feeling desperate.

Some of the people who were in the bank joined in the conversation, some were supporting her school of thought, but some were not. Lucky enough this is a very small bank, and it can hold a maximum of just ten people; if it were one of those big banks then I would have felt very uncomfortable. Anyway, we left the bank with my friend, and I consoled her saying that her son would be fi e and encouraged her to embrace her new *muroora*. But every time I meet her, she still talks about it, although now I can see she is a little bit relaxed than some years ago, because she now laughs about it, and she says she loves her grandchildren. She does not talk much about her *muroora*, daughter-in-law though, maybe she needs time.

When I visited one of the countries overseas, I met some Zimbabweans who invited me to a kitchen party for a young woman who was being prepared for her new home. Her husband was also a Zimbabwean. As women took turns to speak and wish her luck, and teaching her how to look after her home, one said: "Th s is what we encourage - *kuroorana vematongo -marrying from the same geographical area*. Th s was followed by ululations, whistling and loud music and dancing.

But what do we mean by *matongo* - the ruins or roots of the same geographical area. It is a system, which evolves and develops means and ways to guarantee the continuity of a particular tribe or nationality. Even the old people who seem to be pushing it to the younger generation are also part of the system. No one really designs it, but it evolves, as a way to guarantee and ensure survival for one's culture, language, beliefs, and values. *Kunyengana vamatongo - to be romantically involved with someone from the 'ruins/roots' of the same geographical area*, is to create a society with values that will continue amongst one's kith and kin.

Vematongo means sharing the same geographical 'roots, language, historical background, and values.

Kuroorana vematongo is marrying from the same 'roots,' the same origins, and the same homeland.

As a way of ensuring the survival of one's culture some tribes have resorted to arranged marriages, or elders try to fi d ways of encouraging the younger ones to marry amongst their own community.

Farayi M a cultural expert had this to say: "There is little belief in love at fi st sight that it will last. Love is qualifi d in terms of both emotional feelings and material things. What is the husband bringing in the marriage and what is the wife going to bring. If you are part of the same *matongo, amanxiwa* or *ruins/roots,* it is easy to have this information and be able to qualify your love."

That is why in the olden days, elders would want to know whether a future husband was going to look after their daughter. If he did not have a meaningful job but worked hard, he would spend some time at his in-law's home working as payment for *lobola* and also to show that he was going to take care of his wife and children. Th s was called, *kutema hugariri - work in lieu of your lobola/bridal price* - a man working at one's in-laws to show that he is able to look after their daughter and also as a way of paying *lobola/roora - the dowry.* They would qualify him to see whether he would be a suitable husband to their daughter. The same would happen to the women, her in-laws would want to know whether she was going to be a good *umalukazana, muroora* or *daughter-in-law.* Both in-laws would do a thorough check on their families for things like witchcraft, laziness, family curses and so on. Th s was made easier if the families belonged to the same area.

There are traditional customs to be observed in every tribe and this is sometimes made easier if the two come from the same area. Despite putting structures in place to stop intermarriages, this has not always been successful.

A man who came from Mashonaland married in Matabeleland, and when he was introduced for the fi st time as *umkwenyana - the son-in-law* he asked for *amase -* thick sour milk. People were surprised, as this is taboo for a son-in-law to ask for *amase* on his fi st day at his in-laws. They later on grudgingly gave him the sour milk. According to Ndebele culture, a new son-in-law is not supposed to eat *amase* at his in-laws. It is described as *kuyazila - a taboo.* Further, in the Ndebele culture it is not allowed for the son-in-law to sit in the same room where in-laws are eating. It is also not allowed to greet one's in-laws using a handshake; a mother in-law and a son in-law are not allowed to shake hands and handshakes are not allowed between daughter in-law and father in-law. It is said: *"Umkwenyana akamelanga azwe inyama zika mamazala, or umalukazana akamelanga azwe inyama zikababazala - a son-in-law is not supposed to touch his mother in-law nor is a daughter in-law allowed to touch her father-in-law."*

A Zimbabwean man married to a French woman said his father nearly collapsed when he visited them in France, and his daughter-in-law hugged and kissed him. He said that his father, a traditional Shona man, did not know what to do, in his confusion he ended up hugging the daughter-in-law back. When I asked the father-in-law how he took it when his daughter-in-law hugged and kissed him, he said: *Ndakanga ndigere kuvona zvakadero - I had never seen such*! The family traditions had changed, as they now had to embrace the French woman's culture.

Tendai S says not marrying someone from geographical *matongo* got him into problems as he later discovered that the woman whom he had married was possessed by the grandfather (a male spirit). *"Kudoti amai seberayi kuno, wayitenge watopara mhosva - Even persuasively saying, sweetheart come closer, was taken as if I had committed some crime.* It was only when one day the Grandfather *"vaSekuru' - the male spirit* came out and asked for water in a male commanding voice that I knew that she was possessed by a spirit." He narrated his ordeal of how he had jumped out of bed to get water for *vaSekuru*. He told his in-laws about their daughter being possessed by a spirit, and he was told that her great grandfather's spirit possessed his wife. He was told that before engaging in any play they should ask for permission from *vaSekuru*. This did not go down well with him, and he demanded to know why he was not told when he married the woman.

He said that if it was someone from geographical area, the same *matongo* then he would have known about the *vaSekuru* as the geographical *matongo* facilitates family background checks and one can make informed decisions.

Edmore M tends to disagree with marrying someone from the same geographical *matongo* as he tried it, and it did not work for him. He is happy with his fourth wife who is not from the same area, but they share the same hobbies, and this has made their marriage a happy one. He had problems with all the fi st three wives who came from his area, as he was marrying to please the family more than himself. "I had to *kuzvirumura - wean* myself from my community and I said I will do what pleases me." He is happy with his fourth wife.

A woman who married a man whom she had a lot in common with as regards hobbies and work, had a rude awakening when the couple decided to locate back to the husband's home area: "He started going out with women from his home area and comparing me with them. He told me that I was not prepared enough as a woman." She found it difficult to belong and the marriage came to an end.

I spoke to two young women who are in the Diaspora; Mona and Lindiwe about how they feel marrying *vematongo* and Lindiwe said: "As for myself I will prefer to date men of other nationalities while I pray for my Zimbabwean brothers because they seem quite confused about their identity and exactly what they want. Most Zimbabwean women prefer marrying men of other nationalities because there is a general feeling that Zimbabwean men are mostly the same in the sense that they cheat on women. "They seem not to be satisfi d with one woman...I think they like carrying that Zimbabwean 'culture' of *small houses* and most women cannot stand that. They then prefer men from other nationalities such as Europeans and other Africans. Although they may cheat, the general feeling is that at least they will take care of them fi ancially and they respect women unlike Zimbabwean men, who at times act as if there are in a competition of who has acquired more small houses!!" She charged

Lindiwe continued to explain: "However, there are some women who prefer these brothers of mine. We are going to a Zimbabwean wedding next weekend. Such people can relate to each other culturally and at times just like the fact that they will have their roots and a lot more in common. "*Kazhinji vanhu vacho vanoti zvinozobhowa kuramba uchingotaura chirungu kubasa nekumba ndosaka vachizo prifeya Zim to Zim! - In most cases they say that it is boring to speak English at work and at home,* which is why they prefer to marry Zim to Zim! In a nutshell, the advantages of *vanoroorana vematongo - those who marry according to their geographical roots* are the cultural understanding, the language factor, the common factor that they will be both be Zimbabweans out to keep Zim generations going."

But her friend Mona begged to differ: "I am for Zimbabwean men because I know most men regardless of where they come from are into *small houses*. Women who are married or date other nationalities will not fi d out the bad side as these men are able to hide it and it is only known by their own communities. If one is dating a Zimbabwean guy news seem to travel fast in the Zimbabwean community because *tiri vematonga - we come from the same roots*. We hang around together and we speak the same language. Most men from other nationalities only present their good side and one is not likely to fi d out about the bad side because you are not part of their community; you do not speak their language, and you hardly hang around with them."

The meaning of *matongo - same roots -* has changed from its former defin tion, which was mostly geographically based. Today it can be hobby-based, work-based, religion-based, politically based, and so on. People who are into the arts industry might marry regardless of their geographical background because they share that same passion and the same work, and they would like to see the arts industry grow for example. But the most important thing is to know each other in totality and try to cover some of the gaps that did not initially bring you together. If you were drawn together because of your hobbies, work, politics, try to understand the geographical base of your partner. Try to understand how both your families operate, understand each other's culture so that you can have a happy marriage.

The whole idea of marrying *vematongo* is to have someone in your life that you have something in common with. Someone whom you share the same values with because marriage can be empty if it is going to be just *cycling*, and three course bedroom meals, and what do you do with all the remaining hours in the day? What do you talk about? What brings you together, and what kind of values do you share? If there is nothing that you share, the marriage collapses. That is why it is important to marry *vematongo* in its broader sense. There is also the saying which goes - *induku enhle iganyulwa ezizweni - one has to travel afar to get a good knobkerrie* – which means (one has to travel afar to get a good wife or husband)– Yet others would say ukhuni olungaziwayo kaluthezwa – you do not pick unfamiliar firewood and bring it home meaning you do not fall in love with an unknown man or woman and bring them to the family. Take your pick.

Women celebrate life and womanhood to the fullest.

Getting Rid of The *Kanga* & *Mamba* Styles
19 May 2010

In 1997, I went for a *Gender and Journalism Course* in Swaziland. One of our assignments was to go to a nightclub. We went to a very popular nightspot in Swaziland which is well known for striptease shows, mostly performed by women strippers. Our task was to observe and write about the atmosphere in the nightclub, as journalists from the region. I used to hear about these striptease shows, but it was my fi st time to see one for myself. The assignment was made easier by one of our male journalists, who started sweating as he watched the ladies perform. As if they knew that he was not feeling well, one of the women strippers came to him, as if she was going to sit on his head. He shivered and looked very confused. We, the other journalists, and I, looked at him and could not understand how such a grown-up man could be so disturbed with something that we thought was familiar to him. Yes, it was unusual to see such a thing, but his level of excitement and reaction worried us. When the stripper left, we asked him why he was acting like a teenager, yet he had told us that he had three children. He said: "I have never seen this. Th s my fi st time." We asked him: "What about your wife?"

He answered: "In our culture we are not allowed to see the fruit we eat. It has to remain under the *kanga - a Zambia* or *chitenje - the printed cloth that women wrap around from the waistline to the toes, or sometimes from the chest - above the breasts - to the knees."*

We could not believe this and thought he was joking, but he repeated what he had just said, as a way of confi ming it.

A young male journalist asked, "Are you saying that you had all your three children under the *kanga*?" He answered him with a big, "Yes, I did." The group of journalists could not help but laugh. We had a really good laugh. When we went back to class the next day, we handed our report/write up, and our friend was the headline. The facilitator asked him to explain what we had written about the nightspot and about himself, and he repeated exactly what he had told us. He explained, in detail, how things are done in his culture, and what he had seen at the nightclub. He said it very innocently. Life was never to be the same for him regarding how things are done. The *kanga* was not going to be needed. But how was he going to introduce the 'new way' of doing things to his wife. How was he going to tell his wife that, after all, it could be seen? How was he going to tell her that things had changed? Was he going to perform a strip-tease show?

I thought this only took place in other cultures, and yet closer to home we have similar situations. A friend of mine that I had not seen for almost ten years tracked me down and one day she gave me a surprise call from overseas. We went back in time and tried to make up for the ten-year gap. When we were about to conclude our conversation, which had taken almost an hour and half, I could tell that she wanted to tell me something. She said to me: "You know I am tired of living with a *mamba*." I said to her, "I don't get you. What are you saying." She said, "Yes, I have been living with a mamba all these years." I was shocked and surprised, and asked her whether she was keeping snakes as goblins. She laughed, a sad laugh, and then she said: "I wish it was so, then I could send it to get me some money. But it's not." I could not make head or tail of this. There was silence, and then she went on, "You know what, I don't think I know my husband. He is like a *mamba* - a fast-moving snake to me…." I asked her what she meant about that.

She explained" "Before I know it …he is done, and I just feel weepy. I just want to cry and the way he holds me I just feel as if I am suffocating…. I don't know whether that's what he calls love". She was getting emotionally charged.

I nearly dropped the phone laughing. I noticed that the other end of the phone was quiet. I stopped laughing and let her go on: "You can laugh, it is not your fault. Laugh. You remind me when we were young. You still have that laugh." She also started laughing, and then she went quiet. I wanted to continue laughing, but I was now struggling to control myself, because the other side had gone quiet. I asked her why she was not telling her husband that she was not happy with his *mamba style*. She replied: Th s is how it had been for as long as she can remember - more than 25 years! Jokingly I said she should go for an X-ray, as she might have got her bones broken by the *mamba style*. I asked her how she now knows that was not the right way of doing things.

"Are you seeing someone? Who has shown you 'new ways'?" I asked.

"That is why I am afraid of telling him that I am not happy with the way he is doing things. Because he will think that I am seeing someone. He will ask me who told you we were not doing it the right way. What will I say? But you know what, I have never felt good about it but…"

From our conversation I could tell that she had had many things to deal with in the past twenty-five years or so; her career, raising children, wanting to be a good wife and mother - that was her focus. All she wanted was a good home for her children, and she would suppress emotions to achieve that. How time flies! Now all her five children were grown up - some are working, and some at university. She was now left with her husband and, whatever happened, they had to face and confront it without the children coming between them. I encouraged her to build up her guts and to be open with her husband in order to replace the *mamba* with something good. It seemed she was fi ding it difficult to discuss this issue with her husband. How was she going to tell her husband to get rid of the *mamba* style? That what they have been doing for the past twenty-five years has not been right? What if the husband asks how she came to know that it was wrong? Who told her?

If her husband does not compromise, she might end up cheating, or she will stay miserable, and one day she may do the unthinkable. I told her the story of an eighty-year-old lady who one day surprised her family, the *vakwasha, varoora, vakwasha zukuru - in-laws, grandchildren and great grandchildren* and many other relatives. The husband of the old lady had died when she was fi y. A reptile or insect visited the old woman, and it went under her dress. One of her grandsons tried to remove it. She was not amused and asked the grandson to leave it alone. The grandson was worried, but the old lady said to him, "When did your great-grandfather die, young man?" "I never saw him," he answered. He was told to leave grandmother alone and go and play. The grandson left, not knowing whether what he had seen was a reptile, insect, or his great-grandfather who he had never seen. The old lady had gone back, thirty years. She had lost it. She was now in her own world. The *varooras - daughters-in-law* were puzzled. They only commented when they had regrouped, away from the old lady, and said: "*Zvinhu izvi hazvina zera, nhai - There is no age limit to these things of sex.*" Grandmother had had a massage of a lifetime. At least the story thawed my friend, and she laughed. We then said our goodbyes, she was still laughing, and the phone cut. Yes, it was time. We had talked for almost 2 hours.

The challenge the journalist and my friend now face is how to introduce new ways of doing things to their partners? Where does one start, after having realized that, for years, you have been doing it wrong? The source does not matter - whether one saw it in Swaziland, on television, read about it, or just the feeling that one has as a human being - which things have to be done differently. How does one prevent friction and suspicion, and make one understand that all you want to do is improve your love life with your partner? How do these two introduce this delicate subject and succeed in getting rid of the *kanga* and the *mamba*?

A friend who I asked said: "In that room you just become yourself. Pretending can have dire effects on one's soul. You may go out there and pretend things are okay, but unhappiness will be written all over your face. I have always been myself, and I get what I want, and I also respond to what he wants. Th s has been our relationship, and we know how to communicate with each other." She has been married to her husband for 30 years. Th s one is really a care-free spirit.

To my journalist friend, and those who are in the same situation as his, I went on the internet and I found this comment by a David Strovry - *AskMen.Com-Dating & Love*: "Despite rumours, more often than not, women are actually deviant sex goddesses waiting to be released from their good-girl prisons. The main factor when introducing new games to the bedroom is preparation. There should be very few surprises. This means - oh yes, you guessed it - lots of talking… preferably before you leap into bed. Timing is not everything, but rates highly. Educating her is paramount. Making it seem like her idea in the first place is simple genius… if you can pull it off."

Partners should strive to communicate effectively and have a happy love life.

Why It Does Not Pay to Be a *Mamba*
2 June 2010

I have received a lot of mail and phone calls regarding the article, *Getting Rid of Kanga, and Mamba Styles.*

Most of the people who phoned and e-mailed me seemed to confi m what my friend who was going through the *mamba* blues for almost three decades.

Her story opened a Pandora's Box on how couples are living together, and yet do not know each other. Some of the stories are 'unbelievable.' It is amazing how the stories are almost the same: "After 20 to 30 years women become brave enough to tell their husbands that they had been *mambas* all along."

Several men lamented that their wives of many years are only coming out now after living together for 'centuries,' accusing them of being *mambas*.

The question that they are asking is: "Why did it take so long?"

Most of these couples have fin shed raising their children and the women, at this point, are not worried about the consequences. I asked some women why they suffer alone and in silence for all these years.

Some of them said that in the early stages of their lives they tried to talk about it but then they were silenced.

It brings a lot of tension in the marriage, so they would rather keep quiet. But some said it is because of how we were raised as women - to bottle things inside - and wait for the day everything just explodes.

A couple who realised that their marriage was going over the edge after being married for 30 years decided to go for counselling.

It emerged that the woman was also an accomplice, in 'encouraging' her husband to be a *mamba*. During the sessions she realised how she had approached the marriage - being too submissive - and the husband, instead of seeing a human being, saw *nyama yekugocha -braai meat.*

The old lady who gave her counselling encouraged her: "*Kuvewo chikara kana pava panyaya idzodzo - you should also become wild when it comes to it - those issues.*"

I think what she meant was that she should neutralise the *mamba* spirit. The way she addressed her husband was of concern as she addressed her as *Va ...* or *Mr* or *Baba Va... father of...name of their child.*

She said that this alone creates barriers in a marriage and advised them to address each other by their fi st names.

Maybe, because of culture, they could create other lighter/pet names for each other since addressing each other by their children's names created some of the barriers in their marriage.

Now that those same children who they were using as shields are grown up and have moved out, they did not know how to deal with each other, one-on-one.

Most men who wrote to me said they were desperate to try and get their wives who had left he marriage - not physically, but spiritually and emotionally, back.

In the eyes of people, they are married but, between the two, it was over. One man said when married couples allow communication breakdown to go on for too long, with the man thinking that he is on top of the situation, it will one day result in him getting a rude awakening.

An extreme case was of a man who admitted that he was a *mamba* for years, and regrets how he had lost two wives because of his lack of *'bonde etiquette'* - *bedroom etiquette* and he wished he could turn the clock back. But he said that there was a reason why he became a *mamba* - he wanted to create male children - boys: "I was told that if the woman scores before me we will create a girl-child, but I wanted boys.

He went on: "*Unfortunately, despite what I was advised to do, the mamba style in order to create boys, was all in vain and I had three girls instead. I thought let me try someone else, another woman. We had our first girl, but I did not lose hope. My mother had warned me and vowed that I was never to get a boy because it was me who was creating the children, and not the women. She was not happy that I had left my first wife because she gave me girls. She said, 'Ndiwe urikuvadyara vana ivavo. Handiti ndiwe urikuisa mbewu yacho. Haufe wakamuwana mukomana nemaitiro auri kuita'. Hezvo ndiripano. - You are the one who creates these children. You are the one who is planting the seed. You are the one who is creating girls, it is not your wife and, I bet you, you will have a girl with your other woman."*

He explained further: "Yes, I had a girl. I was disappointed. One day I went back to my fi st wife, who had tried all means to get me back. That day I planted a seed, and it came out a boy but, for some reason, I was not sure he was mine as I had not been with my fi st wife for a long time."

"I went back to the second wife, and we had another girl. I gave up. Because of the way I treated her, she left me - I had been a real *mamba*. She even took the kids away - to the Diaspora. When I tried to go back to the fi st wife, I realised she had moved on. I have not seen her with anyone, but she has moved on with her life. I am so lost, I am so lost . . . and, when I visit her, my son is the one who spends most of the time with me."

I asked him, "He is your son now, how did you know? Did you go for DNA testing?"

I was reminding him of what he had previously said about his son. He responded: *Zvirikupiko Sisi? Anobvunzwa here iyeye? Takafana zvekuti...I was just being silly sis-*

ter. We look so much alike. He is just like me."

It was clear that it was this scoring game that had confused him, he had not been sure whether he had scored first, or it was his wife. To him, males were only created if he scored first, but he should have known better.

Some of these stories make people laugh, and cry.

This is how science explains how the sex of a child is determined or is made: Each person normally has one pair of sex chromosomes in each cell. Females have two X chromosomes (XX), while males have one X and one Y chromosome (XY). Half the man's sperms carry the X chromosome and half the Y. If a sperm carrying the Y chromosome fertilises the egg, then a boy is conceived, and if a sperm carrying the X chromosome fertilises the egg, then a girl is conceived, it's that simple. It is the man who determines the sex of a child.

After this brother of mine had poured his heart out, I could feel that what he wanted now was to get back with his first wife.

What I liked about most of the e-mails is that most men who responded to the article are trying to make amends and take responsibility of their actions, and what is disappointing though is that some of the women who feel that their husbands are *mambas* are not forthcoming when it comes to looking for solutions to their situations.

Women take charge.

ARTICLE 16

Unpacking Stormy In-Law Relationships
16 June 2010

The relationship between mother and daughter-in-law is one of the most complicated relationships. Tension, suspicion, competition, and all sorts of animosity often characterise this relationship. Some of the problems that mother, and daughter-in-law create or fi d themselves in are not necessary, they could be avoided.

In the olden days in order to create a positive environment between mother and daughter-in-law, it was advised that they become familiar with each other before the daughter-in-law gets married to the son. Before a daughter-in-law got married a relationship would be created between *umamazala lomalukazana, amwene, nemuroora - mother-in-law and daughter-in-law*. Some of the *omalukazana, varoora - daughters-n-law to be* would go to their *mamazala, amwene, mother-in-law-to be* and show her that they were interested in her son. The mother-in-law would alert her son that there was a woman who was interested in him and this way they would develop a close relationship. That way mother and daughter-in-law would develop a relationship of mother and daughter instead of 'mother/daughter-in-law' typical relationship.

A man whose mother and wife were always at each other's throat asked members of the family and *sahwiras - close friends of the family* to try and diffuse the tension. Part of the delegation was the mother's younger sister who seemed to have a good relationship with the wife and could represent her elder sister. The daughter-in-law explained how her mother-in-law was treating her. Some of the problems were that the mother-in-law would always ask for money, she was controlling, ungrateful, and jealous of the daughter-in-law. The list went on and on. The elderly people who were trying to help them solve their problems asked her to try and understand that her mother-in-law is coming from a different era, than hers. But she answered and said that there were mothers-in-law who came from her era that did not have problems with their daughters-in-law. She was asked to explain some of the things that she was not happy with in detail, and she mentioned how her mother-in-law pays them unannounced visits and asks for money, even during the month before they get paid. She could not explain the controlling in detail, but she complained that she was controlling, and she was ungrateful: "Even if we give her the money during the month, she is still ungrateful." She was asked how she welcomes her mother-in-law when she visits them, and she said she was not able to hide her unhappiness when she made these unannounced visits. She was asked whether she and her husband put aside money for her since they know her problems. She gave an answer, which the delegation was not satisfi d with. When she explained about how her mother-in-law is jealous of her, they were again not satisfi d with the explanation.

The young sister of her mother-in-law asked her to bear with her mother-in-law as she had a very troubled marriage, which might be the result of her actions: "Do not judge my sister too much *muroora. Mukoma wangu akatambudzika, nababa wemurume wako. Iwe unoti nhumbu yese yawaita murume wako anenge aripo, uchimuyemera, muchibatsirana. Kumateneti anenge aripo, musi wekuzvara chaiwo anenge ayinewe. Mukoma wangu uyu ayingoitiswa nhumbu otozowona murume mwana atorumurwa akutomhanya. - Do not judge my sister too much my daughter-in-law. My sister suffered because of how your husband's father treated her. She was not lucky as you, who whenever you are pregnant your husband will be there giving you support. Even when you go to the hospital, and when you deliver, he will be there. Whenever my sister got pregnant your father -in-law would disappear, only to surface when the child has been weaned and already able to walk and run around."* Th muroora did not see why she had to understand this, and she asked: "So what am I supposed to do with such a situation? Am I supposed to get her a boyfriend? She can go and check herself into the old people's home and get one. *Inga varikuchata wani kuma-homes* - people are still getting married in old people's homes." Th s statement was shocking to the elderly people who had come to try and solve the problems, but as shocking as it was, they laughed, and the younger sister of her mother-in-law said: "*Uku ndiko kusekerera nhamo kunge rugare - This is to laugh at problems as if all is well.*"

The mother-in-law was not that old that she could check herself into an old people's home, she looked old because of the problems that she had, had. When she had her fi st child her husband lost interest in her. Even if the elders tried to sit him down and told him that his wife would be back to normal, he lost interest although he would be back when the baby had been weaned and impregnate the wife, then disappear. The elders had explained to him that his wife would get back to normal in three months or even earlier than that, but something terrible had gone wrong in his mind regarding childbirth. He decided to spend his time with women who were not disturbed by childbirth. As a result, the mother in-law did not have many children, she only had three, two girls and one boy. With this background they asked the daughter-in-law to bear with her mother-in-law. The daughter-in-law would not budge and one *sahwira - family friend* said: "How many times have you had your husband?"

She replied: "I have lost count."

Th *sahwira - family friend* continued: "Now your mother-in-law can actually count how many times in all the forty years of marriage she has had sex and you have only been married for ten years and you are saying you have lost count? Don't you think it's too much for her?"

The daughter-in-law reiterated: "That is why I said she should check herself into an old people's home and get someone." The daughter-in-law went on to say that she missed her father-in-law because he was more understanding than her mother-in-law but the *sahwira - family friend* was quick to remind her that *vaiwana zvese zvavaida nebonde - Your father-in-law got everything that he wanted including sex*.

The meeting however managed to resolve some issues, but some were not easy to resolve and maybe with time they would fi d solutions. What at least was resolved was that the daughter-in-law would ask her husband to put aside money for the mother-in-law every month.

Women that I spoke to suggested that the relationship between a daughter-in-law and mother-in law has problems because some daughters-in-law do not take their mothers-in-law as their own mother and vice versa. When these two meet they should remove the tag 'in-law' because it conditions one's thinking that she is not my daughter, she is not my mother. A woman who has a great relationship with her mother-in-law said: "If you are close to your mother what makes it so difficult to be close to your mother-in-law? Maybe they could be both be difficult people, but they must be level-headed enough to drive the relationship and be willing and be prepared to make the other one see the light and come to their senses.

Another woman said most of the daughters-in-law who have a great relationship with their mothers-in-law do not live a pretentious life. Being yourself does not mean you do not kiss your husband when she is around, but you have to be sensitive. Being yourself does not mean you do not display that picture you took on holiday in a swimsuit with your husband, but you have to be sensitive. Being yourself again does not mean you do not go around your house singing when she is around, but you have to be sensitive, and being yourself does not mean you do not tell her that *'amai kana muchiwuya pano munonditaurirawo - mother when you are coming to visit, please let me know?'* You must be sensitive and say and do whatever you do in such a way that does not hurt her. She explained that her mother-in-law was a very difficult woman, who would visit unannounced and demand her son's money, and would make some remarks just to put her down, like: "*Imba yemwana wangu - this is my son's house.*" Ignoring the fact that the wife had also contributed to buying of the house. She explained that her mother-in-law did a lot of things that she could not even start narrating, but she sat her down and told her, her piece of mind in a very fi m but gentle way and even convinced her to be involved in income generating projects: "I leant her money to start her own business and I am the one who now goes to her and 'demands' money and say *'muroora tipeyiwo mari yamurikushanda - my daughter-in-law give us the money you are making,* Playfully calling her mother-in-law a daughter-in-law and switching their roles to make the conversation easier."

It is not all mothers-in-law who ask for money just for the sake of asking money. Mrs Chimutengo - a daughter-in-law had this to say: "There are mothers who when they raise their children especially sons, look forward to being looked after as they would have put all their resources on that child. I think as today's generation we need to understand that and meet our mothers-in-law halfway."

One daughter-in-law said: "I encourage my children to buy my mother-in-law and my mother presents on Mother's Day and to just say thank you *gogo makatizvarira baba/amai - thank you grandmother for giving us a father/mother*." She said, just this gesture has made her the talk of the town and at her mother-in-law's local church and community. But one woman who tried to do the same to her mother-in-law said she was so hurt as the mother-in-law threw away the gift and said: *"Murikuda kuvhariridza kudya kwamunoita mari yemwana wangu.- You are giving me these gifts as a cover-up for your abuse of my son's money."* Th s became a very confusing situation.

Mothers and daughters-in-law who treat each other as mother and daughter enjoy their relationship and are there for each other. A woman whose husband passed away a long time ago, looked after her mother-in-law and for her she is like her own mother.

Mothers and daughters-in-law should try to meet halfway and try to understand each other. Mother-in-law don't put your anger on your daughter-in-law. Whatever you were not able to achieve during your heydays it should not be your daughter-in-law's fault. Encourage the love between your son and your daughter-in-law. You should actually be happy because they will be breaking the circle of what you failed to do with your husband and breaking a circle of unhappiness that the family has gone through is very important for future generations.

Maybe your daughter-in-law is saying in sarcastic manner that you should check yourself in a home and get yourself someone, but if you think you did not enjoy your life with her father-in-law maybe she is right check yourself into a home and get that old *madala - the old man* and have fun. Maybe not necessarily checking yourself into an old people's home but there are plenty of them around if you take your time to look and let your son understand that you have to cover the gap that his father left and be happy. If you are close to your *umalukazana/muroora, daughter-in-law* she can talk to her husband and say: *"Siya amai vafare, isu tirikufara wani - leave your mother to live her life, we are living our lives and, we are enjoying ourselves."*

Mother-in-law and daughter-in-law always remember the biblical story of Naomi and Ruth -Ruth 1:1-5, Ruth 1:6-18, Ruth 1:19-2:2, Ruth 2:1-17, Ruth 2:18-23, Ruth 3, Ruth 4.

I quote: "Naomi knew that Boaz shied away from women. When she returned to Bethlehem after ten years of absence, Boaz was amazingly still unmarried. However, the way Boaz interacted with Ruth convinced Naomi that Boaz found Ruth attractive, but that he just could not muster the courage to propose to her. Naomi took the role of matchmaker. When Ruth sneaked into Boaz room when wine had made him to sleep... and they whispered their true feelings toward each other. Boaz honoured her boldness by praising her support to Naomi her mother -in-law, as well as her coming to him first. Arriving home, Ruth excitedly shared the romantic story with her mother-in-law."

Can sisterhood get any better than that?

Hazards of Cheating in a Relationship
30 June 2010

The response on last week's article; *Hazards of Cheating in A Relationship* was overwhelming. A brother of mine phoned me and said: *"Sisi, nhasi andiende nepepa kumba, nekuti nyaya yamanyora ingandiparire zvimwe. - My sister I am not taking the newspaper home because what you wrote today can cause problems for me at home."* I asked him what he meant, and he said, he had been having problems with his wife. It all started when she had seen him with a female colleague whom he had given a lift. He explained that the woman was a colleague and there was nothing between them; but his wife was just making an issue out of nothing. I advised him to convince his wife that there was nothing between them. He replied: *"Amheno ndikazvigona, asi pepa ndotosiya nekuti ingabva yasimudzirwa - I don't know whether I will be able to convince her, but I am not taking the paper home."*

The next day he phoned me saying that when he got home, the newspaper was the bedcover on their bed, and the wife was reading the article. He knew she wanted to talk about the issue of the woman that he had given a lift too. He said to solve the problem he suggested they use one car (the wife's car), and she would have to drop him off and pick up after work. The wife found that arrangement cumbersome, it would be too much for her, but she made it clear that she did not want to see any woman she did not know or whom she was suspicious of in her husband's car. When I spoke to the wife she said: *"Vatete I have to fight for my man, its winter, andidi kurara ndakabata teddy bear sendisina murume, atorwa. Auntie, I have to fight for my man, its wintertime, I don't want to end up sleeping holding a teddy bear, as if I don't have a husband, when others will have snatched him."* She had a point about wanting to be with her husband during wintertime, as it has been scientifi ally proven that whatever the *leisure room* provides can protect one from colds.

About fi hting for her man, a psychiatrist Dr. Gail Saltz seem to agree with her: "If you sense your partner may stray, then get moving on protecting your union. Ask him more of what he wants with you, sexually and emotionally, don't let him hang out with her without you, don't stay at home angry and pouting and giving him both opportunity and impetus. Tell him what you really love about him."

When I opened my email box it was full.

A woman in her mid-40's wrote: "The reason why women cheat especially in our age group, is that during our prime time, we are given a script of how to act by society, and we do what they want and when the curtain closes, we become ourselves. When I say when the curtain closes, it is when our children are grown up and we are free, we start doing what we want."

It seems they are many women out there who are nursing grudges and are waiting for the day to come. Th s is becoming a serious problem and it is frightening, but this is what is happening, when women have raised their children and they feel they have nothing to lose.

A woman who had a cheating husband and had tried to leave the marriage, but her parents and relatives could not have any of that also waited for her children to grow up. When her children had all left the country to study overseas, she one day left her home pretending that she was going to South Africa. In fact, she had actually gone to the UK, and got a job working as a nurse. She has been in the UK for 8 years, and the husband is still hoping that one day she will come back him. That was her way of communicating, and of ending the marriage.

One other woman wrote: "I enjoyed reading the article you wrote which was in the Herald. Really communication is the best tool to use in all relationships and in any set up, *kubasa, kumba, kupi zvako - at work, at home, wherever*. Most husbands prefer revealing wrong things done by their wives to their *small houses* and the *small houses* improve because they have been communicated with.

Another added: "I must say it's a very educational piece of an article which l found interesting and very serious in our society. Most of the things, and in fact all of the points held or mentioned are of value and need to be looked into seriously. With this day and age, and with our life expectancy so low, high levels of divorces, child abuse, financial crisis etc. l think to reach to a larger population such education is needed to be given to the people. Yes, not all cases will be solved but a few will, and the better. Now-a-days people are not afraid to catch the deadly disease. People talk only of HIV/Aids but there are other diseases which are equally deadly such as Hepatitis B.

Yet another: "Sometimes the way the society labels some way of life *ndizvo zvine effect kuhunhu hwedu vanhu - this is what has an effect to our way of life*. For example, cheating among men *hunonzi hugamba - is said to be heroic* whereas when a woman is cheating *hunonzi hunzenza - it is said to be of loose morals*."

Another writer said: "I seem to be in a tight spot with regards to my marriage and I want to try and save it. I am the one who sort of messed it up and my wife is failing to forgive me. It's so bad at the moment and very soon we might be going for divorce. I still love her."

Dr. Gail Saltz advises: "Adultery need not be the end of a marriage, though it certainly is one heck of a wakeup call. If you are contemplating an aff ir, then there is no question you will be SORRY! Aff irs hurt everyone, including you. You cannot keep both women, so you will be distressed at some point."

A brother of mine who I grew up within Mbare phoned me when he read the article. He was narrating to me what a happy life they now have after he came to his senses and resolved the problems that he had had with his wife which had led to both of them cheating on each other, resulting in her leaving him. In 1995, I met him, and he had just gotten back with the wife who, not only had she left him, but they had actually divorced. When he realised that he wanted his wife back, she was pregnant from another man but, nevertheless, they talked, and he took her back. When he told me this story sometime in 1995, I looked at him without commenting and he said: "I know, like everyone else, you want to ask about the fate of the child my wife is bringing back into the marriage." They had had two boys before the breakup. He said: "Children come from God, and she is my daughter. I love her. I also love my wife, I realised that she is the only woman that I really love." They were later blessed with a fourth child, a boy. The reason that he wanted to be part of the discussion is that he wanted to tell couples to realise and hold on to what they have before it is gone. "Cherish what you have." He said.

Another email I got read: "When she went away for a year, I started seeing some-one else just for sexual pleasure and when she came back, she discovered the relation-ship and also started seeing another man. We both stopped outside sexual life, but the bedroom life is still having ups and downs. If I try to kiss her, she is not interested, even if I try to hold her, she does not want to be held."

All they now do in the *leisure room* is straight *cycling* and nothing else. Why she is letting you at least cycle with her is because the whole thing has become physical and mechanical, so kissing and caressing will be the last things that she would want. It also depends on how you kiss. You might wonder why I am asking this question, but it is important to have proper skills with regards to kissing. It might seem easy, but it is not, and many women get very irritated with kissing. Some women that I have spoken to about kissing say that kissing is like intercourse. Some men rush to put their tongue inside the mouth, and this is irritating.

A friend of mine was sent a book on how to kiss by her sister and when she invited me for tea, she said: "Can you imagine…. my young sister has sent me a book on how to kiss. What is it about kissing that is new? *Kiss i-kiss chete - a kiss is kiss*." I asked her if I could see the book. I read to her some of the tips on kissing and I summarised them:

'*Wash your mouth before kissing. Applying scented gloss on your lips; (munch munch)*

Look at the lips of your partner and love them and play with them. Caress the lips

Take time admiring each other… When you finally kiss take your time before you put your tongue in the mouth.'

I pretended I did not see that she was responding to what I was saying, and I told her I could take the book if she did not need it. She would not let me.

She asked: *"Saka zvinhu zvese zvinotodzidzirwa nhai. So, everything in life has to be learnt?*

I responded: "Yes, and in this book, it also says that when kissing is done well, you and your partner can cruise to another world and reach your destination with just kissing and when you come back it will be siesta time."

So, my brother it depends on how you are kissing her and how you are holding her. *Kudzidza hakupere, ukufunda akupeli - you can always learn a new thing every day, including kissing and holding.*

When you have cheated and you want your partner back, try and do as much as you can to win back their trust, including testing for sexual transmitted diseases.

Cheating Kills Relationships
7 July 2010

According to interviews and talks that I have done, it has emerged that all forms of cheating are as a result of poor or breakdown in communication among couples and spouses.

A wife only came to know that her husband was sending money to his mother when the mother visited them and thanked her daughter-in-law for the money she was given by her son. At fi st, she looked surprised, but composed herself and pretended to have knowledge of what her mother-in-law was talking about. When her husband came back home, she asked why he gave his mother money behind her back, and the husband responded: "If I had told you, you would not have allowed me to give her." That is why he had to 'cheat.'

A woman who sends her parents money every month without her husband's knowledge said she wants to maintain peace in the home that is why she has to cheat and send the money without the husband's knowledge. She said that she tried to rea-son with her husband that her parents are old, and they do not have anyone to look after them, but her husband did not want to understand. As a result of this she has to support her parents behind his back - 'cheat.'

Financial pressures have in some ways led to serious breakdown among spouses. Both men and women say the families' budgets and family business like starting new projects or (something new) sometimes put a toll on their marriages as they end up carrying the discussion to bed. To avoid the discussion, they cut all communication when going to bed, until there is no more communication. Th s creates a void in the marriage, and they drift apart. Financial problems and squabbles and any other issues in a marriage, if not attended to can lead to the breakdown of communication and cause a lot of problems for a couple.

To compensate for the problems or cover the void left as a consequence of the drift they go out to seek solace and they end up having aff irs or other relationships. Most of the aff irs/relationships are for sex and a shoulder to cry on. Some outside the marriage associations can be driven solely for sex purposes.

Th s is coupled with a breakdown in communication and also not understanding sex. A woman that I talked to about this issue gave a very interesting example: "The way sex was presented to us is the same way we were told about giving birth. We were told that giving birth is not even compared to the pain you feel when you touch fi e, the pain was presented to us as not comparable to anything in this world. So as a result, when I gave birth to my fi st child, I was expecting pain *yawusati wamboona - that pain that is out of this world*. The second child it was the same and the third one, I knew *ndakanga ndakunzvisisa kurwadza kwazvinoita* - I now understood how painful it was." She went on: "That is how sex was presented to us, we expect something that is out of this world, until we are tired of going in circles then we realise that it is what you make it with your partner."

Failing to figu e out what one wants and communicating it to their partner has created certain myths in the *leisure room*. When the breakdown occurs each one ends up going their way, looking for what they are not getting or what they think they are not getting in the marriage or relationship.

Some men I have spoken to complain about monotony in the *leisure room*. They then decide to go out and get excitement with other women. They complain that when they introduce 'new ways' of doing things their wives are not forthcoming. However, when I spoke to women, they said it is because of the way these 'new ways' are introduced. They are not happy about the men culturally having an upper hand on the *dancing floor* and controlling the *dance*, but sometimes it is about not being sensitive on how they introduce *new dancing* styles. Consequently, men go to other women, who in most cases are familiar with what they want, and they fulfil their excitement.

Other women complain about their men leaving them for younger women and this leaving a void in their lives. A man who has been happily married to his wife for 35 years explained a bit about these men who leave their wives for younger woman: "These men are the worst lovers but because they want to prove themselves to young women who are still fi ding their feet trying to understand what love and sex is all about. These men are scared of their wives who are now experienced and who will demand what they want. To the young women they will be heroes as they will splash money and show her one or two exciting styles and the young woman is swept off her feet. It is when she starts demanding real love and real sex and quality time, then she is left or someone younger."

Researchers have discovered that; When men have aff irs, they tend to be motivated by sex - new sex, more sex, different sex. Women cheat for many reasons: companionship, romance, more security, and, of course, sex.

Studies show most men who cheat want to experiment sexually and experience the rush associated with 'new sex.' Th s is their way of prolonging indefin tely the early and intoxicating phase of infatuation in a relationship. But men also have aff irs to either avoid intimacy, recover their lost youth, or escape an unhappy marriage.

Men who fear intimacy will have aff irs to maintain power in their relationships. If a man doesn't commit to his lover, he controls his level of vulnerability. Some men cheat in fact to avoid any real intimacy. Intimacy scares them, so they distance themselves from their wives by cheating on them and they don't get emotionally involved with their lovers. Th s way they never have to trust their partners or rely on them. Th s kind of man may also fear confli t according to Dr. Gail Saltz.

Why do women cheat? The simple answer is because they hurt. They have pain related to loneliness, the rejection and betrayal of a cheating spouse, an unexciting and unsatisfactory relationship, or feeling poorly about themselves.

Elaine Sihera a sociologist and lifestyle coach says: "Loneliness is one of the primary reasons that women seek out aff irs or are susceptible to advances. Women who are in an unsatisfactory relationship may feel even lonelier than if they were still single. A partner who is over involved with his work or hobby may severely limit the attention and admiration he gives to his mate."

A woman who was hurt by her husband ended up cheating and when her sons suspected that their mother was cheating with someone whom they thought was the family accountant, they beat up the man. Their father told them to leave the accountant alone. The sons were surprised with the way their father was defending their mother, but if they knew the story how it had all started, then they would have understood but they did not. The story goes like this: When the wife came back home from overseas where she had gone to work for two years to raise money for the family business, she got a box delivered to her with a wilted carrot inside the box. There was a note accompanying the wilted carrot, written; "*Izvi ndizvo zvamainga kumba asikana. Hapasisina. Takazomugadzirisa murume uye ayifunga kuti akangwara - This is what you have come back home to my dear. We fixed this man, he thought he was clever.*" The box came from one of the women whom the husband was going out with.

It is said when playing time came in the main room, there was nothing. The woman tried to have sex using *plastic - condom* since she was trying to protect herself as she had heard about the multiple affairs her husband was having. Nothing materi-alised; the cooking stick had gone kaput.

Although the husband was also suspecting that his wife was cheating on him, he would rather leave it alone, but the children did not have the full picture of what was going on, so they are the ones who felt they were being cheated on.

When the topic of cheating was discussed in one of the hairdressing salons that I was in, one asked a question: "Why do women cheat, why they don't leave the marriage if they are not happy?"

A woman answered: *Zvirinani kuva imbgwa yemuridzi pane kuti uve imbgwa inokudubura mabhini - It is better to be someone's dog than to be a dog, which goes around looking for food in street bins*

Another woman said: "*Amai mwana imbgwa inochengetwa ikabatwa nemuridzi yaba nyama inorohwa kunge ichatotadza kufamba. Saka munenge mahwinei nhai asikana - My dear, when its owner catches a domesticated dog stealing it is beaten and, in most instances, will not be able to walk. What would you have achieved my dear.*"

People in the hairdressing salon laughed and another woman added her voice and said: *"Inokudubura mabhini ikange nani nokuti inotiza - The dog, which goes around looking for food in streets, is better because it will run away if it sees danger."* The laughter continued with no further comment.

Whatever reasons women and men give for cheating; if a woman is caught society is most likely not able to forgive the woman and would rather be sympathetic with the husband. If a man becomes a serial cheater, it is sometimes qualified by society as 'our culture' – 'our tradition' and then later the affair is given a name - *small house*.

A marriage counsellor/therapist advises couples to keep communicating until they understand each other, because cheating is a lot of work: "The strategizing, the scheming, sometimes people have to disguise themselves, by the way they dress, make up, wearing hats even if they do not want, putting on wigs which cover the face, and so on. The places that they go to *musango momborumwa nemasvose, motsvaga kumwe, moenda muhotera mowona murume wako kana mukadzi arimowo mese motiza - one of the meeting places maybe the bush where they are at times beaten by termites, book hotels and sometimes meet their husband or wife who will also be cheating, and they both run away from each other."* We have heard stories of men and women who have ended up exchanging underpants the man getting home in the girlfriend's G - string and vice versa. It is a lot of work." She added: "It is better to talk to your husband or your wife or partner until she/he gets it, that it is worth the try compared to the work one goes through when cheating."

Communication is key to a prosperous relationship.

There's more to Love, Than Control, Fear
28 July 2010

To those who wrote, phoned, sent messages with regards to last week's topic *Children: Innocent Victims of Divorce*. Thank you, I will get back to you in due course. Today I would like to follow up on some responses to the article *Cheating Kills Relationships* which has resulted in the introduction of this new topic.

A friend phoned and said: "You know what, tell your *muroora - sister-in-law* that this might be the last winter that she will be with her husband, if she continues treating him the way she does. Tell her that she will not even sleep holding her teddy bear because it will remind her of her husband and all the other things they used to do."

I asked: "What do you mean?"

She replied: "She is a control freak."

I promised to arrange for my friend to meet my sister-in-law so that she could tell her personally.

We all met as arranged and my friend said: "You do not control a man like that, my sister. How can you be suspicious of every woman your husband gives a lift " There was some silence. My sister-in-law was kind of shocked and felt a little bit challenged. My friend looked at me and said: "Don't encourage her." I did not understand how I was encouraging her, and felt I was just getting caught in the crossfi e.

My *muroora* was quiet for a while, and then said: "Is there anything wrong in me protecting my marriage?"

My friend, with a very serious face, said: "You are not protecting your marriage, you are driving him away." She continued: "Do you know how I got my husband? I got him from a woman who was controlling and insecure. One day she came to work and made a scene, nearly beating up a girl who had been given a lift by her husband. She traumatised the young girl to the extent that you could see her shiver whenever she was talking to the man, even on work-related issues. The poor girl was very innocent, I tell you. One day the man gave me a lift. I had even forgotten that he was not allowed to do that by the wife. Innocently, I got into the car. Again, she came to work and made a scene. I think she had a spy at our workplace. I told her my piece of mind, and she saw that I was no pushover. *Ndakamupeta muswe. I 'folded her tail,' I silenced her.* I looked at my sister-in-law, who shook her head sideways, and laughed. I also laughed. "Now that she could not harass me, she started harassing the husband, at home. As a result, the husband started feeling unhappy and scared of going home. He started confidi g in me on what was happening. He was now looking for solace and comfort.

Th s was not her only way of controlling. She would even listen to telephone conversations that he received at home. She was just insecure. We started getting closer to each other and now we are husband and wife. *Tatozadza imba - our house is full of children*. My sister-in-law looked at her with 'talking eyes,' and then she said: *"Hamusi makanga matotaimira nechekare here nhai vatete? - Isn't it that you had it already planned, or you just manipulated the situation auntie?"* My friend answered: "To tell you the honest truth, I did not have any feelings for him…I did not even have any. If I had, I would have said it. *Ko ndini ndatanga nazvo? Would I have been the first one to manipulate a man?* But it was because of this controlling and insecure woman. She drove her husband into my arms."

My sister-in-law, sarcastically said, *"Mukati zvauya zvega - And you said to yourself 'Here manna from heaven?"*

To which my friend answered, "Yes," confide tly. My sister-in-law then asked what my friend was going to do if her husband started giving lifts to other women. My friend said that she was not going to lose sleep over such a thing. But, before she left, she reiterated to my sister-in-law not to confuse love and control, or control and love.

Th s reminded me of an incident that happened when I was young girl in my home suburb of Mbare. *A sahwira – a family friend* came to our place and called on my mother. She was in a hurry. She said: *"Amai Joyce-wo, ndati ndikuudze shamwari kuti ukanzwa kuti kunemukadzi arova mukuwasha muchimana chino ndini - Mother of Joyce, I have come to tell you that if you hear of a woman who has beaten up her son-in-law in this suburb, it's me.* My mother came out to fi d out what it was all about. She continued: *"Handingaroverwe mwana nokuti zvanzi amhoreswa. Mwana wangu akamuchera mumugodhi here? Handiti akamuona achifamba munyika munevanhu? - I can't have my daughter being beaten up just because she has been greeted, by a man. Isn't it he found her walking in a country which has people?* He did not get my daughter from a mine?" After saying this she went on going where she was going; to beat up her son-in-law, her *mukwasha*! My mother followed her and tried to restrain her and calm her down. She was fuming and meant what she said. When they got to the *mukuwasha's* home, the *mukuwasha* locked himself in the spare bedroom. She fi ally calmed down, and she told her *vanamukurungai – the in-laws* of her daughter, that she did not want her child to be a punching bag for their son. She told them that if he has a problem with his wife being greeted by people then he should go to some mine and dig out a wife who has never lived among people. *"Ngaaende anochera mukadzi wake asingamhoreswe mumugodhi. Kana achida kuita Dhuri (a boxer), ngaaende mugiraundi anyatsonorwa nevanoda zvezvimbokoma" - He can go and dig up a wife from the mines, who will not be known by people, and will not be greeted. If he wants to be a boxer, he can look for those who are interested in boxing and fight them.* The in-laws asked for forgiveness on behalf of their son. In the end the marriage between the two did not last.

When we were discussing this incident with some of my fellow 'Mbareans' who knew the story, one man said: "That man was very insecure. That is why all he could do was to beat up his wife for being greeted. That is insecurity and controlling. A real man is not worried about such things. For some of us, who grew up with our grandfathers around, we were taught how to treat a woman. It does not matter how many men greet her per day, I just know that she will not go anywhere. *Mukadzi aneshamhu yake yaanorohweswa. Haaite ma-black-eyes, but unotoona maziso ake achipenyerera. Ndizvo zvatakadzidziswa nanasekuru* - (There is a stick that is used to beat up a woman with and she will not have black eyes, but you will actually see her eyes shining with happiness instead. That is what our grandfathers taught us). People who were around laughed.

We have heard stories of men who beat up their wives because they have been greeted. Th s becomes such an issue but, to avoid having their wives greeted I think, as my mother's *sahwira - friend* said, "They should dig up their wives from the mines."

A cousin of mine told me a very interesting story of a woman who went berserk when her husband looked at a woman who was crossing the road at the traffi lights intersection. It became a big issue: "Would you not be angry?" She asked. The response: "He was just admiring her, and that is all. The problem with making it an issue is that you start bringing out what he had not seen, and you activate his mind. He might start wondering why you are acting that way, and then start having some ideas. Admiring does not mean you will fall in love with the person. It is just like when you see a dress and admire it, you do not buy it, you are just admiring."

Another friend of mine who was part of the discussion said she had the same experience with her husband who had also looked at a woman, and she had not been comfortable with it, which resulted in a heated argument. She said the husband then said: "I want to give us an exercise. Let us go to the mall, and let your eyes see and admire anything from clothes to human beings. We were to then compare notes after two hours. When we met, I wrote down what he had admired, and he wrote what I had admired. I told of some men that I had seen, he asked me to describe them, and I told him the three men were handsome, and whatever I had admired about them. He jotted this down and he said we would go back there after two weeks. He asked me to describe the men again in two weeks' time, and all I could remember is that they were handsome. I could not describe anything else about them as I had done the fi st day. My husband said: 'You cannot explain because you were just admiring. It is like a menu. When you are given to choose you do not buy everything, because you have specific things that you would want to eat. But if I had made it an issue, then you would be chasing after one of the men now.' I asked him how I could be chasing after the man I had only met at the mall, and he said, 'If we had fought about it, the energies we sent out there would make you meet the men again and then start analysing them and getting ideas, even stripping them naked in your mind.' I laughed when he said that."

She said and continued to narrate what her husband had said, "Anyway those men you saw, it was me, your handsome husband. But you were admiring me through these men.' Yes, I looked at him, and he was the most handsome man that I had ever seen. And he said to me, 'Do you want to ask me about the woman at the traffic lights?' And I said, 'Yes.' He said, 'I have forgotten how she looks like, because I was just admiring, and I know what I want - it's you.'"

This was confirmed by another friend of mine. For some reason, she is no longer interested in Zimbabwean guys, and she is married to a foreigner. I asked her if she does not find Zimbabwean guys attractive at all, and she said, "I admire them. There are times when I see someone and I cannot take my eyes off them, and I say to myself, 'Oh, what a hunk!' - and that is all. It is like you look at a menu, but you do not order everything, you admire some of the dishes, but you do not order. It is the same thing with admiring people - you don't have to order. I already ordered from the menu - my husband - I love him very much. But, you see, I do not have blinkers. I am only human."

Control and love are two separate things, which one are you comfortable with?

The Worlds of Menopause, Andropause
1 September 2010

Changes that occur during midlife for both men and women can cause confusion and anxiety, as when men and women reach a certain age in their lives, they go into new worlds known as menopause and andropause. When women are in their late 40's they start experiencing changes in their bodies. These changes are as a result of the *red woman's* visits disappearing; they start off by becoming irregular - the fl w might be heavier or lighter and with time they completely cease to exist. When the *red woman* stops visiting for 12 months; a woman goes into a world called menopause which is a normal part of life, just like puberty. According to a medical journal: "Menopause is the time in a woman's life when her period stops. It is a normal change in a woman's body. A woman has reached menopause when she has not had a period for 12 months in a row (and there are no other causes, such as pregnancy or illness, for this change). Menopause is sometimes called, "the change of life." Leading up to menopause, a woman's body slowly makes less and less of the hormones, oestrogen, and progesterone. Th s change often happens between the ages of 45 and 55 years of age."

The common signs and symptoms of menopause are:

*Hot flashes:

Hot flashes are the most common symptom of menopause. When you have a hot flash, you'll feel warm from your chest to your head, often in wave-like sensations. Your skin may turn red, and you may sweat. You may feel sick to your stomach and dizzy. You may also have a headache and feel like your heart is beating very fast and hard.

Help for hot flashes:
- Turn your thermostat down. Sleep in a cool room.
- Dress in layers, so you can remove clothing when you get too warm.
- Wear cotton and other natural fabrics that "breathe" so you don't get overheated.
- Use cotton sheets on your bed.
- Drink cool water or other beverages when a hot flash starts.
- Get plenty of exercise.
- Find out what triggers your hot flashes and avoid them. Spicy foods, alcohol, tight clothing, and hot humid weather are some common triggers.

*Vaginal dryness:
During and after menopause, the skin of your vagina and vulva (the area around your vagina) becomes thinner. Your vagina also loses its ability to produce as much lubrication (wetness) during sexual arousal. These changes can lead to pain during sex.

You can use an over-the-counter water-based sexual lubricant (such as K-Y Jelly) or moisturizers for the vagina area (such as Vagisil) to ensure sex less painful. You can also talk to your doctor about the benefits and risks of using prescription oestrogen cream for vagina changes.

*Urinary tract problems:
You're more likely to have bladder and urinary tract infections during and after menopause. Talk to your doctor if you have to go to the bathroom often, feel an urgent need to urinate, feel a burning sensation when urinating or are not able to urinate.

- Headaches, night sweats, trouble sleeping, and tiredness are other symptoms.
- Trouble sleeping and feeling tired may be caused by hot flashes and night sweats that keep you from getting a good night's rest.
- *Weight gain. *Many women gain weight during menopause. A healthy diet and exercising most, if not all days of the week will help keep you fit. (www. revolutionhealth.com)

Medical research has discovered that men also sometimes suffer from the same midlife symptoms that are often associated with menopause. Although the debate continues, medical evidence strongly points to the existence of the *andropause* - the male counterpart to menopause. While it is not as obvious an event as the menopause, men do suffer from declining hormone levels as they age.

With menopause, women's sex hormones decline rapidly over several years, usually in their '50s. The decline in sex hormones in men starts from their '30s but decreases much more gradually.

As one doctor, Dr Tony Vendryes, on radio POWER 106FM explained: *"Women fall off a cliff, while men sort of roll down the hill. After the age of 30, today's male may lose up to two per cent of the function of his testicles each year. Up to 50 per cent of otherwise healthy men over 50 have low levels of testosterone."*

"An increasing amount of evidence points to an aging-related hormonal change in men that corresponds to the hormonal change in women known as * menopause*. Some call it "male menopause," which is not entirely accurate but still gets the point across: Much the way women's oestrogen levels drop after a certain age, men's testosterone levels decrease with age. Testosterone is also known as androgen, and many doctors prefer the term "andropause" for this male condition."

Menopause involves a sudden and dramatic decrease in oestrogen that marks the end of a woman's ability to conceive a child. Men, on the other hand, do not lose the ability to father a child. Men in their 80s have fathered children.

Still, andropause is in many ways similar to menopause. The symptoms are remarkably similar to those experienced by women in menopause, including moodiness, fatigue, weight gain, depression, decreased sex drive, decreased muscle mass and bone loss. (www.MedNewsReports.com<http://googleads) (http://www.mednewsreports.com/NightSweats/)

A woman might lose interest in activities to do with the *leisure room*; this might be psychological or associated with health issues. Some women believe that when the *red woman* stops visiting them it is not safe to *cycle* or participate in any other forms of playing with their husband or partner.

Dr Louise Foxcroft encourages women not to continue with old-fashioned beliefs about menopausal: "*We need to stop repeating outdated assumptions about menopausal women', new research suggests that women in their 40s might be having the best sex of their lives. Well, wake up, what's new?*

Older women have always known this but keep pretty quiet about it because of the mud that is hurled at them if they speak out. Look at our society's emphasis on youth and beauty and the way it despises signs of age; witness the furore when an older woman behaves in a sexual way and lets on that she still likes sex and wants it.

A quick glance at the history of female sexuality reveals the roots of this potent taboo. The idea that older women have little or no interest in sex can be traced back to the 19th century and beyond. Some doctors recommended that women gave up sex completely when they hit 40 and believed that love should be banished forever from their hearts once they were approaching menopause. Drugs such as camphor were prescribed to help with unwanted sexual urges. Women of our grandmothers' generation were even thought of as insane for loving sex. But today we can say that sex is better when you are older because of experience, independence, relief from the risk of pregnancy and, frankly, my dear, just not giving a damn."

While there are women who when they reach menopause, they become more interested in the *leisure room* activities as this is the time, they know what they want, some men are not keen on playing with their wives or partners when they go into menopause, as the men might not be aware of their menopause status - andropause. Some men would rather date younger women who unfortunately their blood will be at its boiling peak and the old man might not be able to fulfill the needs of the young woman. The old man ends up taking some aphrodisiacs like an overdose of Viagra or go to the popular 'Mupedzanhamo Market' for an equivalent of Viagra. (*Mupedzanhamo Market* is a popular market for all sorts of Viagra concoctions/ aphrodisiacs in the Harare, Township of Mbare). We have heard stories of men who have died while in action as it becomes overwhelming for the body to perform, and the heart fails to keep up with the pace induced by aphrodisiacs.

An old man who decided to date a younger woman had to sustain the relationship by taking aphrodisiacs, but one day it backfi ed. Th s way he was assured that he would satisfy the young woman and feel like a 'real man.' He said: *"Tuvakomana twake twese nditukunde, tusa tombo svika pedyo naye - I want to outdo all her young boyfriends so they do not come near her and completely take over."* Th s is according to those who narrated the story.

While there were busy in action the old men's heart stopped beating. When he was informing the Almighty and his Ancestors that he was on his way, the young woman must have thought she had done a splendid job, but just minutes later, the young woman was left with a cold corpse in her arms. The kicks were not for enjoyment but there were for kicking the bucket. Dying. The old man had achieved one thing though: *Tuvakomana twake twese akatutandanisa - He had chased away all her boyfriends*, as she was to spend years going from one traditional healer to the other, *'Kuti abviswe munyama - in order to be cleansed.'*

Age gap might not really matter in a relationship depending on the circumstances, as long as you are prepared to meet each other halfway in whatever you do.

The old man had taken it too far, his body wanted to take it easy, but he forced it to the limit and his heart could not take it anymore; it stopped beating. Playing is supposed to make the body relax and not to strain it. Men should also start taking it easy when they go into the world called andropause and go for milder ways of playing.

According to the site wwwdoublemenopause.com: *"All midlife couples face turbulence. It is a matter of degree and preparedness that makes the difference between those who separate and those who compensate. By sharing our goals with our partner, we can make the quest for healthy longevity even more fulfilling and life enhancing. By achieving optimal living as a couple, each partner can become each other's coach and can harness the unique, irreplaceable elixir that love has to offer."*

If your partner has gone into menopause or andropause and you have not, please meet him/her halfway; were there is love there is a way - you will fi d ways to make each other happy. Just massaging your partner sends shock waves all over the body and that way they can reach their wonderful destination and come back to you alive and relaxed.

Despite ailments and discomforts that come with midlife changes or crisis such as menopause and andropause one can still live a healthy and have a happy life.

Secrets and Issues of Virginity
15 September 2010

I have been receiving emails pertaining to issues of secrets in marriages and how this has destroyed and led to unhappy matrimonies. Some of the issues are by men complaining that when they married their wives there were not virgins and were not told the truth and later to fi d out that they had been lied to in order for the woman to get married. Some say that they were not only lied to about issues to do with virginity but also discovered much later in their marriage that their wives/husbands had out-of-wedlock children and children during marriage that they are secretly supporting.

Here are some of the emails:

A man wrote to say he had an interesting story, but he wanted assurance that his name would not be published, and I gave him that assurance.

• *Ndatenda zvangu amai. Dambudziko rangu ndeiri. Ndiri mukomana tichikura pane musikana akanga aine mwana wake wandakadanana naye ini ndisingazive kuti ane mwana wake. Pandailodger vakamufururira kuti asadzokera kumba kwavondikagara naye. Kana neni handina kuita dambudziko nazvo nekuti ndaimuda. Avanepamuviri ndakazoziva kuti akanga aine mwanawake. Ini ndakanga ndisinakumborara nevirgin girl kusvika ipapo. Hapana zvandakakwanisa kuita nekuti anga atakura mwana wangu saka ndakagara naye. Takaita mwana mukomana,tikaitazve musikana, iye zvino tavenemusikana zvakare. Asi munozivao hapanamurume asingadi kumborarao neVirgin.Ini nazvino zvinondidya moyo. Ndakudanana nemusikana ane about 26 years iye anoziva kuti ndine mukadzi, ini ndichimuudza kuti mhuri yangu ndinoida. She is willing to do it ndiwo mukana wanguo. Mungati ndinopaita sei. - Thank you mother. My problem is some time ago there is a woman I fell in love with, I did not know that she had a child. One day when she came to visit me, she did not go back to her home, she fell pregnant. We had a baby girl, then a boy, then a girl. But I had never slept with a virgin girl. As you know there is no man who does not want to sleep with a virgin. This eats me up. Now I am in love with a 26-year-old woman, she knows that I have a wife and three children. She is willing to do it with me and this is my opportunity.*

What do you think? I have replied to my son, but he has not yet come back to me. Please someone out there help him.

Here is another letter:
* 	*First and foremost, I would like to say that I enjoy your Herald columns very much. Sisi, I am a 45-year-old married father of four. I love my wife and family very much and together we have achieved so much. Honestly, I would not change anything about my family life for anything now. However, there is an issue that has been haunting me for the rest of my life and I would like to off-load it on you for some help. When I married my wife, she was not a virgin. At that time, we briefly talked about it, and she said this had been caused by sporting activities at school, not sexual intercourse. To be honest, it was not an issue to me then. However, later in life, this issue kept creeping back into my mind and still does so up to today. For example, even if we are watching television, and the word virgin is brought up, one can actually feel the tension in the room between us! In my mind, all I am saying is that she did not tell me the truth, therefore, I am wondering why she could have lied to me. Sisi, this issue is eating me. I have brought it up once or twice with her and her story does not change and these further eats me up! Sisi, I am not saying that she has been up to anything suspicious - no. If anything, she is the best thing that ever happened to me, but this issue just sometimes clouds my feelings and respect for her. Don't tell me to sit down and talk to her because I have done that before, and I get the same story. But the story is just unbelievable. Sisi, does sport destroy virginity to the extent that when you have 'secret entertainment' for the first time, you just glide in? What can I do to get this sensitive issue out of my mind? Please help, I am getting out of my mind.*
*

Yours,
Baba T

This was my reply to the writer:

My dear brother,
I know we all have wishes and dreams in life, and for you one of your dreams was to marry a virgin. But not all dreams will come true, and you did not get one (a virgin). And you also think that she is not telling you the truth how she lost her virginity. It is true that a woman can lose her virginity through sport. Why do you think she is not telling the truth? Let us say she is not. What you must also understand is that sometimes women lose their virginity in very painful circumstances and for them to forget that episode they would rather coin a lie which will help them to 'heal'. I have heard of women who lost their virginity to a close member of their family, and they lie on how they have lost it in order to protect the whole family or they are raped, and they never told anyone about the rape, so they would lie about it.
I think you must be grateful for having a good wife as you say this is the best thing that has ever happened to you. Breaking virginity is a one-day aff ir and then what?

I have received emails from men who married their wives as virgins, but they are not happy at all. As much as it is encouraged for people (both men and women) to keep their virginity we should also bear in mind that they are unfortunate circumstances that people fi d themselves in and they lose their virginity. What you are feeling my brother is in your head and you really need to remove it and enjoy what the Almighty has given you; a good wife and four children. You also have to be careful that your wife is aware of what you are going through and one day she will move on, maybe not leaving you physically but you will grow apart, and it will be very difficult to bring her back from the world that she will have gone into. Women are very patient people, but when they move on, they move on. Count your blessings and love and enjoy what you have. Life is too short.

All the best
Sis Joyce

Baba T replied:
Dear Sisi Joyce.
I think you have helped me to put the whole thing into perspective. I have weighed my blessings over the not-so-blessings, and you have helped me realise that I have more blessings than anything else. I am now calling my wife to tell her how much I love her and how blessed I am to have her. I have not done this for a while now.
Thank you and God bless you.

Regards,
Baba T

But why do men want to marry virgins? An old woman that I interviewed said, "It was/is to do with status in the community for the two families - the one who marries a virgin and for the family were a virgin is coming from. It brought joy to the two families when people say - *mwana wekwanhingi akabvisirwa 'mombe yechimanda - so and so's daughter's husband paid a cow to confirm that she was a virgin – mombe ye-chimanda –cow for chimanda.* That was not all, the family of the husband would also send people early in the morning to take a full blanket and a full coin to the doorstep of the girl's family. When the parents woke up in the morning to open the door, they would see the blanket and the coin, confi ming that their daughter was a virgin. If she was not, then they would make a hole in the blanket and also a coin with a hole in the middle (there were coins like that up to the 70's), this would be a shame to the family of the daughter who was not a virgin when she got married".

But some chose to disagree, "I think that men just think it is cool to be the fi st one to penetrate a woman. It's like they've conquered something, done something that no one else can ever do after them. It's like a (weird) source of pride, knowing that your woman has never been with anyone else. In reality, her past doesn't matter to any man who is comfortable with himself."

Another woman said: "Have you not heard men say *ndinechipwanya ma-bhonzo changu, my chicken in the basket*, meaning a young delicate woman? It is about conquering."

However, there are men who love their wives regardless of not having defl w-ered them. Th s reminds me of a story which happened in the 70's; this is a story of true love. A man who married his wife and paid whatever was supposed to be paid including '*mombe yechimanda*' and one early morning sent his relatives to take a full blanket and a full coin to the doorstep of his in laws, who would see it in the morning as soon as they opened the door and this would confirm that their daughter was a virgin. This went well as he had done his part as a *mukwasha* - son-in-law. One day the man was approached by a man who said to him: "*Inga uri bharanzi chairo! Ungabvisire 'mombe ye chimanda' munhu wandaiita chikorobho changu, asi akatosona kani? Chakanga chirichi korobho changu chiye. You are such a fool! How could you pay 'mombe yechimanda,' to confirm that your wife was a virgin and yet she was my 'broom' who used to clean my 'floor'? Did she go for surgery to piece it up or what?*"

He boasted but the man replied, "*Inga uneshave rehurombe chairo waikorobhe-sa ne-'velvet', manje 'velvet' iye ndakayiyendesa ku-'dry cleaner' ikabuda 'shine', saka ndakabvisa chimanda - You are real low class, how could you use velvet to clean your 'floor', you see what; I took the velvet to the dry cleaner and its shining, that's why I paid 'mombe yechimanda'* [the cow to confirm that she was a virgin.] Velvet material was in fashion in the 70's.

(Velvet was expensive to make before industrial power looms became available. It is thus considered for the elite class and associated with high status.) The man looked stupid as he thought that using the women's sexuality to destroy her would spoil things for her, but it did not. Yes, the husband knew that his wife was once in a relationship with the man who had approached him. He married her also knowing that she was not a virgin, but he loved her, and he wanted to 'protect' her, from his family, her family, the community, and society. The woman says her husband has never brought up the subject, no matter what. It does not even crop up in any of their discussion, she said: "I thought one day when we are angry with each other he would bring it up, but he has never."

Some think this desire for a virgin is perfectly okay, as long as we recognise it for what it is, a sexual fetish. When I asked the writer Baba T, if I could publish our communication, he said: "You can publish the letter and if it helps someone out of a burden like what I had, then glory to God!" To my son who has not replied to me; maybe you can learn from your uncle, Baba T.

Virginity Is Not the Issue
22 September 2010

The article on secrets and issues of virginity generated a lot of debate; with the emails that I received we can go for weeks talking about this issue. But next week we have to go on to another topic. Here are some of the responses from readers to last week's article.

• *Your article on virginity was spot-on, Men are dying because of this sexual fetish, and it is indeed a sad reality. The sooner they realise that they are killing the nation in pursuit of this fetish the better for the nation building. Men need to be responsible and spare a thought for the future, asking themselves what they want to leave as a legacy when they die. Certainly - not a trail of heart broken, HIV infected girls and loads of fatherless kids. Your article ought to help one or two men out there and hundreds of girls can be saved from these men!*

• *Thanks for the wonderful column, keep up the good work. Allow me to comment a bit on the issue of men who say they wish to sleep with virgins, the question is how they (men) or we expect to get virgins when we go on a virgin hunting spree and after that we dump them for various reasons. Women are not goods that you feel you can use and after that you throw in the bin. The reasons why most men don't get virgins and for them as well they won't be virgins is that they sleep around too much, in the hope they are going to meet a virgin. This will see most of these men taking the virginity of most women and at the end of the day they don't marry these women. That's why you find most women who are not open to their spouses or husbands about how they lost their virginity, it is simply because they could have been fooled by their boyfriends whom they trusted so much that they end up losing their virginity in the name of love and trust. So, ALL men who rather stand tall boasting they would love to sleep with virgins I would love to hear them saying they are also VIRGINS themselves otherwise this claim does not hold much water. I rest my case*
(You can publish my name auntie)
Thank you
Tafadzwa T Madzimbamuto

• *I am 30 and still single. In 2005 I went to a kitchen party, and I got drunk, and I did not want my parents to know that I was drunk since I'm the first born and I did not want my siblings to follow that road. On my way home I thought its better I went to my boyfriend's place to rest for a while and continue with my journey home after sometime maybe ndinenge nda - I will be sober, but that was the mistake I made because I got raped by my boyfriend and after I asked what he did and the implications, he asked me to stay with him but I could not because I did not want to stay with someone who does not respect me and my principles. I did not report the case because I was very ashamed, my sister I blame myself for this. The guy destroyed my life because he knew how much I respected the principle of remaining a virgin till you get married. I could not tell anyone, not even my friend because I was ashamed of myself. Anyway, I dumped the guy that day and I do not speak to him until now, but after that I slept with the next guy I dated because I felt there was nothing to protect but now, I cannot sleep with the guy I am dating because I feel it's wrong. Now I blamed myself for what happened 5 years ago, and I feel very responsible for that. I hate myself and keep asking why I drank that day. Now it's been 2 years since I had sex and my problem is I do not know how to get past that experience and move on because I still want my virginity and I did not get to feel how it feels to lose it properly. I do not know what to tell my parents because they believe I am still a virgin. I cannot live with a lie because it's haunting me. I want to pass through this, but I cannot because I feel responsible that I did not protect myself that day. I cry every night because it is my secret. I told my boyfriend and he asked me to tell at least my mother because he said he will pay mombe yechimanda when we get married. He is not worried that I am not a virgin but the fact that it's killing me inside and it's affecting my relationship with him.*

- *Thank you for your articles especially this one on virginity. I am a lady aged 35years of age. I got married to my husband when I was 19 years old, and I was not a virgin. I lost my virginity at the age of 7. I was raped by my cousin brother an issue which my mother and sisters knew about, but I did not disclose this to my husband. This issue caused untold suffering in my marriage life because my husband never trusted me, and he became very possessive of me such that he became very physically abusive. My husband started dating other women in search of a virgin and has since married another woman (I guess she was a virgin) who has a child for him, and I believe he has several children as well (with virgins I guess). This did not go down well with me, and we divorced. I managed to tolerate the physical abuse but to tolerate the two - kurohwa and barika - being beaten and in a polygamous marriage, I couldn't. His excuse of dating other women was that because he was hurt so much when he discovered that I was not a virgin, and he has never forgiven me for that because he says he was a virgin when he married me. Because of his violent nature I kept it a secret of who raped me and blamed it on my ex-boyfriend who also dumped me because I was not a virgin. I later told him the rapist when the rapist died (am not sure if he believed it or not). During the course of my marriage, I never cheated on my husband, and I tried all my best to be a good wife (ever since all we had was each other) but zvakashaya basa - it did not help the situation. To all men out there, ladies can lose their virginity even before they know what sex is all about, I lost mine when I was 7. To all women out there chengetedzai vana vechisikana mudzimba umu because hama dzedu ndidzo dzinodistroyer future yevanasikana vedu - please look after your daughters because it is our relatives who destroy the future of our daughters.*

Victim of rape.

•   *What an enlightening article on the male fetishes with virginity! I am glad Baba T saw the light and has restored things with his wife. Virginity is like a balloon - one prick and it's gone! A few seconds yet one spends their entire life giving themselves a headache over it, please keep on giving such enlightening topics to help out our brothers. Pamberi ne velvet! - Forward with velvet!*

•   *I don't normally write like this but what irks me is the fact that men want to marry or sample virgins, yet they are not virgins themselves. When I got married, my husband was a virgin, but I wasn't, and he knew that, but he loved me beyond my lack of a piece of hymen.*

Just questions for some brothers out there Does a hymen make you laugh after a hard day at work? Does a hymen cook, clean and bear children? Does a hymen respect you and your whole clan? I do not condone sex before marriage, but mistakes happen, and people learn and repent. Guys, if you want a virgin, be one yourself.

•   *Allow me to air my views on this social intercourse you opened on the issue of Secrets and Issues of Virginity. For a start I am a virgin bachelor, and my dream is to marry a virgin as well, anything short of it, granted feelings change, but I don't think I will be a happy man. While I accept that some girls lose their virginity in very unfortunate circumstances, we must also note that the majority are giving away their virginity in acts of sexual immorality, which brings home my point. Once a girl loses her virginity this way it takes time for her to realise the worth of her womanhood. In the meantime, any relationship entered before her marriage will in most cases involve sexual intercourse. Being a Shona, Zimbabwean and a Christian, my values, culture, and beliefs have hammered in me the importance of marrying a virgin. I wish I could quote elsewhere for the sake of others but the Bible (70% of Zimbabwe are Christians by the way) in Deuteronomy 22 vs 20-21 says "If, however, the charge is true and no proof of the girl's virginity can be found, she shall be brought to the door of her father's house and there the men of her town shall stone her to death. **She has done a disgraceful thing in Israel by being promiscuous while still in her father's house.**" Please underline the last sentence of the quote. I think it's a disgraceful sin for both boys and girls to have sexual encounters outside marriage. This should be the message. Otherwise, we are preaching to the community to forgive those who intend to commit sin and letting go the would-be sinner. Forgiveness should come second.*

•   *I am not married yet, but this is a very sensitive issue. If you marry someone who is not a virgin the moment you think about it, you will go wild. Some men* would opt to revenge by having small houses and this is another source of domestic violence though it might not be put on the table by men as to why they are being difficult. This issue haunts every man if I were a woman, I would value my virginity more. If you sleep with a woman and she is no virgin there is a very high probability that you will leave her unless she has told you. Most single guys who sleep with virgins tend to marry them. The vicious cycle is that: a) They lose their virginity to married men, b) Married men are on the look for virgins because their wives were not and this vicious cycle repeats itself, so value your virginity my sisters because men's behaviour towards this issue cannot be changed.

- *In my opinion, virgin or not virgin it doesn't matter. I am a young man of 21yrs. Why is it that we judge women when it comes to virginity, what about men? Who is judging us? It's being selfish I think my fellow men are just selfish when they think if they tie the knot with a virgin their marriages will be secure, they are missing the point. Marriage is not about marrying a virgin; it is about two people who are in love and want to spend the rest of their lives together. What if you take a virgin who is arrogant, dirty, moody, and annoying? Let us not judge women, and secrets are poisonous in relationship. Women tend to keep secrets so that they secure a relationship, if he finds out it is over, be honest from the start!*

- *God abhors sexual immorality because this sin outside marriage connects the spirits of the two who become one after sexual intercourse. That explains why either a man or a woman feels injured when one is not the virgin they wanted or when one cheats. You will be surprised that even for women, they would also prefer a male virgin, for the very same reason that men abhor the thought. Let it be made clear that young adults and married people ought to know that every sexual encounter with a woman/man that is not your wife/husband connects you to her/him and renders her/him to be your husband or wife in the spirit. Remember that the Bible says that whatever you bind on earth so in heaven it is, yes these become spiritual husbands and wives, because we bind them through the act of sex; an astonishing level of ignorance to this fact that is in many of our young adults and married couples.*

I have not even published half of the emails I received from readers on this topic which means it needs to be further discussed, but we would also like to give other topics a chance and we will come back to it some other time. You can continue to send us emails on this issue.

Letting Go, Painful Necessity
6 October 2010

Letting go is not easy but necessary. Letting go will free us from unnecessary burden and keep stress at bay. Holding on to relationships which are not working, failing to let go our children when they reach a certain age is pointless as it has some negative effects on our health and personality.

Why is it so difficult to let go? It is difficult to let go because we tend to get attached and we cannot imagine living our lives without the person we are failing to let go. Priya Florence Shah who manages India's fi st portal for empowered women and blogs about self-improvement and spirituality emphasises why it is important to let go. "One of the hardest things for any person, man, or woman, is letting go of a relationship that's not meant to be. We are often attached to the illusion that this person is "the One" for us, and that if we don't have him or her, we'll never fi d somebody new. Holding on to disappointment, hurt, blame, anger, resentment, and bitterness, we convince ourselves that "all men are jerks" or "all women are bitches."

A friend of mine told me a very touching story of how she was able to let go of her partner when she discovered that he was seeing someone else. They had been in the relationship for about five years, and it was going well, but it seemed at some point in their relationship things started falling apart. He had started seeing someone. They broke up, and the man invited her to the wedding which she accepted. When she told me that she went for the wedding I could not believe it. She explained why:

"Yes I did because I wanted closure." She continued. "When I got to the wedding, his new partner maybe 15 years younger than me, came to me and said I have heard from my husband that you are a very special person in his life, and she hugged me." She narrated, I looked at her and did not know what to say, I held her hand as to comfort her, she went on with the story, "Later on my ex-partner came and introduced me to his new wife formally, and the new partner told him that we had already done our introductions. The young lady excused us and he, my ex-partner, said to me 'You are very special to me, and I also told him he was also very special to me."

I asked her how she felt about the whole experience, and she said: "Maybe I was prepared for the whole experience, because when I travelled to where the wedding was taking place, we had sat down and talked about ending our relationship, it was painful. It was not easy, it really hurt me, but I had to accept it. I think that day I cried a lot with him and even when I got home. Th s is what he wanted, and I had to let him go." I sighed and shook my head and said to her, "Are you okay? How do you feel now?" She said, "You know what if you really love someone you will always love them. I do love him in a different way now than I did before, he will always be in my heart, but I had to let him go."

I said: "You are a very strong woman, you seem to have gotten over it, with so much ease."

She answered: "Sometimes you just have to let go and move on and fi d peace." She told me of how she would cry all night for days until she accepted it, it was not easy, but she got over it.

Priya advice: "It takes a lot of tears, hard work, and introspection to break the chains of the past. But it's worth every moment! The feeling of freedom and contentment that you experience is just awesome. Getting rid of your anger and hurt will help you stop blaming others for your pain, and allow you to see your former partner as they really are - a wonderful,

sensitive human being with the capacity to love, to care, and to hurt just as deeply as you. It will allow you to love life again, to see the beauty in every experience, to be non-judgmental and open to new relationships. No time spent in a relationship is ever wasted. Every experience is a lesson and only when you learn the lesson will you progress to the next level. So, stop beating yourself up over all the years you 'wasted' with that 'loser."

One day my friend came home for tea and had invited some of our friends, and it seemed the story had taken a new twist. She said that one night at around 2.am the ex-partner phoned and when she received the call at that hour of the night she was confused. She answered the phone, and it was him, it was as if someone had risen from the dead. "We greeted each other and after that there was some silence and I had to ask if everything was alright and he said, 'I failed to sleep, I have been thinking about you and every time I think of you I ...' Before she fin shed the sentence our young sister who had also come for tea said, "Oh no, oh no how can he?! How can he make you his *mubobobo* he is sick! ('*Mubobobo*' is a concoction that is believed to make it possible for a man to be invisible or otherwise allow him to have sex with a woman without her knowledge).

The Drama Queen as we call her, was not amused. We all looked at each other and laughed, and when the Drama Queen was done, she fin shed her sentence and said: "He said that he wakes up at night and cries every time he thinks of me." Our young sister said, "I thought he was using you for his whatever......but cry let him, and next time when he wants to cry tell him to wake up his wife not you." The Drama Queen did not mince her words.

It seems while my friend had let go of her partner he had not, but what my friend said was that one thing that she was not going to do is to be his mistress, she had let go and had moved on.

According to Priya Florence Shah my friend seems to have made a wise decision, as Priya explains, "If it didn't work, it was probably not meant to be. You can't force someone to love you, just as you can't force commitment or marriage. These are stages that should happen naturally when it feels right for both people. Contrary to popular opinion (and sad love

songs) love is not meant to hurt. If you're in pain, what you're experiencing is not love, but attachment or codependency. Too often we fall in love, not with our partner, but with the IDEA of being in love. It's best to let go of a relationship that's causing too much pain. Instead of wallowing in the past and writing your own sad love song, do your inner work, get rid of the anger and disappointment, and get on with your life. Let go of your partner with love, so you can move past your hurt and learn to love again."

It is not only in 'love/romantic' relationships where people fail to let go, some parents cannot let go of their children when they are old enough and responsible enough to look after themselves. A friend of mine went to visit her daughter in America, the daughter was graduating and when she came back, I went to see her and asked her how she had travelled and how the daughter was doing. I also met her sister who had visited my friend. She said that she had travelled well, and she had a great time with her daughter, she took out some photos that they had taken to show us. As we were looking at the photos there was a guy who was with her daughter and when she looked at the photo, she was not happy. I asked her who the guy was, and she said: "I was told *ukuthi nguye umkhwenyana* - he is my future son-in-law." She sulked. "What is the problem?" I asked.

She said, "You know what when I was introduced to him, I thought to myself, *ukuti shuwa nguye oyabe esenza izinto kumtanami, ngezwa ....- just to think that he will be doing things to my daughter I felt...*"

It was as if she was feeling goose bumps and we laughed with the sister and the sister said, "*Kanti wena umama wakutshiya, uhamba endodeni, umtwana nguye otheni. Ngiyabona usukhohliwe njengoba umkakho wafa sokukudala. - Mother let you get married to your husband and let your daughter go, maybe you have forgotten since your husband died some years ago.* The sister was trying to cool her down, but she answered, "You cannot compare this one to my husband. What is the comparison based on?"

We had a good laugh, but we could see that it was all to do with not being able to let go. Yes, it is difficult, but very necessary.

I was watching a Nollywood film; a mother who could not let go of her son, she did not approve of her daughters-in-law, she poisoned the first one and she died; and when she tried to poison the second one it did not work, and she drove away her son.

Letting go is important because when you let go of those you love when they come back to you, you will laugh, and cry and they will bring new experiences into your life, and you will both grow in leaps and bounds spiritually and everything else will follow.

This Game Has No Formula, But…
27 October 2010

Choosing a life partner is one mystery which has not been understood, because there is no formula on how to go about it. You might try to do it the way your parents did it but might not work. Your parents may encourage you to do it the way they did it, but this might not work but cause friction between you and your family. The choosing of one's partner is led and influenced by various factors, which can work for one and not the other. It is purely instinct which leads the heart, the heart is also sometimes led by what it sees, how it has been conditioned. Some people shock their families and the community when they chose their lifetime partners.

When Sandy fell in love with John who unfortunately did not fit into her family's structures, her parents almost had a heart attack. No one supported her 'crazy' idea even her sisters and brothers. She had passed her Form Four – (O Levels) with flying colours, which was in the late 70's and got herself a job at the bank. Those days this was one of the best jobs, which were opening up for black people and having such a job was the talk of the township. *"Kuti mwana wekwanhingi ano shanda ku-bank - To say so and so's child works at the bank was a big deal."* It became the talk of the township. Her boyfriend had only gone as far as Form Two since he could not get money to continue with his education. But the bank teller loved her man, unconditionally. Her parents tried by all means to discourage her, but they failed, she decided to get pregnant and eloped with the guy, still they could not accept him as a *mukwasha-son in-law*. When he came to marry, they said it was their daughter who had given him money to marry. He had decided to get a menial job so that he could pay *lobola* to his in-laws but for them he was low class who could not raise that kind of money.

Since they refused the money, the daughter decided that he stops working because the main reason for him to work was so that he could pay for his *lobola*. The wife sent him to school – to night school and during the day he would look after the children. The family wondered what it was that she had seen in this man and when people were discussing the grandmother could not also believe what it was with her granddaughter and she said, *"Chiyi chaizvo chaarikuvavarira muzukuru wangu, no-kuti zvatinoona hazvisi zvingapengese mhunu, toti mheno zvirikutsi.- What is it really that is making my granddaughter lose her head, because what we see does not warrant someone to lose their head. Maybe it has to do with some of those hidden things."* At least she brought some humour to this situation which had become such a pain in the family. People laughed and she continued: *"Ndirikuda kuendako ndinozviwonera kuti chiyi chaizvo. I want to go there [where they stay] and see for myself what could it be."* Since the family had cut her off, the parents were not on talking terms with her. The grandmother thought her visit was going to help the situation by visiting her granddaughter and talking some sense into her.

When the grandmother got to her granddaughter's home, she found the husband of her granddaughter doing housework and looking after the children. The grandmother was not happy to see a man doing housework, she even forgot what she had gone to do; to scan and look for hidden things. Instead, she found herself helping the man with housework.

The love between the two changed how the grandmother had perceived them. She encouraged the family to support her granddaughter and her partner. She realised that the two had found each other and that is what mattered; it had nothing to do with what people saw or did not see with naked eyes.

It was not only her family which was against her decision of going out with *ka-poto - a nobody*. She lost friends, who preferred man who had good jobs, or who were rich. When she phoned me recently from abroad where she is based with her family she said: *"Vese vaye vaindiseka, vachida ma-Alfa Sud, ma-Citroen, ma-120y, ma-March One, vanondiudza ma-story anonzwisa tsitsi ekuti motokari dzacho vaka-zombodzikwira? - All those who used to laugh at me preferring men with Alfa-Suds, Citroen's, 120y's and March Ones, they tell me painful stories and they say they never got to ride those cars."* She is happy that she followed her heart and did not give in to peer pressure.

"Shamwari inini ndakazvi-polishira ngoda yangu ndega, pandinenge ndawona pa-siri right ndinopolisha ndenga - My friend I looked for an unpolished diamond and I polished it myself, to my liking." She said proudly."

"But how did you know that he was the right one because some do exactly what you did, send the husband to school and go out of their way to help in the name of love but they get a raw deal at the end." I asked

"I don't even know how to explain it, I don't think there is anyone who knows how to explain it, but you feel it. You know this is the right one." She explained.

She is not the only one who went against the grain to get a husband. I got a letter on the same subject, and it read; "I have been married to my husband for almost 20 years now, but my sister-in-law seems not to be accepting me like others have. I used to work for her as a housemaid and fell in love with her brother whom she was staying with. She was very angry when she discovered that we were dating and tried to break us up, she could not believe that her brother a graduate could fall for a housemaid like me. When she realised that she could not break us up, she fi ed me, and the brother looked for a place to stay and asked me to move in with him as I did not have anywhere to go. I had come to Harare to work and raise money to continue with my education. The sister told the family about us and tried to plant a bad seed to the rest of the family, but one day the parents of my husband visited us when they heard I was pregnant and discussed with my husband that if this is what he wanted then we were supposed to get married, which we did. At fi st some members of the family accepted me grudgingly but later on they took me to be part of the family, but my sister-in-law, I used to work for has not. When we meet at family gatherings, she makes some comments to just make me look stupid and most of them to do with my being a housemaid, one day she said: *"Mumwe nemumwe ngaite basa rake raanoziva, ma-housegirl ngaaarongedze atitsvairirewo mumba - each and every one should do the work they are used to do. Housegirls make sure the house is looking smart."* I really would not have minded if we were in a good relationship, but this was all to spite me. I have proved myself by going to school and doing some courses and I am now running the family business we started with my husband, and it is doing well.

There are times I feel I should just tell her off, but I restrain myself. I did not take her husband, and her brother was single, I wonder what I did wrong. When is she going to accept me? When is this fi hting going to stop? What should I do with this situation?" I asked her if I could get other people's opinion and she said it was okay as long as I did not disclose her name. I asked my friends what they were reading into the story.

My two friends had this to say:
"Unoziva chiyi tete vake i-type iye inofunga kuti ivo ndivo vanofanira kufara vega, you know that attitude yekuti ndisu chaivo isu. - You know what - the sister-in-law thinks she is the only one who has the right to be happy you see. She never thought her maid would attract her brother and actually fall in love and get married."

The other friend added to what she had said: "It is amazing how the universe works, it gives according to the way it sees fit, and those who think they are more special than others have always had a rude awakening."

"What is she supposed to do?" I asked.

"Nothing really, nothing. I think the *vatete - sister to the husband*, is just an unhappy person and the *muroora - sister-in-law* is just a victim of her unhappiness."

One of my advisers said: "But she should continue to reach out in a quiet way and enjoy her husband that the universe gave her."

When I asked my friend who stayed with her husband despite her family being against it and the woman who used to work as a house maid and fell in love with the brother of her boss, why there were so brave to go against the grain, they had the same answer; they knew they had found their lifetime partners.

There is neither formula nor explanation on how to choose a lifetime partner, but you know - that this is the one.

ARTICLE 25

Virginity And Ugly Face of *Chiramu*
3 November 2010

I have been trying to avoid this topic (on issues of virginity) for some time now, but it keeps crying that I talk about it, stories cry to be written and be heard. Since the fi st article I wrote on the topic, I have received emails, phone calls and visits. As I have said in my articles that it is a story that will be with us for some time.

I received a call from a man who said that getting my phone number was not easy, he said an email would not explain what he wanted to discuss with me that is why he had phoned. I told him that it was fi e we could talk over the phone, but he said that he would want to see me, that was the only way he could discuss what was bothering him. I agreed to meet him. He came to my offi . He looked very distraught, and he mentioned that he was happy that I had agreed to meet him. It took him time to tell his story and he looked very disturbed. He did not know how and where to start, I then suggested that he send me an email, but he said he was not strong enough to write down what he wanted to discuss with me, but he would try to talk about it.

He pulled himself together and then he began: "The story you wrote on virginity, I have a story which I would like to tell you that has been worrying me for years, but I don't know where to start." I told him to just start from anywhere.

"I have been married to my wife for almost 23 years and we have 4 children, but when I married her, she was not a virgin. When I asked her, she did not give me a satisfactory answer in fact she did not want to talk about it. Our relationship has been strained since the day I discovered that she was not a virgin, and I don't even know how we have managed to have four children. One day my wife said she would like to go out there and see how other men are? I was very disturbed and hurt by what she said."

I asked him why he was hurt by what his wife had said and yet since the day he dis-covered that his wife was not a virgin it seems there has been no connection between them. "Yes, my sister we are like strangers, but I did not expect to hear that from her. I must say that in our *secret entertainment life* I do not know her for all the years we have lived together, I fail to hide my anger that I have as a result of the virginity issue." Yes, the anger and pain were written all over his face.

"So, it means the two of you have never been connected, there has always been this barrier - the virginity issue between you." I wanted to understand.

"Yes." He answered, "Our relationship is just deteriorating further, but I never thought she would tell me that she would want to have other men, I felt my manhood challenged. Although I know we have never really been…"

"Have you ever felt her?" I asked and he did not answer. It was as if he was in another world and then I explained: "What I mean my brother is –when you are connected with your partner, just one touch, you feel something, you feel a wave, a sensation." He came back from the world he had gone to, and he said, "Actually not."

"So there has been nothing between you, and what you have been doing for year is that you have been sending *Thombi/Ntombi* and *Bhoyi* to work, and these two are very obedient and you have been forcing them to go to work. (*Thombi/ Ntombi* is girl for Ndebele/Zulu and slang for Shona who have corrupted it to thombi instead of ntombi in Zulu/Ndebele and *Bhoyi* is for boy both in Ndebele and Shona but in this context *Thombi/Ntombi* is a vagina and *Bhoyi* is a penis and are used in disguise sex talk). *Thombi/Ntombi* and *Bhoyi* have managed to bring you four children from their work, but what you have been doing is causing so much pain between the two of you. Imagine if you were beaten to go to work almost every day, how would you feel? The moment you went into that main room Thombi/*Ntombi* and *Bhoyi* knew their job description and sometimes did not wait to be forced but just did their job without the 'two of you participating,' that is why you never felt her, and she has never felt you. She does not know you. You are not connected to each other than those two Thombi/*Ntombi* and *Bhoyi*. It is not surprising that from that lifestyle, you have brought unto yourself stress related illnesses." He looked at me not knowing what to say, and he sighed, "Have you ever gone for massage my brother?" I asked in order to drive my point home, he answered, "Yes." I continued, "There is a time when the person massaging you will say, 'I can feel a knot, there is big knot here and he works on that area and when that knot has been dissolved you feel relaxed." He nodded his head in agreement.

I continued with my explanation: "One of the purposes for *secret entertainment* is to dissolve unseen lumps which are in your system, which a massage parlour cannot detect and instead for years you have not been able to do that, you have been creating more knots in your system. Your system is clogged. As I mentioned that if you are connected just one touch will send a wave into your whole system and those knots will dissolve, purifying your system, but instead you have been contaminating your system and now your wife cannot take it anymore. Imagine the knots in your body right now. Is it worth it? Just because you could not forgive her that she was not a virgin when you married her?" He could not answer. His eyes were full of tears, and he shook his head sideways, looked down and he exhaled. There was silence for a while, and he said: "You are right my sister our marriage has brought us pain."

There was silence again and he said: "I wish she had told me the truth, maybe I could have helped her, because now I know the truth and I only wish she had told me.

It was her sister's husband who broke her virginity." He sighed again and he looked confused. I was also confused.

"Oh, no!" I exclaimed.

He told me how he had come to know: "Her younger sister had visited her elder sister's husband and he tried to force her. When she refused the man told her that she was very stupid. Who did she think she is, if two of her elder sisters gave him sex, who is she to refuse him. While he was fighting to force himself on the young woman, he told her that for the six years he had been staying with the other sister she was just 'as good as his wife.' This was too much for me, the fact that I had been looking up to this man as my big brother, I feel betrayed."

"Have you asked your wife?"

"Yes, I have but she becomes defensive."

I advised him to tell his wife's family so that the *babamukuru - brother in-law* could be held accountable, because I believed once he had fin shed with the sisters, he would go for any female member of the family since he was clearly a monster.

He informed me that the young girl had told her parents about the attempted rape, but the family had dismissed her and said it was *playing chiramu - a friendship between a sister-in-law and her sister's husband.* Unfortunately, no one wanted to take her seriously. Having no one to turn to she decided to tell her brother-in-law, whose wife was also a victim which is how he found out about his wife's experience.

It is amazing and unfortunate how some *babamukurus - brothers-in-law* have abused the whole family and other female members of the family, some of whom they are supposed to see as daughters.

We went back to the problems that he was having with his wife as he wanted some advice on how to handle this situation.

"What do you want out of life my brother, just life; let us forget about all that is going on. What do you want from life?"

"I want peace and happiness." He said.

"That is very important, it is important to have peace and happiness in whatever you do. Your situation will not be able to provide for that unless you are willing to talk about the issue of virginity with your wife and close that chapter and move on with your wife or alone. You need peace and happiness, and it is only you who will create an environment which will give you the best of life."

He nodded his head in agreement and asked me how he could make it possible to achieve a fulfilling life. I advised him to talk to his wife and come to some understanding if they still wanted to be together or to go for therapy with his wife.

It was time to go. I walked him to his car while we were talking, he said: "Th s situation has contributed to my high blood pressure. My doctor asked me about my life, and I told her about my family and children, and she wandered what the problem was since I had a seemingly perfect family... but I am unwell because I did not tell her what I just told you."

"Yes, I knew that with the way you have lived your life you are bound to have a stress related illness. Do something about it and live a peaceful and a happy life."

"I will try to talk to my wife and come back to you." He said.

As we said our goodbyes, I wished him all the best.

ARTICLE 26

Matchmaking as Old as Humanity
1 December 2010

Some day will be together... Someday we'll be together. Say it, say it, say it, say it again ...

Th s is the song I sang for my friends who had come to bid me farewell as they were travelling abroad. The wife was going to give a paper at a conference and the husband decided to accompany her so that they could see their children who were based abroad. They would be away for a month. I sang this song as I was accompanying them to their car.

The wife also joined me, and we did a duet: *"Vasikana makundifungisa kachana. Zvamunetenge ma-Supremes acho. - Girls, you remind me of the good old days. You sound just like the Supremes."* Said the husband.

"Say it again..." we continued with our song. Yes, *vasikana - us girls* had really gone back in time, we became like teenagers. While we were singing the song the husband said: "You know what you remind me of a friend who used to love this song, *Someday Will Be*

Together, he would write a letter filled with this song to his girlfriend." The wife then answered; "Oh yes John and Patty. You know those two were just meant to be together. *Kufunga kuti kudanana kwavakaita vasingatombozivana - When they fell in love, they did not even know each other.* There were really meant to be together."

I did not understand this, and I asked: "What do you mean they fell in love not knowing each other?" Then they told me the story, it went like this - Norbet and Sandy (my friends who were telling the story), were asked by their friend John to get him a girlfriend. Sandy organised one of her friends who was at school in Mutare. She gave John her address and he wrote a letter proposing to her. She did not respond to the fi st letter, but when she fi ally responded John could not hide his joy, but the distance between the two affected them, and he used to play the song *Someday Will Be Together*, a number of times per day. When he was listening to this song it is said that he would sometimes cry thinking of his girl.

"We would ask him, *'Ko urikuchemeyi iwe chukazi wanayo? - why are you crying and yet you have your girl.* Said Nobert, Sandy sarcastically added: *"Muranda anga afunga mbenembe -the guy was thinking of his girl.* I had not heard the words *mbenembe* and *muranda* for a long time. Th s is the 60's,70's slang which has since been replaced. I had a good laugh, and it brought a lot of memories. In one particular instance John was crying because he had just received a letter saying that Patty was no longer coming to Harare for holiday and instead she was going to spend the holidays with one of her aunts in Mutare. He could not wait any longer he just wanted to be with her, just to hold her. The song *Someday Will Be Together* used to bring him hope and solace, although he would also listen to songs like *Tears on my Pillow* by Johnny Nash or *Say Something* by the Hurricanes and the endless list of love songs of the 70's, but that song: *Someday will be Together* was his theme song.

The duo is said to have been very creative, these songs would be followed by illustrations; people running towards each other and hugging, illustrations to accompany *Tears On My Pillow* would be those of the two sleeping on a pillow in separate worlds crying, but to bring hope they would be drawings of them sitting in the park holding each other and having a picnic. Yes, then, people were creative, they would express their love through writing and art. Words like '*take my mistakes as your kisses!*' and the other one would answer, '*I will always love you no matter what.*' Oh boy, oh girl, which was some contract to be fulfilled.

"When John and Patty fi ally met, '*Takawonerera - We saw wonders.*'" As my friends would say. They accompanied John to *Musika Bus Terminus,* and they showed him his girl Patty. Norbet recalled: "We introduced Patty to John, they hugged and kissed, and tears rolled. Patty even forgot about her suitcase which we had to collect from the conductor who had called Patty's name several times to no avail. When they collected the suitcase Patty and John were nowhere to be found. They had gone for a photo shoot at Muronda studios."

But how do two people who have never seen each other fall in love? My friends said, "We cannot rule out the spiritual component and that they had put their trust on us as their friends that we were going to do what was in their best interests, we wanted them to be happy just as we were."

My friends are such a happy couple and I wondered whether these two were also a happy couple like them. The wife answered:

"They are still married, they are happy, and sometimes the wife reminds us of how we connected them...." While Sandy was narrating her husband Norbert interjected and said: "I am happy you said the wife is happy that we connected them, it seems when the wife talks about us connecting them the husband becomes very uncomfortable...I don't understand my friend, what is wrong with him?" Sandy answered: "But *iye Patty wacho anombozvitarisa here izvozvo,* I think *murume anenge akufunga kuti anozonzi akanga asinga gone kombising* [*Kombising* is slang for *ukukhombisa-kunyenga - proposing love to a woman*) - *But Patty does not really mind, I think the husband feels embarrassed that people might think he could not approach/propose love to a woman on his own.*" The husband laughed and said, "*Ko ndiye atanga kunyengerwa mukadzi, ungabva wagona zvese, ukagona ka kuita murume kwacho ndizvo zvikuru, sezvatirikuona...-* He cannot do everything by himself, what is important is when you get the woman be a real man as he is, that is what is important…" We could not help it but laugh. He continued, *"E-ka ndosaka mukadzi wacho achititenda, kubatsirana, ungabva waita zvese wega pasi pano pakazara vanhu kudai - Yes that is why the wife thanks us. You cannot do everything in this world and yet this world is full of people …"*

We continued to laugh.

How can one do everything in a world full of people; family, friends, colleagues, institutions you name it. All my friend was trying to say was that there is nothing wrong if you get a husband or wife through friends or family. They are people who do not have the skills to propose love, it does not mean that they are dull or stupid, they are not cut out for that, but they need someone in their lives. Are they going to live a lonely life because they will be laughed at because *avagone kukombisa - they can-not propose love* if they are those who can do it let them do it and the two of you can enjoy being together. I know a lot of people who are happily married, and they were connected through a go-between. Today they are different ways of connecting people and lovers. Some are using the internet - various social media platforms. This shows that society has always recognised go-betweens as a way of making it easy for those searching for love to find each other.

In many families, communities, institutions they are individuals who are known for being go-betweens, they make it their prerogative to see that they hook up people. Their approach differs depending on the situation and they can be successful or not. I was recently told of a grandmother who introduced her granddaughter to a man in the diaspora where she once lived. When other relatives including the father of the young woman asked to see the photo of their in-law to be, the grandmother and the granddaughter could not make available the photos. The man sent money to marry the young woman but remained a secret until the day of the wedding, when he came from the diaspora to be introduced to the family. Some relatives did not approve of the wedding and wanted to cancel it, but the grandmother and the granddaughter stood their ground and made sure that the wedding went ahead. The

reason why many relatives wanted to call off the wedding was that the man was much older than the woman, he was over 60 years old and the woman 25 years old. There were also rumours that the grandmother had gone out with the man while in the diaspora. However, a *sahwira* – a close and recognised and respected friend of the family used his authority to break the impasse and the wedding went ahead. He said:

"Siyayi muzukuru ayende kunochengeta zvinhu zvaambuya vake, chakaipa chii? Let the grandaughter go and look after her grandmother's things. What is wrong with that?" Some relatives also felt that if the woman is happy then they should let her wed the man.

The radio is also being used as a go-between to link those who would want to spend a life together as husband and wife or partners. Radio station, Kaya FM's reality show intitled '*2 Strangers and a Wedding*', saw a Zimbabwean woman Rudo Dumbutshena and David Malindi getting married under masks and that was their first time ever to meet. The Sowetan reports, "The pair first recited their vows before Reverend Brits, and exchanged rings, before removing their masks. They were already bride and groom before coming together face-to-face with each other for the first time ever. Expressions of happiness and appreciation were noted on both of their faces by the congregation. Rudo looked stunning in a strapless gown, while David was dashing in a pin-striped dress suit. The newlyweds were then formally introduced to each other by their real names - Rudo Dumbutshena and David Malindi. Speaking shortly after the ceremony Dumbutshena said: "I am feeling very excited and am looking forward to the future. It has been a journey and a half."

When asked what she thought of Malindi now that she had seen his face she said: "He is lovely, and I think that I made a good choice". Malindi, feeling totally overwhelmed about the event, said: "I am so excited. I have been looking forward to this day - anticipating what

she looks like but it is her spirit that I fell in love with. "She has a warm spirit and just by listening to her voice I was expecting to see a beautiful person. She is a lovely person and words cannot describe how I feel."

The ceremony resulted from Kaya FM's social experiment. Unfortunately, the match making did not work, after six months Rudo and David called it quits. Musical group Malaika's Bongani Nchang (who was with Tshedi Mholo), had warned: "It's very risky and adventurous at the same time. They should just keep in mind that marriage is not a contract but a covenant. They must be willing to love each other despite their differences. There's no *chechela moraho - looking back*."

The whole idea was to bring together two people who are looking for love and companionship. Different institutions in society feel it is their responsibility to facilitate those who are in search for love, sometimes it works but sometimes it does not. Those who feel they cannot approach the person they love or need help to get someone to share their life with, should not be ashamed to get help from go-betweens, family, friends, the community, institutions, internet, reality shows. As my friends said, "You cannot do everything alone in a world full of people."

ARTICLE 27

Generation Gaps, in-Laws, And Marriages
15 December 2010

THE gap between the young and the older generation can cause misunderstandings between the age groups, but this should not be the case. The two can actually learn from each other and close the gap. The way the old and the new generation were raised contributes to seeing things differently.

A colleague said that what she admires about the new generation is that they do not go round in circles when they want something compared to "our" generation, the "older" generation.

She gave an example of how when we want something we will say, "*Ndanga ndi-chida-I wanted to...*and today's generation will say, "*Ndiri kuda ku-I want to...*

That mentality of not being decisive regarding the older generation particularly women is unfortunately what they take into their marriages, but some young women know exactly what they want.

The way the different generations view marriage often results in clashes between mothers and daughters, mothers-in-law, and daughters-in-law, *ubabakazi lomzukulu wesifazi/vatete nemuzukuru sikana - aunts and nieces.*

A friend of mine has been having problems with her muzukuru - her niece Rudo, because of the way she conducts herself in her marriage.

She invited some friends and her elder sister to try and talk sense into the young lady after her husband's relatives approached her as the aunt who accompanied her to her new home and reproached her for Rudo's behaviour. The aunt tried to discuss the in-laws' concerns with Rudo, who gave all sorts of excuses.

It was then that the aunt decided to invite a few friends and relatives, including an elder aunt. She explained that Rudo's in-laws had complained that Rudo was not a good *muroora - daughter-in-law* because she did not want her husband's relatives in her home.

The elder aunt asked Rudo to explain.

Rudo bluntly said that she did not want too many people in her home because she was trying to know her husband well and wanted the two to be left alone. She also said that too many people in the house would restrict some of the things she does with her husband.

The elder aunt asked the niece to explain some of the things that she was talking about are.

Rudo replied: "Like being really free with my husband, doing the things that we really love to do…"

The aunt who had called the gathering was not amused and she asked Rudo, who was clearly going round in circles, *"Zvinhu zvakaita sei zvisingade vanhu, muzukuru une lucky fani kuwana murume sewako - Things like what my niece? Which do not want people? You are so lucky to get a husband like yours!"*. Rudo replied and said, "He is also lucky to have me." The elder aunt intervened and said that they did not come to fi ht.

She asked her niece again to explain the things that she did not want visitors to disturb. Rudo shocked us all when she said she wanted free movement in her house, like moving around in her birthday suit; and that she even cooks in her birthday suit, which is why she wants to have space in her house. When we were busy marvelling she continued, "Yes, we cook in our birthday suits with my husband."

One of our friends marvelled and said, "No, you don't?"

"Yes, we do." She said and continued . . . at fi st he (her husband) was not comfortable but now we prepare food in the kitchen together in our birthday suits and it is real fun."

The elder aunt asked what they would do when they started feeling funny.

"That is the whole idea to prepare ourselves for the big thing… it can be done anywhere in the house," Rudo boasted. The younger aunt was not happy although the elder aunt and the friends seemed to be enjoying what this young woman was saying.

The elder aunt laughed and said: *"Romance dzenyu dzekumasendiraini dzazo-chalenjwa manje - The romance you used to have in the centre-lines or greenways - masendiraini has been challenged* [*masendiraini* was a word which was used in the township [Ghetto] Mbare to explain greenways which separated some of the houses - romantic excapades used to take place at the *masendiraini* mostly at night). *Masendiraini* was like a lover's paradise, a lot of things took place at *kumasendiraini*, sports, games etc.

The friends could not believe that the elder aunt compared this young girl's love antics to the puppy love of kissing and touching which took place *kumasendiraini* during her days. As if this was not enough, Rudo, who had now assumed the role of the princess or queen of romance, told us that when her husband was promoted to an executive post, she had to choose the furniture for the offic and arranged the offic to her liking. She said she did this so that when her husband gave excuses of coming home late because he was working, she would just go to his workplace and turn the offic into a massage parlour and when she is done went back home leaving him to work with renewed energy and she would also go home with new energy.

When the old-fashioned aunt made an issue about Rudo's antics at the husband's workplace, she reminded her of her husband who had turned his offic into a Sodom and Gomorra and when he died the wife was shocked by what she found - pants, condoms, and sex toys.

Rudo was not going to leave room for that.

The elder aunt then asked Rudo when she was going to have a child to which Rudo replied that she needed time to know her husband as they had just been married, for three years. Rudo said she did not want a situation where she would end up with two strangers in her life - her husband and her child.

It seemed all the princesses, queens and goddesses of romance were speaking through Rudo.

Some African cultures discouraged friends and relatives from making frequent visits to newlyweds' home as they are supposed to be given time to find themselves and understand each other.

Jealousy Could Spoil Your Xmas
22 December 2010

A jealous husband nearly got himself into trouble with a *hwindi - a conductor on a minibus, a kombi, a form of public transport* when he saw his wife walking with another man. He trailed them from a distance and saw them buying biscuits by the roadside.

The man gave the biscuits to the woman whose husband was following them. The husband then tried to walk faster so that he could catch them "in the act". The man who had bought the woman biscuits decided to give her the Five South Africa rands, change from the biscuits, he said: *"Chitorai zvenyu mari yacho mutengere vana mas-weet - You can have the money and buy your children some sweets."*

The husband arrived while the man was handing his wife the R5, he seethed with anger as he had followed them from a distance: *"Ho ndizvo zvaunoswera uchita nhai, nhasi ndakubata kunyengerwa mabiscuits netu R5 - So this is what you spend your time doing. How can you exchange it with biscuits and R5?"*

The wife and the man who had given her biscuits did not understand what was going on and they looked very disturbed.

"Muri kuti chiiko? - What are you saying?" The wife asked her husband. *"Saka ndiyo boyfriend yako iyi? Uri very cheap. So, this is your boyfriend, you are very cheap!"* Shouted the husband.

The man was shocked and did not know what to say. The wife then answered, *"Tanzi tibatanidzane na-conductor...The conductor has given us a dollar so that we can look for..."*

She did not finish explaining, the husband was fuming and cut her before she could finish what she wanted to say. *"Kubatanidza kwekutengerana mabiscuits, nekupihwa mari yekunotengera vana masweets - how dare you giving it away for a packet of biscuits and sweets".*

They had a heated argument and the wife decided they go to the *hwindi -* minibus conductor who had given them a dollar so that they could look for change to pay the transport.

The husband asked for an explanation and was told what his wife had told him. He did not believe the *hwindi* and thought he was friends with the man who was with his wife and said, *"Ndinoziva sei kuti muri kutaura chokwadi, pamwe ishamwari yenyu, yamuri kuvhariridza - How do I know that you are speaking the truth, maybe the man is your friend and you are covering up for him."*

Other *hwindis – bus conductors* ganged up when they saw one of them in trouble and ordered the husband to leave or they would deal with him appropriately. They asked him how he could ill-treat his wife like that.

When he saw that he was going to be overpowered he left and said, *"Muzviregere izvozvo zvekutsvagira vakadzi vevamwe varume - You must desist from your behaviour of match-making married women with your friends."*

When he was leaving the *hwindis* said, *"Amai mukanorohwa muuye pano mutitaurire timugadzirise murume wenyu – Ma, when you get home and this man beats you up come and tell us and we will teach your husband a lesson."*

The man just became emotional for nothing, and nearly landed himself in trouble by jumping into conclusions.

In another case, a birthday surprise that a husband was organising for his wife did not take off smoothly as he had planned because the wife became suspicious of her husband's behaviour.

The husband had to work hard to present his wife with a birthday surprise of a lifetime. When the wife came across a receipt which had suspicious items, she had her head spinning. The items were: mama lie bling (US$28,00), black power of love (US$25), Little heart (US$26), black stars and heart (US$22.70), rosa heart (US$30,65), svat heart (US$25,54) Girlie Girl (US$20,90), Cod Squid (US$31,99), melting heart T-shirt (US$24) vibrating ling . . . (plus remote) (US$42), KY jelly (US$3,99). When she got to the last one; Va-Va Voom Boa (US$16), she felt her head spinning it went va voom, she wondered what that could be. The items came up to a total of US$300.

She did not know whether to ask her husband or not, but she did not want to seem as though she was spying on him. She was very disturbed and could not hide it. She looked for the items on the receipt in the bag, but she could not fi d anything. However, she put back the receipt where she had found it.

She confid d in her friend about the receipt and the friend advised her to talk to her husband and ask for the items on the receipt. She was scared that it would seem as though she was spying on him. She then took the receipt and went to show her younger sister so that she could get more advice on how to handle the issue, but the sister asked her to calm down.

The sister knew that the husband was organising a birthday surprise and she did not want to spoil the surprise. She tried to cool her down. It seems she was unsuccessful, she then suggested that they go on the Internet to search for the items one by one. They searched. While there were on the fi st item, she could not take it.

The sister as a way to cool her down suggested that maybe it was not her husband's receipt after all. It could have landed into his bag by mistake, and yet she knew very well it was his. As she continued to try to calm her elder sister down, the young sister assured her that she was going to investigate where the items were, but in fact, she was trying to buy time as the birthday was just around the corner and she did not want to spoil the surprise.

The day finally came and the husband packed his surprise bag and asked his wife if they could go out. They flew to some hotel where he had booked a room. He wished her a happy birthday and told her that they would be at the hotel for three days.

The wife said that she had not packed anything. The husband sarcastically said, "*What did you want to pack, oh, let me guess wanga uchida kupfeka zviwaya zvako or maparachute ako - you wanted to put on those very loose unattractive pants of yours.*"

He went on:

"*You know what, whoever designed those parachutes or zviwaya I don't have kind words for them, ndauya nembada lingerie, chaidzo kwete zviwaya - I brought you nice lingerie not zviwaya and ma-parachute - those lose pants like parachutes.*"

He opened the bag and each item that she had seen on the receipt was for a particular day and for a particular purpose.

He gave her one *mbada* – vibrating lingerie to put on and they went for dinner, he had his remote control that he was playing with while they were having dinner.

The wife did not know what hit her. Had she continued searching on the Internet she would have known what was happening? She started sweating and could not finish the food, yes that was the whole plan. They went back to the room. It was a beautiful evening.

The three days were great. She had an amazing time! Had it not been for her sister who calmed her down she could have spoiled this wonderful surprise, by jumping to conclusions.

This festive season surprise your partner; give her/him a surprise trip into the world of love. Surprise! Surprise! Please don't spoil the surprise.

ARTICLE 29

Communication - Key Tool in Thriving Unions
29 December 2010

Revisiting some of the stories which generated debate.

I hope you are enjoying the festive season!

I would like to look at some of the stories that got people talking and generated some debate in this column; *Girl, You'll Be a Woman...Soon; Learning to Be a Chef and Win; Treat Goose and Gander Equally; Mating Game Go on Play Your Part; Kanga and Mamba Styles; Secrets and Issues of Virginity.*

What came out of these stories was that there is a need for couples, partners to communicate, respect, have trust, and love each other. What also transpired from the discussions is how the family, community and institutions should create a balanced society in order to have happy families and unions.

The article on; *Girl, you will be a woman, soon* – was/is about the fi st visit from the *red woman* - most girls do not know what to do when the *red woman* (fi st periods) visits them as it is not talked about openly in many families.

Th s is when a girl is supposed to be welcomed into womanhood and be educated on what the *red woman* requires. The *red woman* needs attention, if she is not handled properly, she can cause chaos in a woman's life – the *red woman* can cause imbalances in a girl's life at school, at work and the way she socialises.

Long time ago in African societies the visit of the *red woman* was celebrated by the family and the community, as it was seen as a good thing and the girl would feel that what was happening to her body was supported, accepted by the community, her family and she became balanced.

The article encouraged girls to celebrate the *red woman* the fi st time she visits them; turn the house red, wear a red dress, collect red fl wers, eat red sweets, red cake and allow sisters, mothers and grandmothers drink red wine for to celebrate womanhood.

Amongst the letters that I received a single parent a father, said it was now going to be easier for him to educate his girls about menstruation.

The story of a *broken cooking stick* (erectile dysfunction) was one of the stories which got people talking. A man who had a *broken stick* started acting in a strange way and would get home very late when his wife was asleep to avoid being asked to perform his duties in the main room. He did not even eat the food that the wife had prepared, he became just impossible so that the wife could not even talk to him. The wife thought that he was seeing someone else. She decided to inform the family of her husband, she went to the elders and told them what was going on, and as evidence she took the food that her husband had not eaten for days to show the elders, they advised the wife not to leave him food anymore. The husband then went to the elders to report that his wife was not cooking for him, they asked him whether he was *cooking* for his wife. He seemed confused to what the elders were trying to say. They were disappointed that he did not understand what they meant. He was told very clearly that if he does not carry out his duties, the wife was also not obliged to honour hers.

He was confused, but they were serious. They said it was only when he had fulfilled his duties that they would talk to him. He accused them of following practices that advocated for men to cook, and he declared that he would not allow it to happen with him. But the elders stuck to their guns.

Realising that they were not going to be intimidated by *umntwana abamzalayo, nemwana wavakabereka* - their own child who they gave birth to he complied and asked how he was going to learn how to *cook* at his age.

They sat him down and revealed to him that his wife had registered her concern about his behaviour, that he was getting home late and that he had stopped eating the food the wife cooked and that was why the wife had stopped cooking for him.

It was only when he had done his part of cooking and presented a report, and the elders would take it up from there. They said they expected a report from a top-class chef that certainly included a three-course meal and not a paltry sandwich.

They said a three-course meal would mean a starter, the main dish, a desert and if the meal was as good as they expected, it would be followed by a siesta.

A good chef will also see that he serves his food in a good environment, the room in which the food is served should just make one salivate, the table, the tablecloth, the lights, the music, and everything else. A good chef would follow up to see whether the food had been good. If the food had been good, those eating will acknowledge by nodding their heads as a sign of satisfaction but at the same time not wanting to be disturbed.

It is only then that the chef will know they have done a good job. Realising he was cornered; he broke down and explained that his *cooking stick* had broken a long time ago! That was why he was playing hide-and-seek with his wife. The elders gave him some herbs to drink and in addition advised him to consult a medical doctor. Soon after, his engine was roaring, back on track.

He went on to prepare one of the best three-course meals that was followed by a siesta. When the elders visited their home there were no signs of malnourishment. The cuisine was rolling!

Because of lack of communication the wife might have thought that the husband was seeing someone and yet it was because of his broken stick that he was acting weird.

Communication is the backbone to every successful union, but some couples resort to silent communication which can complicate things - bring problems to the union, as one ends up assuming and trying to think what is happening with their partner. Lack of communication brings anxiety, which results in confli ts and may end up in physical fi hting. It also contributes to numerous health problems.

A *broken stick* is not something to be ashamed about, men should learn to communicate with their partners so that they know what is going on and seek help. I received a lot of letters from males with *broken cooking sticks* or *weak cooking sticks* who needed help.

A story of a man who wanted to bewitch his wife got people talking and opening up on new ways of making the *leisure centre/main room* alive and bringing variety to the ways they had been used to.

I gave a talk to some women and when we were discussing about *bewitching* (oral scx) an elderly woman was not amused and she was very angry and left, but other women and especially the young women said they wanted to discuss the issue as this is what they were now doing and it is another way of breaking the monotomy to what they had been used to - the missionary way.

A woman who did not understand what her husband was trying to communicate to her raised alarm when she phoned her husband's brother and said: *"Babamukuru munin'ina wenyu arikuda kundidya ...brother in-law your brother wants to eat me..."* which the brother took as bewitching. The brother thought that his younger brother had become a witch and told his other brother to go and see what was taking place, they went with their wives to solve this issue.

When the brother was asked where he had gotten the bewitching spirit (to eat people) he could not say anything, but his eyes were full of tears. Then the wife explained. Her sisters-in-law took her to a room where they had a serious talk with her and said how they wished they had such a husband as they only saw it on DVD's and read about this in books.

A woman who let her husband bewitch her for years did not understand how this gave him pleasure but one day she tried it, and it was great! She said: "It is advised that when your partner introduces a new way of doing things discuss it and try to meet them halfway." I received a lot of emails on this topic some wanting to understand more about *bewitching*, some saying that it provided an alternative to the way or *cycling* they had been used to.

In another article, an elderly woman had to cool off her friend who was not happy by the way younger women in church were behaving by not sleeping at funerals, but her friend asked her not to worry since they are old and could not *cycle* and young women could cycle. She said: *"Nhaiwe unozvinetsereyi, uchiri kugona kuchovha bhasikoro here regera tirare zvedu isu kumariro vanogona kuchovha varare zvavokumba - Why are you worrying yourself about us we can no longer cycle, let us sleep* here at the funeral and let those women who still can cycle go and sleep at their homes." The old lady was right, I got letters from young couples who felt they could not sleep at funerals three days in a row as they needed to *cycle* with their husbands. *Cycling* is said to be good exercise and it is also a way of *purifying blood*.

When I wrote the article; *Treat Goose and Gander Equally*, some did not understand why widowed women and divorced women needed partners, although some understood the importance of *purifying blood*, purifying blood is necessary to both men and women. It is also important to old people. Have you not seen old people who when they look at each other the next thing you see; tears rolling down their cheeks? They will have taken each other to a world afar and back.

After giving one of my talks an old woman, I think in her late 70's came to me and said, "*Mwanangu wataura nezvezera repakati, nezvemazera echidiki, ahuna kutaura kuti vezera redu toita sei? Baba vako varikumba ndingavatange ne-bewitching (kuroyana) vanoti ndaita sei, kuchovha bhasikoro hatichagona, uchanyatso gadzira chirongwa chevezera redu - My daughter you talked about how the middle and younger generation can entertain themselves in the leisure room, but you did not talk about our age group. Do you think I can go and tell my husband about bewitching he will be shocked and as you can see, we are old and not able to cycle. Please come up with a programm for us the old.*" Those who were around laughed but she was very serious, and I promised her I would be back for their age group. Purifying blood - if it is possible should be an everyday thing.

A Zimbabwean doctor based in South Africa Dr Shingai Mutambirwa was quoted on *3 Talk* a Talk Show presented by Noleen Maholwana-Sanqu, explaining how important it was to purify one's blood, at least twice a week. In this article, I mention a man whose wife had passed away, but it seemed he did not have anyone in his life for some time, an uncle asked why their son was not thinking of remarrying or having someone in his life. The aunt who had been asked replied: "*Musazvinetsa zvenyu anako kwaanoenda kunosukurudza ropa rake - dont worry he goes somewhere to purify his blood.*" Then the uncle was happy that at least his brother's son was 'normal' because he goes somewhere to have his blood purifi d.

It became apparent that divorced and widowed women also need their *blood purified*. If blood is not purified, it has some consequences to women's health just like it has for men. Who wants to go around with contaminated blood? It is a health issue. This made many people understand why widowed and divorced women had the right, just like anyone else, to remarry or have a partner, in order to have their blood purified. However, it is more fulfilling if one has a partner that they truly love. Be aware of sexually transmitted diseases so that you will know what to choose from the *leisure centre*.

It is through communication, respect, and love that we will have happy communities, families and unions and live a fulfilled life.

Have a blessed Happy New Year!

Virginity No Passport to Happiness
5 January 2011

Last week we could not summarise all the stories that generated interest and debate in this column. We could not do it last year and we will not be able to in this one either. Some of the stories are:

- Get Out of Your Box – Celebrate Womanhood,
- There Is More to Love Than Control, Fear,
- Getting Rid of Kanga and Mamba Styles,
- Cheating Kills Relationships,
- Good Dads Mould Confide t Daughters - Rebecca Chisamba's Father,
- The Worlds of Menopause, Andropause,
- Dyslexia; Real Life Challenge,
- Virginity And the Ugly Face of *Chiramu*,
- Generation Gaps, In-Laws, and Marriages
- Letting Go – A Painful Necessity

The article *Letting Go - A Painful Necessity*, discussed how to let go gracefully and move on – An example was given, of a woman who was brave enough to attend her ex's wedding in order for her to fi d closure. Finding closure prepares for one to move on and let go of the past - you don't have to be enemies because you have ended a relationship. From this story a number of people learnt how to let go, but some are still struggling and fi ding it difficult to let go, although they are trying to. It is not easy letting go but it is necessary. Some readers who responded to the article were having problems moving on even if it was clear that the relationship could not be resuscitated from the intensive care. One woman admitted that her marriage was beyond the intensive care; it was dead, but she could not let go.

Generation Gaps, In-Laws, And Marriages - Th s is a story of a young woman who did not want her husband's relatives visiting as she wanted to move around in the house in her birthday suit. She and her husband would cook in their birthday suits that is why she did not want her husband's relatives in the house as this would restrict her from her freedom. Her aunt could not understand this because of generation gap.

Another article which generated a lot of interest was - *Children, Parents, Switching Roles*. When children have reached a certain age, they sometimes take over as parents. One of the stories in the article is how a couple got together because of their children who did the match making. Recently I was watching a television show - *Who Wants to Marry My Dad* - an NBC-produced reality show that aired in the summer of 2003 and 2004. The point of the show was to have the children pick out a new bride for their father to propose to and marry.

Women competed for the affections of a single father - with her three daughters calling the shots and issuing a series of challenges. Before the contestants meet the man in question, they have to endure a round of lie-detector tests, leading to eliminations and furnishing the kids with plenty of useful information on those who remain. In the African culture when the girls swap roles with their father they are seen as the mothers-in-law, and a mother-in-law in endulo/pasichigare - in pre-colonial period and even now in some families she organises a wife for her son. Th s was/is to avoid confli ts between the mother-in-law and the daughter-in-law. In this case in which daughters are helping their father to get a wife it is also to avoid confli t in the home, in case the father brings in a woman who will not be compatible with his daughters. The father wants to create a situation in which his daughters will feel they are part of his life. This also includes sons.

I felt sorry for the father in, *Who Wants to Marry my Dad?* When he got attached or in love with one of the contestants but unfortunately the girls had their reservations, and the woman was sent parking from the show. The father and the woman had fallen in love and when they were parting, they both could not control themselves they cried and the father that day did not want to continue with the show. Although the girls had not found what they wanted from the woman whom their father had fallen for, they also cried when she was leaving. They talked it over and the father understood, and the next day they continued with the show. What all this is saying is that 'love' on its own might not be seen as bringing about a happy family because if the father had gone ahead and used his authority as a father then his relationship with his girls could suffer and he did not want this to happen. He wanted to create a situation where all parties are happy, even if he will get a woman whom he really does not love but the one that the girls will have Okayed and love can always follow, and love can thrive in a healthy environment.

Some cultures believe love is based on respect, trust and being there for each other, they call this practical love and the other love we are used to, to them saying it is fantasy love. When we were discussing this with friends, they had mixed feelings. A man got married to a woman whom no one in the family approved of including his children. One of his daughters decided that she was not going to sulk forever and decided to accept the stepmother. The stepmother was to teach her a few tricks about life, which she says became helpful in her life as a woman and later in her marriage. In our conversation she said: "My father left my mother 15 years ago and married another woman whom the family associated with loose morals because of how they had met. They called her and some still refer to her as '*mukadzi wemabhwawa - a woman of nightlife.* They say that, that is where they met and they still love their nightlife, for the 15 years that they have been together they make it a point that they go out at least once a month. In the meantime, my mother has become the most bitter and angry woman." She sighed, and then continued "One day I overhead my mother talking to her sister my aunt and said how he (my father) could leave me for a low-class woman, when he married me, I was a virgin, and yet he decided to leave me for that woman. I felt so sorry for my mother and hated the woman my father had married. My aunt encouraged her to continue praying and one day he would be back."

She explained how her mother has been praying, fasting for the past 15 years and she believes that one day her father would be back in her arms: "But I do not see this happening. My mother has become a bitter and angry person and she is failing to move on."

When her father relocated to one of the neighboring countries, she and her siblings joined him together with his new wife, she said that she decided not to continue sulking but to accept her stepmother; she said that she ended up admiring her stepmother's life compared to her mother, who ended up taking her anger on them. "Because of my mother's life I did not see the benefits of being married as a virgin, because despite my mother having married my father as a virgin, he left her for a woman who was not a virgin, and they are happy. I have learnt to live for myself!"

Her sentiments were echoed by women who thought women who had lost their virginity were being portrayed as victims. One reader wrote: "Not all women who have lost their virginity are victims, I lost mine with my eyes open and I knew what I was doing - exploring my sexuality!"

I inquired whether she had introduced some of the things she had learnt while exploring her sexuality to her husband and confide tly she said: "Yes I did, and my husband has taken it as his copyright!" She seems to be having a good time. I asked her, "Were you not afraid of diseases, during your exploration time?" She answered, "I used protection and we both went for tests, I think that is what people should be worried about."

A letter from Amai Tatenda; "There are some trends I have noticed in the discussions of womanly virginity. First of all, there seems to be this theory that somehow when a woman is not a virgin upon marriage, then she "should explain herself" and most explanations feature the woman as a "victim" of rape, or some other catastrophe. Th s is a myth--which is very oppressive to women. Why is it so difficult to think that a woman's loss of virginity could perhaps happen voluntarily? Just because in our patriarchal society, women's sexuality is controlled and should only be expressed after the men (woman's father, and her husband) have made some transactions - right? That way she has male approval to "mate.""

Does she owe her husband her virginity? NO! She does not, that is why per Shona culture a man only pays *mombe yechimanda - a cow which is paid for a virgin by the husband* in the event that he fi ds her in her pure state. But, because families, and particularly fathers are greedy, there's a lot of pressure on girls to be virgins. Th s way the family not only gets the extra beast - *inourayiwa - which is killed -* is as a symbol of the fact that 'her virginity has been taken.' Also, the father gets to feel he has done the good "macho-thing" of "protecting his daughter from vultures." My bottom-line is that – why do women feel like they owe men their virginity? Is it not oppressive to think this? Unfortunately, our cultures so highly prices virginity--but also please bear in mind how this concept or state of being is so temporary and so elusive. It doesn't even protect the virgin-wife from the husband's philandering ways. Once the husband has "drilled you" he moves on to 'drill others.' Not to mention the fact that, virgin-wives themselves, don't always remain true to those who 'drilled them.' Women, do not tolerate men who pretend to value you based on the state of your bodies - that is objectifi ation in its purest form!!!! You owe no one an apology for losing your virginity when you do, and however, if you do - this is your decision to make and yours alone! In the event that this power is taken from you, and you are raped and lose virginity - then actually, you shouldn't feel guilty at all because actually, you are owed the apology and you shouldn't be giving one!

Women please let's take control of our bodies and lives *ndapota hangu - I beg you.* Relationships are about love, about the whole person - not a tiny little membrane that partially obstructs a person's vagina. Love the whole person, and if someone cannot do that - get this: they are not worth your time!!! Get rid of them!"

Issues of Virginity topped the list as I am still getting emails on the issue Some three weeks ago, I was invited to give a talk on a number of issues including most of what I write about. A woman came to me and said, I am so happy to meet you, but my friend would not have felt the

same. *Pamakanyora nyaya ye issues of virginity, shamwari yangu yakati - 'chimukadzi ichi chandivhiringidzira zvinhu zvangu, nyaya iyi yakambonetsa mumba medu, asi yakanga yanyararwa iye zvino yakutangwa pamusana pechimukadzi ichi. Shamwari yangu yakatsamwa zvekuti - When you wrote the article – Issues Of Virginity, my friend said this woman has spoiled things for me, the issue of virginity was a problem in my marriage at some point in time but it has not been talked about for some time now, and this woman has decided to ruin things for me with her article as it will resurface. My friend was very angry."*

The aim of this column is to discuss those taboo issues in order to help create a balanced society – let us meet halfway.

There's indeed life after Divorce
12 January 2011

Last week's story covered several topics which were responses from the readers, they commented on most of the topics and also about a woman who has been praying for 15 years to have back her husband who has married another woman.

She could not stomach that her husband decided to marry a woman of 'loose morals' according to her as she had been married a virgin and the woman was a 'nightlife' woman.

Because of the bitterness and anger that she derived from the divorce, she became unpopular with her own children as she was now taking her frustrations onto them. Her own daughter ended up being closer to her stepmother whom she saw as a happy person; 'caring and loving.' The woman failed to move on without her husband, her world was her husband, she could not see how she could go on without him, but in the process, she was losing herself and chasing her own children away. Most of the people who remarked on the story, felt the woman needed some help in order to let go and move on. The way our institutions are structured was cited as making it difficult for the woman to imagine that there was a world out there without her husband. Cultural beliefs were also mentioned as playing a pivotal role in this whole issue; how a woman is raised and what is expected of her. If she accepts to move on and to let go, how she is going to face up with her new life which will require that she may need to look for another partner or she will be labelled a woman without a husband - these are some of the thoughts.

How does our society help this woman to continue living a normal life? A pastor who decided to remain anonymous said, *"Isisu kuchechi kwedu tinokurudzira mukadzi kuti kana muchato wapera, wadimburwa, namata Mwari akupe mumwe murume, kana uchida kuroorwa patswa.*

Tinokurudzira kuti mukadzi anamatire hupenyu hwakanaka, zvinozogona izvo kumuunzira murume akanaka nemamwe makomborero - In our church we advise the divorced woman to pray for a good husband and we also encourage her to pray for a good and happy life, whatever it brings, it could be a good husband and other blessings. It is actually a sin for this woman to be praying for her husband to come back to her. The husband is now married to another woman, and she is the one who is now a home breaker, because their marriage was ended, and they divorced. She is free to marry, what she is holding on to is not love but control and she has created a fantasy world in which she is still with the man and when she wakes up from the fantasy world reality hits her- This is the reality of life, it does not matter what happened, at some point she just has to let go. We sit down with such people and explain to them, that, such is life, and they should move on and not become bitter and angry."

We were discussing the issue with my friends a couple, and the husband blamed the so called 'culture' on why the woman was failing to move on and reminded us of a story which he told us some time ago, of how women are controlled in all aspects, he said: *"Muchikutondera here nyaya yandakakuudzayi, ye –tomato sauce? - Do you still remember the story that I told you – the tomato sauce story?"* We laughed with his wife. He repeated the story and this time elaborated a bit: *"The way women can be controlled is unbelievable, starting from their appetite for food, kana a simple thing like kuriyha tomato sauce uchikurambidzwa kwakuzoziya kuzipa kungoita zvimwe zviro - If a woman is not allowed to enjoy eating food, something as simple as tomato sauce - that is if one likes it, how on earth will she even be expected to think of how appetising 'other things' are."*

The story of the tomato sauce started when he visited his uncle and aunt in Chipinge, there were served rice and chicken and they added tomato sauce which they had brought as part of the grocery for the couple. Everyone else added the sauce to their food except their aunt, and the *muzukuru* (the man who was telling us the story) took the bottle of the tomato sauce to add in her aunt's food, but she indicated by shaking her head that she did not like it.

Th *muzukuru* asked why, and the aunt answered: *"Kwazi ayiriwi neakadzi peya, ingoriwa nemadhodha. -* was told *it is not supposed to be eaten by women, it is only for men."*

Th *muzukuru* asked why and she said: *"Kwazi tingobude ngazi yakawanda pakuteera tikariyha, ndeyemadhodha - If a woman eats tomato sauce she will have endless periods, and a lot of blood will come out during menstruation"* she explained. The *muzukuru* could not believe that his uncle could be so mean, and he assured his aunt that it was safe to eat the sauce.

"Murikunyeperwa ndisekuru, aiyisi yaa-yisa (madhodha) basi, inoriwawo nemadzimai mbuya, haisi ngazi, zviro zvingoriwa namadzimayi, inobanaka, namburayi muzwe - Uncle is lying to you there is no such a thing, women can also eat tomato sauce, it is not only for men."

His uncle was not happy, his eyes said it all when he looked at him, but the *mbuya-*aunt had the *muzukuru* to protect her. He was giving this as an example to show how women's minds are controlled starting with small things and he said that that's why this woman has been praying for years because she does not know what life is.

I spoke to some young adults whose parents divorced and have been either affected or have come out strong from their parent's divorce. What were their comments on the young woman who seemed to have chosen her stepmother over her own mother?

They all had mixed reactions; one young woman said, "It does not matter how bitter and angry my mother is, I will always be there for her, I cannot choose another woman over my mother, even if she is taking the bitterness and anger on me."

But her friend who also came from the same situation decided to disagree, as she just wants to live a life and not to be bitter and angry: "I don't think it is choosing the other woman over her mother but she is only human and sometimes the bitterness and anger weighed heavily on her and she got closer to her stepmother, 'unconsciously'." They are also those who thought the divorce might not have been handled properly, which becomes a problem to the children as they end up taking sides, which is an unhealthy situation. Parents are advised to help kids understand this situation: "Tell kids who are upset about the news that you recognise and care about their feelings and reassure them that all of their upset feelings are perfectly OK and understandable. You might say: "I know this is very upsetting for you. Can we try to think of something that would make you feel better?" or "We both love you and are sorry that mommy and daddy have to live apart." It is recommended to parents to remove anger and bitterness in order to be able to move on and also help their children to move on with them.

The woman who has been praying for 15 years and others like her are advised to rise above this challenge and become good role models for their children. Structures should be put in place to help particularly women to learn to let go and move on, the family, church, and workplace and dating agents - the society as a whole.

ARTICLE 32

Of Piknini Madams, Full Madams, Super Madams
19 January 2011

Sometime in the early 1990s I had a meeting with a woman who was in her late 50's at some institution. I asked for her offic at the reception where there were two women and one of the women at the desk gave me the number of the offic and told me that the door was written: 'Miss so and so... ', she wrote all the information on a small piece of paper.

While I was going to the offi , I realised that I had left my diary at the reception, I went back to collect it and the two women were discussing the woman that I was go-ing to see. " ......that woman is a real *mazakela - a woman who is not married and who does not seem to be getting married anytime soon, do you think she will ever be a Mrs*?" I pretended I did not hear what they were saying, and I collected my diary. It seems they continued with their discussion because as I turned my back on them, I heard one of them saying, "*Ndiwo unonzi munyama chaiwo... That is what I call bad luck.*"

When I got to the offic of the woman that I wanted to see, she was humming a tune and in good spirits, I could feel good vibes in this offi , positive energies com-pared to the women at the reception who did not have respect of this woman, old enough to be their mother.

When I went back home, I asked myself how such a respectable woman could be addressed by a title for *picnin madams - young women*, it did not make any sense. Th s woman is being treated as a young woman who uses the same title as a teenager - Miss. She is seen as *picnin madam - small or young madam*. It seems it is not the age which defi es women but titles which usually come with their marital status.

Th s is when I saw the beauty of our African culture which addresses one accord-ing to their age, when a woman reaches this age - of the woman I had gone to see - she is addressed as amai (mother), whether she is married or not.

Sometime ago I met a young man, and he greeted me he said, "*Makadiyiko Amai Jenje* - How are you mother Jenje?" I did not recognise him, and I asked who he was. He had grown up in Mbare and he knew our family. When he met me, he did not ask the question that I have heard many women being asked. " *Ko makunzi ani? - What is your name now*?" Meaning what is your marriage name. This question makes women who are not married very uncomfortable, and it is done deliberately to make them feel that way.

Now that I have grandchildren my grandchildren call me Gogo Jenje of course some call me Mai Makwenda. I am happy that my identity which comes with my fi st surname has not been destroyed.

A number of women today feel the same way, one day I met two young women who felt that they would like to keep their fi st surnames; " I am doing my PhD and soon I will be Dr So and So....., I would like people to know kuti *ndiri mwana wekwa nhingi, ndinodawo kusimudzira zita rekumba kwedu kwete revamwe vanhu* - when I become Dr. So and So I would like people to know that I am a child of so and so (the family were I was born), I want to be associated with my fi st surname not just my husband's."

Her friend explained how her surname is becoming extinct as they are few sons in their family, and she said in the whole of Zimbabwe she knows of only three families who use the surname: "I will not watch my family name disappearing even if I get married I will continue with my surname to save it from extinction."

When I was discussing this with some young women, they said they do not understand how a young man of 18 years old is addressed as Mr. (a full man) and not Master picnin baas - *small boss* and yet they (women who are 18 years old) continue with the Miss title.

While we were discussing I realised that the young women would also want to be recognised as full women, for instance one said, " We should stop using Miss title and graduate to a title that qualifies us to be a full woman like Ms." She lamented how most of the forms/stationery in many institutions do not include the Ms title which forces one to use either Miss or Mrs.

Because of how the Mrs Title has been presented; as dividing women, even those women who are married are preferring to use a uniting title like Ms.

Some of our institutions use the divide and rule method to weaken women using these titles. A sister of mine paid me a visit to tell me how she had been treated by some members of the Mothers' Union *UManayano/Ruwandazano/Chita*. She was very disturbed by how she had been treated, *"Nhai amainini iko kusava nemurume kwangu kwabva kwanyanyoipa kukadiyi?"* My young sister is my not being married such an issue [in this instance she calls me amainini – auntie, which is what her children would call me as a way of respecting]. I could feel her pain in her distressed voice. I asked her what she meant and said: *"Ndingaudzwe nemwana anezera nemwana wandakabereka kuti andigone kupfeka bhatye nekuti andina murume? Nhai amainini, kusava nemurume kwangu kwabva kwanyanya kuipa kukadiyi? Andisati ndambo nyadziswa zvakadaro? - My young sister how can a young person almost the same age with my daughter tell me that I cannot be a full member of the Mother's Union because I am not married. Is my not being married really that bad?"*

There was silence, I did not know how to answer her, and she continued with her story: *"Nhai amainini zera renyu iri ringandiudze kuti andigone kupfeka bhatye - amainini, I cannot believe that a young person of your age can say such things to me that I do not qualify to be in the Mother's Union.*" I was of the same age as her fi st daughter and her young sister who was/is my friend that is why she addressed me as *amainini* (young sister).

She was a good mother who had raised her children well and her young sister, educated them single handedly after a divorce where she came out with nothing, but continued with her life, worked for her children, and instilled in them positive values about life.

She was very angry how this young woman could judge her on the basis that she was not married, she said, *"mukadzi uyu ndirikuda kumufumura - I want everyone to know what kind of a woman she is.* (The grapevine had it that she slept around). Obviously, she was angry that is why she said this. I cooled her down and said: " Sisi let this woman live her low life alone, don't let her change you, the good person that you are, don't let her do that."

It is said that women who like to flex their muscles on other women using the Mrs Title are in very unhappy marriages. A woman made me laugh when she said, "*Mumachira ndimo munebasa, avawane zvakakwana, hakuna zviriko ndosaka va-chipedzera vamwe vakadzi shungu, kunyanya vasina kuroorwa, vanobva vafunga kuti ndivo vanotora huchi hwese - In the blankets [between the sheets] that is where the problem is, some of these women are starved that is why they end up taking it on other women, because they think that these women particulary those who are not married are the ones who take all the 'honey' from their husbands.*"

Another woman who was told that she was not fit to be a full member of the mother's union of her church because she was not married took the women to task as she went to the highest authority in her church to justify why unmarried women were not allowed to be full members of the Mother's Union.

"*Ndakatakura Bhaibheri ndikaenda kumukuru kuru wechechi ndikati 'nhai baba ndirakidzeyiwo vhesi rinoti mukadzi asina kuroorwa haapfeke bhatye, ndakabva nda-vataurira nyaya yaMary Magdalene. - I took my Bible and asked the man of the cloth to show me where it was written that a woman who is not married cannot be a full member of the mother's union. I told him the story of Mary Magdalene. I asked her which story of Magdalene she told the man of the cloth as they are many stories that I have heard. She said that she reminded the highest authority of the church that despite Magdalene not being married, she was the first to see Jesus when he resurrected.*"

Because she knew her rights as a human being, she was allowed to be a full member of the Mother's Union and so was my sister. One wonders why women use titles, (Miss, Ms, Mrs) to divide them, even in the church.

An unmarried woman who tried to be a full member of the Mother's Union but later decided the hassle was not worth it, said this division is caused by the structures laid by the society which the church is one of the gate keepers, "Some of these Mrs women are made to think that they are superior than all the other women, that is why you find that, even a woman young enough to be your daughter can show you some disrespect because according to her she holds a ' superior ' title which almost every woman live for. When these women are talking to me, they see a little girl in me a Miss as I am to acquire a proper title that they have. Women should not be divided by these titles but instead learn from each other and support each other."

ARTICLE 33

Show Affection, But …
23 February 2011

Recently while I was in South Africa, I was invited by a friend to her house and other friends for tea. The tea was that township tea which is prepared with water and milk, and it is left on a stove to simmer for a while, and you sit down to drink it not on chairs. One needs to set aside time for this kind of tea, you cannot drink it in a hurry. Stories with this brand of tea, get on very well, you can chat and talk and forget there is what is called time in this world.

Th s is what I miss about township life, sitting outside with friends, eating outside. I have observed that in the 'suburbs' people rarely sit outside; they eat inside their houses while watching TV. It seems these big houses have become like mini prisons.

Anyway, this was a lovely morning. As we were drinking our tea her son and his wife, *muroora/malukazana* her daughter-in-law and her grandchild came to visit, and we were introduced. The son left us and went to join his brothers, but the *muroora* remained with us and the grandson. The grandson was known as Junior, he was given his grandfather's name, the late husband of our friend who had invited us. We continued with our tea.

Junior started getting restless and wanted to play, but there was no one to play with. He sat on his mother's lap and said to the mother, *"For you baby."* He kissed her on the chin, the mother embarrassingly tried to stop him quietly and like typical of children he was not to be stopped, he continued. *"For you baby kani mama - please mummy."* He laughed and the mother said, *"Unopenga here Junior - Are you mad Junior?"* We continued to drink our tea, you know the kind of tea *hobvu - thick tea*, and with such entertainment it became even more appetising.

We continued talking as though we did not hear what Junior had said. He went on this time with a loud voice, "I said for you baby. For you baby. For you baby!" His voice was becoming louder. Th s time the mother ignored him, and we looked at each other with talking eyes, we were all communicating different messages. Junior was not going to be ignored, *"Mama awunzwe hele ndati for you baby - Mother are you not hearing me? I said for you baby."* The mother shook off her head sideways in disbelief at what Junior was saying.

An elderly woman, the aunt of our friend, was worried that Junior was becoming restless and why the mother was not answering him when he said, 'for you baby.' And she naively or she seemed, she asked: *"Ko mupindureika zvaanenge achida kana ati 'for you baby'" anoda kupindurwa achiti chiyi. - Why don't you answer him? How does he want you to answer him when he says, 'for you baby'."*

We all looked at each other with talking eyes again and we did not know how to answer the old woman. (Some said we could have told the old lady that it was the same as they used to say in the olden days – *mahobo ako andakakuchengetera –these are the things I have kept for you."*

In the meantime, Junior was now beating up the mother, "For you baby mama, for you baby" He was crying and laughing, the mother ended up laughing and one of our friends said: *"Nyaya dzenyu dzekutaura zvinhu vana ava vachinzwa, amenho zvenyu, chimudayirayi ka tinzwe anditi zvanzi nagogo (the aunt of our friend) mupindureyi. - You see, this is the problem of saying some of these things while these children are listening. He is saying answer him."*

The tea we were drinking nearly chocked us with laughter. Junior was getting really frustrated and he was no longer polite, he decided wrestling was the language his mother was going to respond to, he became a John Cena. He started jumping on his mother's lap and would say, "John Cena! John Cena!" One of our friends commented, *"Hezvo zvazo svika kumakata, makuitwa chiJohn Cena- ka. - Oh, dear he is now John Cena. It's bad."* Our *muroora - sister-in-law* was so embarrassed that she excused herself and went to do some work in the kitchen, Junior remained, now wrestling with the grandmother our friend.

What Junior had done was translated by others as a way of showing how the father loves the mother and when he says, 'for you baby,' they go into a love zone, either by kissing or do other things. What frustrated the child is that the mother did not respond, smile, or show some appreciation of what Junior was saying, as she would to the father, and then he decided to go the John Cena way.

Th s is how other couples communicate to each other, when the other fails to answer to their request they become the John Cena's of this world and they become wrestlers. Why some partners fail to respond to 'for you baby' might have something to do with the environment, bad timing. How do you get what you want from your partner without becoming a John Cena?

There were several lessons which came out of Junior's - 'For you baby' story. Some felt that adults should be careful what they do in front of children, saying things like for you baby would result in the child saying it at wrong places. But some chose to disagree and said that parents should show affection to each other so that their children will understand what love is all about. They would make sure that they do not go far, in front of the kids, but can pat each other, kiss, and call each other romantic names that would not be a problem.

The love which parents show to each other also goes to the children. Th s is what some parents had to say: "I have 2 boys, aged 4 and 6 and yes, my husband and I do kiss in front of them, not full snogging. The younger one will always go eew to get a reaction from us, but the older one will tell him we are allowed. For example, dad comes in from work, kisses/cuddles his children or they hug him fi st and then he does the same to me, the only difference is I get lips and they get cheek or forehead. They already know that they are not allowed to kiss anyone on the lips not even mum or dad, even my 4 year old will tell me my lips are only for his dad. I believe there is nothing wrong in moderate affection, I never did see my parents displaying any affection to each other. If we can kiss and hold hands outside, I see no reason why we cannot do the same in front of the children."

Parents should be careful not to do those other things in front of the children. Although some parents try by all means to hide it but some of the language, they use might not be smart enough and the children become curious. A joke has circulated for years of a child who was asked by her teacher, 'what is the last thing that your parents do or say before you go to bed?' and the child said: "My father says to my mother *dzimayi rambi tidle zvinhu - My wife switch off the light I want to eat things.* (Th s kind of jargon might make a child curious and want to see what it is that the parents eat at night which may confuse them).

Junior's story also teaches lovers good timing – when to say and how to say romantic words to your lover and how they are likely to respond. If your lover does not respond favourably maybe because of the environment or because of what they are going through, do you become a John Cena, (be angry and force them to understand what you are trying to convey to them). What do you do if she/he does not understand what you are trying to convey? You fi d other ways of communicating and make sure you apply more love to how you approach the whole issue and not to say to her/him – 'You don't understand if it was so and so would understand, that is why I end up going to her/him'.

It does not matter how slow someone is in trying to understand what their lover is trying to communicate to them, but if it is communicated through love and one is persistent then the other will fi ally be part of what you wish for.

When communicating something to the one you love and they are not getting it, watch out for distance or space, you are better off using ways which will not take up their space and then they feel as if they are suffocating. Write them a letter even if you live together, email them, compose a poem for them, a love song, last week we sang along to some of the love songs, buy them fl wers, cook them the best dinner, do whatever you can do to persuade them without causing any harm. Buy that nice lingerie and those toys as presents. Go out of your way to impress!

Some might wonder why space is important – no matter how much you love each other there are times when you just need space from each other – simply because you are human beings. When one is in such a mood show them, you miss them and try and joke about it, in a manner that you understand that they will come around. But this moody business should not be an everyday thing, then it would be a problem which only a psychiatrist or psychologist will have to deal with.

Let us end the Valentine's month with love. Blow a kiss for your lover and say – For you baby!

ARTICLE 34

We Value Your Comments and Contributions
2 March 2011

I have not responded to comments, contributions from readers for some time now, new stories kept coming up. I would like to let you know that we value your comments and contributions. I have received emails and calls from readers of this column on stories going back five weeks; *There Is Indeed Life After Divorce; Of Picnin Madams, Full Madams and Super Madams, When Parents Find It Difficult to Let Go, Sing Along to Love This Valentine* and *Show Affection but Out of Children's Sight.* The recent one on; Showing affection but... How far do you go showing affection in the presence of your children... raised a lot of interest and readers had different views on the issue.

One reader was of the view that parents take children for granted thinking that they are young and therefore they do not recall what they see. She would like to advice parents that a two-year-old child is intelligent enough to remember and mimic what they see, from parents. Th s is the time when they are shaped to understand the world around them and they might get confused if messages, actions are transmitted in a wrong way. Th s could have a negative impact into their adulthood.

These sentiments were echoed by a young father of two whom we shall call Tinashe, whose experience affected the way he relates to his wife. When he was growing up his parents got divorced, and his father remarried. His stepmother would sit on his father's lap and feed him in front of them and when they looked in wonder to what the parents were doing the stepmother would say, *"Asi amusati mambowona vanhu vachidanana? Chiyi chamurikutarisa, budai muno! - Have you not seen people who are in love? What are you looking at, get out!"* He would take his siblings and leave the room. When he visited his mother during the holidays, he would tell her, and the mother comforted him and his siblings and advised him that they should ignore it and try not to be in the room (lounge) when this happens.

When I discussed the behaviour of these parents with my friends, they felt the woman was very insecure and she wanted the children to feel that their mother was not loved or did not know how to show affection to a man. One friend said this woman had her own problems which she was trying to cover with misguided love, "Showing off to your stepchildren that you are in love with their father more than their mother is very cheap. Real love does not hate others especially innocent beings like children whom she was supposed to protect. She had serious issues which needed to be dealt with by a therapist."

The man who was part of the discussion blamed the man as a weak father who failed to protect his children and thought this man was very childish, as he himself would have not let any woman feed him in front of his children as a way of showing off as this is how he saw it. *"Ndiyo inonzi love yechibharanzi manje. Unoita baba verudziyi vasingagone kumiririra vana vako* - That is a foolish kind of love- what kind of a father who cannot protect his own children."

Yes, Tinashe felt he was not protected, this was abuse as one of the readers would like to call it 'passive' abuse that children suffer from insensitive affection by parents. He says that now that he is married, he cannot show affection to his wife, sometimes just touching each other and some of the simple things like hugging and kissing. "I become so uptight, and I fi d it difficult to demonstrate love to my wife. I feel sorry for my wife who is a good person and deep down I love her, but it is sometimes difficult for me to show her affection."

Parents can show affection around their children, but it should be sensitive and make sure they are not hurting their children. Showing affection, which is filled with love, and considering how those around you feel helps children to understand what love is all about, and that they carry that into their adulthood.

The article, *Of Picnin Madams, Full Madams and Super Madams* got people talking. Here are some of the emails that I received:

- Very true some people think that every female should be married by a certain age and treat those who are not married like lesser people. I am not married and am enjoying my life at 38 I do not care for such people who belittle others because they think by now, I should be called Mrs. I don't let their thinking or what they say affect me. I do not live my life for other people but for myself.

- Thanks a lot, for the article referred above of 19 January 2011. I really enjoyed reading it and I guess most women did so as well. I am also one who is affected by the same situation, where society judges one with her marital status and think they can disown that person. The society we live in is very cruel. Th s boils down to church where fellow women are not comfortable in your company, but when it comes to *kupa, donations*, etc for Church, they expect now that this group of women (singles) should be at the forefront. They want to benefit from us and yet they don't want us to be part of them. It also begins from the church where if one has to be accepted in the Mother's Union, the teachings are all centred on marriage. One lady at a workshop of single parents (both man and woman) said, at her church: *"varume havatodi kuona vakadzi vavo - men do not want to see their wives talking to single women, hanzi unodzidzei from them ivo vasina varume (what do you learn from them since they do not have husbands."*

- One lady also said that *kuChita chavo* (Mother's Union) one year, it was led mostly by single women, and *Ruwadzano* (Mother's Union) that year *vakaroorwa vazhinji* (those who were married) dropped because they felt that the group was filled with too many single women - imagine.

  At my church I am called as *Mai/Mother*... which I am so used to, at fi st it used to offend me, but now I am used to, and I also refer myself the same way. Thanks a lot for the article, and for other articles they are so interesting, eye openers and revealing.

- I loved today's issue of the Herald titled "Of Pikinini Madams, Full Madams, Super Madams" the HERALD January 19th. Thanks for educating the society about issues the society itself has helped to bring about. It was not like that in the beginning! You couldn't have highlighted it better than you did. Ultimately, us, the women are responsible for this cancer and one way or the other each of us if not already affected, will be affected by this cancer. Up to 18 years you are *pikinini madam*, you get married you become Mrs. - full madam, you stay longer in the marriage, and you even become - Super Madam. Along the way you lose your husband and suddenly your title changes, relationally everything changes, other church members are no longer comfortable with you holding positions in the church. Worse still if you are divorced, believe me, no one is interested in the circumstances that led to the divorce, you revert to the title of *pikinini madam*, unfit to be part of Mother's Union in the church and therefore relegated to back benchers.

- I am divorced with two beautiful kids. I thank God for these kids are well mannered and exemplary. When I visit my mother in the rural areas, *Vana ambuya vemuraini - the grandmothers in the area*, and other relatives whom we had not seen for a long time would always mistake other children to be my children because of their dress and behaviour, *'Ah ava ndivo vana vako here muzukuru, inga vakura - Are these your children my grandchild? They have grown*" and when I then show them my real children, they are stunned and ask "*ko murume wako ari kupi, where is your husband?*" They all expected my kids to dress and behave "in a certain way" in conformity with my title as "Pikinini madam." See!! Children are affected as well. Each time I have made it a point to tell them straight away *kuti, handina murume - to say I do not have a husband*, and my mother would feel embarrassed. I did not feel any embarrassment at all, I was merely stating a fact.

- This discrimination that women are facing is not only happening at the workplace and at church alone, but also within families as well. At one point at a family funeral, I was asked to prepare food and bath water for my young cousins" husband by my Aunties while his wife was sitting in the shade with other super madams.

"*Mainini motoona kuti babamunini venyu vadya uye vageza - young mother [in this context] please see to it that your brother-in-law has bathed.*" ...and this was at my own father's funeral.

WITH THE LORD's help, I have done well for myself, I love the person that I am and the situation that I find myself in, and I believe that I am not a lesser per-son just because I am not married. This attitude in women has made me despise marriage, what's the point, "you a *pikinini madam* today tomorrow you are super madam and again you switch positions back to *pikinini madam*, either through divorce or death. What's the point Joyce!!!

• I love the Lord so much, I love praise and worship but somehow, I feel comfortable as a back bencher, because that's where society has placed me. I am such a quiet member of the church and I fi d it difficult to interact with other church members after the church service because of this cancer that we as society continuously help to generate.

• I have been following your articles in the *Herald*. Madam its good, but I think in your conclusion you must put yourself a comment *yezvakanaka - good things* at the end of the column. Look, on my opinion or in our culture's opinion *kuroorwa nekuroora kwakanaka, kuzvichengetedza kana uri mwana kwakanaka hanzvadzi* - to get married or be married is good my sister, looking after yourself if you are young is good my sister. Virginity is not a passport to good life and Mary Magadalene was the fi st to see Jesus despite not being married. So, my dear journalist researcher I think if you quote all these kinds of things, it's good to fi - ish with good conclusion which educates the society. Don't try to protect *zvinhu zvakaipa* - bad things. Thanks.

My response - On virginity not being a passport to happiness it is what some women feel, women who have been short changed as virgins are bitter and, in this instance, it was the daughter who did not see the benefits of keeping her virginity if her mother did not benefit from it and her stepmother who was married not a virgin was a happy woman. Th s is a fact, and many women are going through this ordeal. It is up to the society to correct this and until then we will have people who complain and would want their voices heard.

Mary Magadalene was the fi st to see Jesus despite not being married. Married women should not think they are superior to unmarried women that was the reason for that example. Women are encouraged to close these divisions of *picnin madams*, *full madams*, and *super madams*.

There is no individual superior to the other and as women we need to promote sisterly love instead of creating and having these divisions. Most human beings would want to have a partner in life but because of circumstances beyond them they do not and that should be respected.

I also got emails and phone calls mostly from my friends who were commenting on the article; Sing along to love this Valentine, we went back in time and they reminded me some of the songs that I had forgotten; *Shumayira* by Dr Footswitch, *Chipo Chiroorwa Tipemberere* by the Green Arrows, *Calling Your Name* by the Eye of Liberty, *Behind Closed Doors* by Diana Ross, *Mid Night Train To Georgia* by Gladys Night, *Baby You Can Drive My Car* by the Beetles, *Leaving On A Jet Plane* by Peter, Paul and Mary (Composed by John Denver). We sang these songs with my childhood friends at a certain joint and we went back in time. Bring out your song books and let us sing. *Cause I'm leavin' on a jet plane. Don't know when I'll be back again. Oh babe, I hate to go ...*

It Takes Two to Tango, Play Your Part
23 March 2011

It is essential for couples to understand each other.

My 70-year-old *muzukuru - grandson* - although he is much older than me, phoned me and said he wanted us to meet.

These are some of the things that I enjoy about our culture. When I was young there were older people who used to visit our home and address me as *ambuya - grandmother*.

I still remember when, I must have been eight years old, there was this very old man who used to visit our home and the respect he showed me made me feel so uncomfortable as he would address me as *ambuya* and recite my totem as he greeted me while clapping his hands.

He would say: "*Makadiiko Mukanya; Makadiiko Chinamhora. Greetings Mukhanya, Greetings Chinamhora.*" (Mukanya and Chinamora are my totem names)

I would feel so embarrassed that an old man like him could show me so much respect, yet it was supposed to be the other way round. I later got used to it as more relatives addressed me that way, and I kind of felt put in a place of authority. That is the uniqueness of the Zimbabwean culture that everyone has a role that they play from childhood to adulthood. I am trying to explain this to some cultures who would be surprised how a 70-year-old person can be my *muzukuru - grandchild*.

Anyway, my *muzukuru*, had something burning that he wanted to tell me. When he phoned me, he had mentioned that he enjoyed the article that I wrote last week. When we fi ally met, he was going round and round in circles. He greeted me using my totem and asked how the family was doing which I also did.

He then referred to last week's article and said, "*Ambuya makaita basa nekunyora kuti vakadzi vaite ma-exercises. Ndanzwa nekufondoka ambuya. Kana ndiite sei ndinongonzi hapana zvandaita. Ndoti ko unoda kuti ndiite seiko, unongonzwa oti, 'handisi kunyatsonzwa parere mwoyo'. Iwo musi uno ndakazoti ndingangofa ndenga ndikati ka toita 180 degrees munhu wakayowera, izvozvi muzukuru wenyu ari kuto kamhina.* - Grandmother you did well to write the article on "sport"; it's not just for men, you encouraged women to exercise. I am tired of being the one who does most of the work in the leisure room. It does not matter what I do; your granddaughter, [his wife] does not appreciate my efforts. She is forever complaining that she does not get satisfaction. Just recently I said to her we have to go 180 degrees, for her to get that satisfaction, she actually cried that I was breaking her and as I speak, she is limping.*"

Some of the reasons could be lack of *exercise* and some could be that she is not comfortable with that particular way of doing things.

When I visited my *muzukuru's* wife, she was very comfortable to discuss what had happened and said to me: *"Ambuya zvema 180 degrees takazviita tichatemwa dzinobva ropa. Hazvisirizvo zvinoita kuti zvinhu zvifambe, chete muzukuru wenyu akaoma musoro, mumwe musi muchanzwa kuti afenda, nekuda kuzviita mukomana. Chitema here kuti nditi handisikunzwa parere mwoyo. Panechiyi chatisina kuita nhai ambuya, tichazvinzwa, vanhu vanokura, zvinhu zvochinja. - Grandmother the 180 degrees styles: we did them when we were still in our prime time, it is not the 180 degrees which makes playing pleasurable. Your grandson thinks that he is still young, one day you will receive news that he has collapsed because he is trying to be like a young man forgetting that with age things change."*

What she meant is that as you grow old you are not as athletic as you were and one should try and look for other ways of making each other happy, meeting halfway.

I pointed to the fact that the husband is worried about her not *exercising*, and she only exercises *kana azvimbirwa - when she has eaten and is too full.*

She laughed and I ended laughing too, she sighed and shook her head.

"Kuseka nhamo kunge rugare. Muzukuru wenyu arikumbo nyanyo dyeyi ngaan-dipowo zvarikudya, zvinobva zvamupa ginger yakadaro, kutoda kundityora mukadzi mukuru, ndiudzeyi kuti vanhu ndinovaudza kuti ndirikugamina ndakaita sei? - One can laugh at problems as if she is laughing about something good. What is it that your muzukuru is taking he must also give me, so that we can be at the same wavelength. Tell me ambuya what do I tell people who see me limping?"

She told me that she has been buying books and they would read a chapter and try out what was in the chapter, but for some reason my *muzukuru* was fascinated by a certain chapter which seemed not to come out of his head.

She said even if he has read some of the chapters which explain how at a certain age one needs to take things easy and other ways have been introduced but for some reason, he seems to be more interested in being a bionic man.

We have heard of people who have had heart attacks in the process and yes at a certain age people have to take it easy.

Some couples that I know have been helped by reading books, which educate them on this subject of *leisure*. After reading a chapter they do their homework, until the book is fin shed. Not everyone needs to read books some just improvise and have had a fulfilled life.

In past articles we also discussed the importance of communicating as a couple and couching each other, this helps to meet halfway and minimises confli ts behind closed doors. Playing is just not physical, it should also be understood that it is very spiritual, feeling for and loving each other is very important for a couple to enjoy being together.

The 180 degrees which is part of the missionary way of doing things is not the only way to fi d pleasure, but some people are stuck in the conservative ways, and they end up bringing misery during playtime.

It is essential for couples to understand that each and every part of the body can be used for *leisure*, it should really be leisure and not pain, from the head to toe, all that is a *leisure field*, and it is up to the two of you to explore and bring joy to your love life.

Exploring other ways of doing things in the *main room* brings the two of you even closer as you laugh and joke about sometimes not getting it right, until you get it right.

You can do absolutely anything in that room, as long as you do not hurt each other, and as long as it is for enjoyment; go for it.

A friend of mine was approached by her niece who wanted advice. The niece complained about how the husband wanted her to be a model in some costume, but she felt that it was for those women not her a decent woman. I have never understood why women think that if they are in that room, they should be decent. What is decency?

He wanted to admire his wife, and what is wrong with that. It also seems that women associate real pleasure with loose women. *Playing* is *playing* and if you lose your mind in the process and become a child the better, then you go to a world that you have never been. It is fulfilling.

I asked the aunt who is my friend what advice she gave her, and she said: "I told her that she should also buy her husband some costume and have him on the ramp - call it Catwalk romance!" I laughed, and I repeated: "Catwalk Romance!" She said: "The way you have responded is the same way my niece responded but the advice worked."

After our meeting this elderly couple had real fun and became more open to each other, and did not need to go missionary, they discussed other options. Taking time to understand and appreciate your partner is vital to a happy marriage.

A colleague of mine asked me when we met recently about me revisiting *the Kanga and Mamba*. He said: *"Joyce imbodzokorora Kanga and Mamba, vanhu varikurambana mudzimba umu - Joyce why don't you revisit the Kanga and Mamba story, do you know that people are divorcing at an alarming rate."*

A female journalist intervened and said that I had revisited the subject, but he said it was not exhausted enough and it needed more information. He reiterated: "People do not know their partners in these marriages that is why they are collapsing."

The story of *Kanga* and *Mamba* was about a couple that had been married for years but did not know each other. The *kanga* story was about a man who had never seen his wife fully unclothed as she was always covered by the *kanga - a wrap* and when his eyes were opened that he could after all see it, he could not believe it, after having three children under the *kanga*.

The *Mamba - a snake that moves fast* was a man who had been married to his wife for 25 years and because of his *Mamba* style the wife did not know him.

Get to know your partner and you will have fun!

Communication is central for couples.

Mix of Tradition, Modernity is Key in Marriage
27 April 2011

An elderly couple came to my house one day, the man is in his 80s, and the wife is in her late 70s. They had told me that their granddaughter was getting married sometime in December. I thought they had visited to confi m the date and remind me not to forget. But there was more to their visit than just to inform me of the pending wedding ceremony.

They had come to collect some seeds of a particular tree in my yard. They said they were going to use them to help prepare *ribbons* (a traditional way of elongating the labia) for their granddaughter's big day. The granddaughter had gone past the stage when she was supposed to have done that but had shown lack of interest at the time when most of the girls her age group were doing it.

"Vana ava unoti uchivaudza kuti hupenyu hunodanzwi unonzwa vakuti 'gogo ndezvekudhara izvo, - You know with these children when you are telling them about life, they will tell you that grandmother that is old fashion." She said as she was picking the seeds.

"Iye zvino ndavekumhanya mhanya kugadzirisa zvinhu, kuti iwo muti uyu, mumwe wandakazonotora kumusha wekuputa kwako. - You know when you are telling children about life they don't want to listen, you hear them saying that is old fashion grandmother. Now I am running around trying to get all sorts of herbs, this one and the other one I went to collect in the rural areas which she is supposed to smoke."

The husband laughed as he gave her some of the seeds that he had picked, which were drier than the ones that his wife had collected. *"Chiregai kuita BP, modzi idzi. - Don't get worked up, here are some seeds."*

They had raised their granddaughter after their daughter had passed away. They were obviously ecstatic that she was getting married and were proud of their success. She had lived with them from the age of 11. Th s time the granddaughter was willing to prepare herself before her marriage; to do what many girls nowadays either shun or do grudgingly.

But a few decades ago, it was a must to prepare *ribbons*. Women in most Bantu-speaking areas are expected to *pull the ribbons* as part of marriage preparation and also for a woman to be in touch with their sexuality and *enjoy sex.*

Some cultures in Zimbabwe believe that dried seeds of certain bushes or trees help to make it easy when stretching or *pulling ribbons* preparing the woman for playtime.

However, I would like to encourage people to consult with elders, or doctors on which roots or portions to use, and how to use them and if they are safe as some concoctions can cause inflammation in that part of the body.

Traditionally, *ribbons* were pulled just before a girl was visited by the *red woman* (menstruation), around the age of twelve or thirteen, but now women are visited by the *red woman* at around ten years of age.

It was widely believed that the *red woman* made the labia shrink, hence the preparations had to be done before the *red woman's* arrival. (But now it is done either after or before the arrival of the *red woman* depending on the age the girl is visited by the *red woman*; age is important as the girl is supposed to understand what she will be doing and why.)

A cousin of mine, who was with me when this elderly couple visited, was curious to know whether it was still possible for her the granddaughter to prepare the *ribbons* at the age of 26.

She sought the advice of the elderly woman, who told my cousin that it was possible, but it was going to be slightly difficult. She would have to work extra hard and use multiple concoctions including some that are inhaled overheat while the others would be rubbed on the parts to be pulled before she starts *pulling the ribbons*.

My cousin was not particularly interested in the one that is inhaled through smoking. The elderly woman invited my cousin to her home, so that she could explain to her, as that needed more time. The pulling and preparation of the *ribbons* was and is still very big with the Zimbabwean community, although they are some who are not into this practice.

A colleague of mine who lives and works in the UK, found that some women from Rwanda also practiced the same. "I was on duty the other night, working with two ladies, one from Rwanda and one from another country in Africa. The other lady, started to complain that women from Zimbabwe, were taking their husbands away. She was actually labelling us as loose women."

I asked her were they not retaliating by going for Zimbabwean men. She laughed and said that she would never dream of having a relationship with a man who was unclean, uncircumcised because in their country such men were viewed as boys.

The talk drifted to circumcision, and then I remembered a friend of mine, a Zimbabwean man who had a girlfriend from another African country, saying that he had ended the relationship because the lady had repeatedly asked him to be circumcised at the age of 43 because he was dirty, he lashed out at her that he would never do that to please a woman who had a "flat screen" who had no *ribbons* and that he would only marry a full woman with intact *ribbons* as long as his index fi ger.

"While I was surprised to fi d out that the practice was also common in as far as Rwanda, it gave our colleague food for thought because she had looked at us as loose."

A historian explains how men used *ribbons*: "Th s was done for us men so that in case a woman did not want to play that day a man was not supposed to force her to have sex but persuade her by playing with her *ribbons*. With *ribbons* a man would never go wrong because eventually the woman would mellow down and respond."

I asked the views of a traditional healer, who added to what the historian had said: "Depending on the situation, one would wait until the woman had gone to sleep and then start playing with the *ribbons* while she is asleep, this would slowly bring her into the playing mood that is if the man does it right."

Th s means that *ribbons* were not only meant to please the man, but also to increase the pleasure in the woman, especially if she could be aroused in her sleep.

The elderly couple who came to my house also supported this notion. Sekuru said, "*Waitonyatso bata zvakanaka uchinyengerera kwete kutswinya, kana mukadzi ainge anechakamushatirisa aibva atoita hasha dzakanyanya. Nzira yacho yaibva yatovharwa, waitenge wakungotenderera kunze kwechivanze. Waitoita kunyengerera chaiko. Maoko kana aive neman'a waito nyika mumvura inodziya kuti ambopfava, wozoazora mafuta enzungu! - You had to do it well, nicely, not rough, not as if you are pinching the woman, because if a man did not do it well, let us say the wife was angry then she would really lose it and the path would be closed, it would be like you are going around a closed homestead, the path would be closed. A man was supposed to do it right, if your hands/fingers were not smooth then you were supposed to soak them in hot/warm water to soften them and then apply peanut butter oil.*"

Ribbons - labia minora - are said to carry the greater part of a woman's pleasure spot together with the clitoris. The labia minora (inner lips) are inside your outer lips. They begin at your clitoris and end under the opening to your vagina. The labia minora are the two inner folds of skin that surround the opening of the vagina. The labia minora are part of the external female genitals, or genitals present in individuals assigned females at birth, which also includes the *mons pubis, labia majora, vaginal opening, hymen,* and clitoris. It is one of the very sensitive points in a woman's body. The man was required to buy beads for the wife to thank her for the *ribbons* or *kushonga,* the beads were called *gomwe.*

The female relatives of the young woman would also give her some few beads, which would anchor the waistline, and combined with the *gomwe* would provide music in the *leisure room* when having sex.

The use of music in the *leisure room* is encouraged. One day I was watching model Tyra Banks on television, and she asked three couples what kind of music they play during *leisure time*; one couple said jazz, the other one said they play rock, and third couple said they created their own music.

Beads created music during *recreation time*. To further prepare the young woman the paternal aunts gave the bride-to be what was called *chinyu* - a bottle-necked gourd, which she filled with some ointment that she would use to oil members of her husband's family during the *bathing ceremony - kupa mvura yekugeza.*

She would use the remaining ointment for massaging her husband. When the woman died the *chinyu* was supposed to be buried with her.

I interviewed two elderly women on how a young woman was prepared for her marriage, and they concurred that *chinyu - the gourd* could be used today to put oils for the couple to massage each other before and after playtime), thereby bringing the couple closer other than just mechanical play where the man forces himself on the wife, and then sleep straight afterwards.

Th *chinyu* can be used to improve playtime. An aunt told me how they would have *nyora - special incisions* and that the incisions were done in such a way that they were bumpy and when touched during *recreation time* they would send waves throughout the body.

The incisions were applied in strategic places. There are women who feel that although the preparation of a woman might seem as done to please men, actually women were empowered in the sense that they controlled their foreplay.

One woman who decided to remain anonymous, said: "Women directed play in the leisure room, by being prepared for it, they knew what they were going to do in that *main room*.

"You can only control what you know. Today's young women go into that room not knowing what they are going to do, and they become very unhappy, because it is only the man controlling, calling the shots." Women could use *ribbons* to empower themselves in many ways.

I will explore this topic further and discuss it in other articles.

I asked the couple whether men were also prepared for playtime, sekuru explained: "*Taidzidziswa, asi zvedu zvakanga zvisina kuwanda sezvemadzimai. Chimwe chataidzidziswa kugusana, zvaikurudzirwa zvikuru. - We were taught, but not much as what women were taught - one of things we were taught was how to shave each other.*"

An aunt explained how it was done: "*Kazhinji mukadzi aitanga ndiye kugusa murume asi kana murume akugusa, waingoita reza yekutanga yepiri wooona Jakopo akuda kutamba, motombomira moona nezva Jakopo mombozorora mosimudzira kugusana kuye, rwepiri inenge yava nguva yangu Jakopo tinenge tapedza naye. - The* woman would shave the husband fi st and when it was the husband's turn it was just one razor and the second 'Jakopo' would want to play. So, we would attend to Jakopo and take a break and then when we are done with Jakopo we continue." (Jakopo is a word in this context used to mean the penis, meaning that Jakopo (penis) would be erect wanting to have sex).

A young woman told me a story of how she was having endless fi hts with her family because she did not believe in the *preparation of ribbons* as she was told by her medical doctor that it was not healthy.

Gogo disagreed with the young woman and said she and generations of women who engaged in the preparation of ribbons did not have any health problems, adding:

"Dai Zimbabwe ichine vakadzi nhaiwe, dai takapera kufaka tese, tese - If pulling or stretching ribbons was not safe healthy wise, then many women would be dead by now, then Zimbabwe would not be having women by now."

While we should uphold some of our cultural practices, perhaps medical scientists should help us to achieve this in a hygienic and safer way rather than discrediting some of our cultures.

From the discussions I have heard with many women, both in Zimbabwe and abroad, *women's ribbons* enhance pleasure during playtime and are part of sexual and reproductive health. A friend of mine told me that in the UK some Zimbabwean women continue the practice and they use concoctions sent by courier.

There are elderly women who are instructing young girls on how to do it. In the past it was easy for girls of the same age group to convene at an elderly woman for instructions on how to *pull the ribbons*. Those were the days when people lived communally in the townships, rural villages, and mines. Unfortunately, in the so-called suburbia, where people don't usually share information of this nature, the practice is dying.

Let us preserve some of our cultures, and challenge modern scientific research to work with tradition to improve some of our practices so that they are carried out in safe environments just like male circumcision, which is now carried out in the hospitals.

NOTE: Actually, circumcision was a practice carried out in Zimbabwe and a lot of African countries during the pre-colonial era but was stopped with the advent of foreign religions and teachings.

ARTICLE 37

Let Us Clarify It for You
4 May 2011

I have not responded to your interesting e-mails for a while and want to answer all your questions this week.

The responses to last week's article alone have also been overwhelming and readers had different views on the topic *Mix of Tradition, Modernity is Key in Marriage*.

Some readers felt that I should have just said it as it is, and this is not the fi st time that readers have expressed such sentiments. Here are some of the emails:

- *Hi Joyce, I trust you are well. I take it from your piece Herald is also meant to educate the "modern" generation. I don't think they will understand what is meant by "pulling the ribbons"; I think you should have spelt it out. Some of them will no doubt ask their elders what it meant and what it's all about, but the majority will be totally bewildered. Why not just spell it out?*

My Response:

The reason why I don't really spell it out, is because this is a family paper, and the information might fall into wrong hands - those who might not be able to process the information in an informed way. I deliberately use jargon language so that couples, families, friends, and parents can explain to their children in a more informed way and also discuss these things amongst themselves. Anyway, my brother as you say, let me spell it out, *"pulling the ribbons"* is the *pulling of the labia* to prepare for womanhood or marriage, to those who are into this practice. The *ribbons* are mostly used for sexual pleasure - to please the woman and the man. The *pulling of the ribbons*, it is one of those ways of enhancing sexuality just like other ways which we have discussed and that we are yet to discuss in this column.

A woman who was also having problems understanding the article had this to say:

- *I was lost and I kept reading ribbons and ribbons and I kept asking what ribbons are? It took me a long time to understand what you were talking about. This is interesting, it's sore when you are older, but that thing is elastic it stretches to whatever length you want.*

My response:

I am happy to know that you understood at the end and thank you for explaining the way you have. While there are some who prefer that I spell it out, some prefer the subtle way of writing.

- *I like the way you put it Joyce because, as Africa, there are things we do not put across directly then the platform can go into any hands - since you cannot use fore-warnings like PGA etc, as with films. But what I also like is the fact that, as Africa, we are communal by nature - and your articles encourage social discussion and debate as we try and find out from each other - and that stimulates further discussions, thereby helping knit the social fabric. Asking those around does not kill - we learn from each other.*

A woman who read the story expressed her displeasure and wrote:

- *I believe that humans are created normal, why disfigure yourselves with these sad myths? It's like the other Africans who circumcise girls for the same sad beliefs (to please a man). This pulling is a very painful process for the girls, and those ribbons become swollen and painful when rubbed often. This act is senseless to me.*

I sent this to some readers of this column to comment and here is one of the comments I got.

- *God made one of us unique as individuals, the very reason why authorities use fingerprints to distinguish between different individuals for different purposes but, in the final analysis, distinction has to be made between mutilation (which may be removal or de-sensitisation of a part) and enhancing (which may exaggerate, but leave structure with original feelings but giving the owner the potential to feel good or even show off in appropriate situations). So, in my opinion, ribbon-making (good or bad to some, depending on upbringing and exposure) is no different from fingernail extending, or momentarily pain-inducing practices like: tattoo-making, hair plaiting, plucking of eyebrows, piercing (ear-ring/nose ring/lip ring/belly button ring/genitalia ring, etc), and all sorts of figure-enhancing surgery. If we are to talk disfiguring which deviates from how we were created, then we may as well lead a laissez faire life where we just "let it be" - then we will stop activities like shaving - (both upstairs and downstairs). At the end of the day, simply because our world has become outrageously democratic, it all boils down to choice - one does what they want with their body.*

A contribution from a woman who is into this practice - "pulling of the ribbons" wrote:

- *Hi Joyce, I read your article and have some contribution(s). Yes, I grew up in rural area of Zimbabwe and as young girls (up to 13yrs) we would go to swimming and take a small break and went kuseri kwemagarden (behind the gardens) and do the ribbon pulling – and started swimming again. Those who were older within the group would tell youngsters and newcomers what to do. Now don't you think that the issue of climate change (one of the many reasons) has contributed negatively to this practice? All the madzivas (rivers) have disappeared. On the other hand, the platform where we can draw attention and make some changes is within our own country. In other Western countries, integration courses have by denouncing the ribbon pulling practice. And because we like the practice, we are forced to do it secretly. I did a course in pre-modernity, modernity, post modernity and trans-modernity and all the issues and references are related to developed countries. During the exam I gave examples of Africa and my own country, and they could not let me fail because I was giving real examples. I can write books over this issue but ... what is our starting point? Would like to hear from you.*

<u>My Response</u>:

- Our starting point my sister is here, we need those books as I have also started writing a book on *Sex in The African Context* and how women should understand their bodies before anyone comes into their lives. We need to document these issues, to document and pass on the information, oral traditions have gone this far but we need to start harnessing everything that we can get hold of and to document it in more dynamic ways; writing of books, making of documentaries, film, have schools, clinics that discuss these issues. Get rolling my sister, time is not on our side.

- I got an e-mail which encouraged me to start a school to teach these issues, yes, it is important to have a school and also a clinic. The emails I receive from readers wanting to understand certain issues have also encouraged me to study sexology in order to understand this subject from a scientific oint of view.

There are some who felt that women were getting a raw deal from this whole thing - *"pulling of the ribbons"*.

- *For starters when are women going to be their true selves? It's all about pleasing men. It's as if women are sex objects. I know of women who despite having these ribbons are divorced and some without them are still married. Some are stuck with these ribbons which are a permanent reminder; the modern guy does not know what to do with them in some instances. Please women be yourselves.*

I also discussed with friends, sisters and those who follow this column. A woman who read last week's article said:

- *"I think when you wrote the article you mentioned that the pulling of ribbons was encouraged so that a man could play with them and persuade the woman to engage in play time. I don't see anything wrong if women feel they want to do this to bring happiness in the leisure room. This practice obviously was passed in some parliament long time ago, and for a bill like this to be passed it meant that everyone was involved men and women, but our society being patriachal it had to be okayed and announced by a man. There is no way this could have been successful if women were not part of it, whose ribbons were men going to play with if they did not include women. Someone must have touched that part of the body and what came out of it was something - the leisure room must have lit up, just like once upon a time a gynecologist while examining a woman touched what is known today as the "G" spot. If a man does not pass-through Port "G" when navigating this can up-set a woman. Women should not feel as sex objects if the pulling of ribbons makes them happy."*

Another woman felt that women should not be negative about everything that is "introduced" by man, if they can benefit from it, they should make the best of it, and most women are part of this practice because they benefit from it.

She also advised women who do not feel they do not want to pull the ribbons not do it, it has to be about choice and for a woman to be able to choose they need to be empowered.

We have discussed and encouraged women to be empowered in this column, as that is how they can live fulfilled lives - women need to empower themselves in order to be able to choose whatever they want in an informative way.

Sentiments were raised on how some felt that the introduction of *ribbons* to young women will give them ideas of wanting to sleep with men, but some chose to disagree that this should be part of a broader spectrum of sex education; educating girls and boys to understand their bodies and take care and look after their most prized possession.

Girls should be taught to love themselves and love their bodies, be proud of them, understand them, not to wait for men to tell them how beautiful they are.

They should have some sort of pride instilled in them and this is done during the time the girl is initiated into womanhood.

When Miriam Makeba went to sing in a shebeen she would sing a song - *Into Yami Ngiyayithanda* (I love my thing), so that people in the shebeen would know that she had not come for men, but to sing and of course to drink beer.

The Nguni song goes like this - part of the lyrics:

"Into yami ngiyayithanda noma injani, into yami ngiyayithanda . . . ngiyekeleni ngento yami, ngiyekeleni ngento yami, into ngeyami, into yami, into yami - I love my thing, I love my thing . . . please leave me alone with my thing."

Here Miriam Makeba is saying singing in a shebeen does not mean that I have come to look for men please do not touch her even if she is getting drunk.

ARTICLE 38

Cheating, Agent of Misery, Death
1 June 2011

Last week I mentioned that I was going to be a moderator on a panel discussion; *Why Do Women, Men Cheat*? It seems to be a hot issue these days, dominating the head-lines. People have always cheated but why has it become such a topic now, maybe as a friend of mine said on that day that we human beings we are civilized animals but our being animals is brought out by the way we deal with sex. However, we still want to become civilized human beings, which is why we always want to try by all means to come up with solutions not to be the uncivilized animals by having multiple partners through cheating.

While talking to people on the issue of cheating before and during the Wednesday evening discussion, one could see that if there was a way out of cheating people would prefer not to cheat. A man who was quiet throughout the discussions decided to say his true feelings and asked everyone who was participating whether they have considered that cheating is genetic? He was very serious and wanted some answers, but since this has to be backed by scientific evidence, it was difficult to help the man, people could not help him much. But he continued to
drive his point home that cheating is a hereditary problem.

Dialogue between couples was cited as one of the stumbling blocks. One man said that he was having problems introducing new styles and joking with his wife who always refers to whatever he does as *zvekubhawa ne zvechipfambi: things from the beerhalls and prostitution.* He said: "*One day I tried to introduce something to her, and she said to me, asi manga muchitohura...kuita musikanzwa - you must have been up to mischief where you were.* Just kissing and holding my wife in public or in front of the kids is an issue. *Ndoita seiwo veduwe?* - What should I do?"

A woman intervened and said that it is sometimes the way women are socialised, their sexuality is too controlled and when they get married, they carry on with that controlled mentality. "Women don't want to do what they think is for prostitutes."

But another woman decided to disagree and encouraged women to be free when they are with their husbands and partners. She told of a story that she read of a woman and man who started cheating because they were not getting that excitement at home. She recited the story she had read in the magazine, "When there were travelling to wherever they had booked a hotel, in the remote areas, far away from the meddling crowd, they would sometimes stop the car and play and by the time they get to their destination they would have had real 'fun.'" A sister intervened and said: "Why is it difficult for us to do the same with our husbands than to cheat. Why don't we stop the car when going kumusha to the rural area and say *baba vevana ngatimbo …my husband let us …you know*"

But a visibly shaken woman said: "*Unozvitangira papi nanaMuseyamwa?*" - *Where do we start with these husbands of ours [mentioning their totems?] One of the totems – Museyamwa.*"

A brother poured his heart out and said: "I am here now but ask me where my wife is?" The gathering asked where his wife was then he started to narrate his story: "I have never understood my wife, if I ask her to accompany me to social places like these she refuses and

she says she is going to church. Then I come alone here and meet other women. What do I do?" He said that her wife is not an outgoing person, and this has created a rift between them as he is an outgoing person and he has always extended invitations to his wife to accompany him to music shows, social clubs but she seems not to be interested because of her church. The man seemed very worried, and he looked very unhappy when he described what he was going through. "*Ndinoita sei nenyaya yakadaro?* -What do I do with such an issue?"

Not sharing the same interests can contribute to fractures in a marriage. A friend of mine shocked me one day when we were discussing about his parents' marriage which never worked and we had always thought that it was the other woman who had broken the marriage, but he shocked me when he said that her parents were not compatible: "When

that woman came into my father's life it was already over between them and fortunately, my mother married someone and both of them are happy." When he was young, he did not understand this, but he decided to be honest with the situation and what led to the divorce of his parents; it was incompatibility. Compatibility is a serious issue with couples, which is why it is encouraged to know each other well before getting married or deciding to settle, as incompatibility can lead to cheating and fi ding happiness outside the home. There were those who did not bit about the bush but explained why they cheat and somehow, they have been pushed to cheating.

A no holds barred intervention came from the fl or – a man stirred the gathering and almost brought the house down: "I am happy that there are women here who will help me to answer this. *Inini - Me*, I am a 'happy eater,' and I am having problems as I am not allowed to 'eat,' that is what I want but you fi d that someone is not interested."

While he was still explaining some women in the audience interrupted him and said: "*Ha ibva iwe happy eater, happy eater chiyi, in ndinoda iye Mazvimbakupa chaiye haikona happy eater, happy eater chiyi ichocho. - Heater, happy eater what? I want the real thing. I want the real Mazvimbakupa, happy eater, happy eater! What!?*" The man was not intimidated by the women who had jeered at him, he continued and said:

"*Ndati, I said*, I am a happy eater and *ndizvo zvandinoda izvozvo - that is what I want*. These are the problems I am facing, and I end up going to other women."

Meeting halfway was encouraged as a way to accommodate each other and trying to understand where one is coming from. A man encouraged variety in the *leisure room* and said: "*Veduwe, oh please*, we are tired of this missionary. Missionary, missionary, always as if we are going to end up with collars, like priests, let us have variety. If the brother wants to be a happy eater give him a break!" It seems the *happy eating* is becoming very popular; couples feel this is a way of giving your all to your partner and being one in the true sense. "It is a way of accepting my partner whole heartedly," he said. I referred to the article I wrote on *happy eating*, but I used a different name – *bewitching*, which encouraged couples to meet halfway.

When the discussion was offi ally over people continued to discuss in groups and suggesting new topics. A woman who is tired of dating cheating men has decided that she will have relationships with married men as this way she will not feel committed to the relationship, as all she wants is to have a good time and the man can go back to his wife. Someone asked her whether that was not cheating, but she defended herself that no one will be hurt in the process we will all be giving each other what we do not have, and it is a win-win situation. Someone warned her that right now she might be in space where she is saying that she does not want to be committed but she will be surprised that as they continue to see each other they might end up having other ideas. She was also warned that such aff irs have a way of coming out in a very surprising way and the other partner will know about it and someone might be hurt.

To summarise the one and half hour heated debate a brother gave advice to couples that in a relationship you cannot get 100% of what you want: "No matter how you introduce variety, excitement in a relationship you cannot get 100% satisfaction, you can get 80% and still want to have that other 20% somewhere." He posed a question: "But honestly are you going to risk, 80% for 20%?"

That is food for thought.

It was a hectic week for me, because after the Wednesday discussion I gave two more talks, and one was for couples who were on retreat. I was impressed that couples were going out to discuss issues that affect them and want to fi d solutions, maybe as my friend said, so that they can remain human beings, civilized animals.

The other group was fascinating as I met young men and women who are taking charge of their sexuality in an informed way. I was amazed by two expecting women who said that they were going to play until the day of giving birth, one made us laugh when she said: "Actually, it helps the child to just slide."

It might be called *playtime*, but it is one of the basic needs in life and it has to be taken seriously, the good Creator presented it to us in a peculiar way which is scientific and creative, depending on what is working for you that day. Is it not great that one can play around with it and get the result that they want, relaxation, unwinding, a way of showing love, creating another human being, etc. It is because of its multifaceted nature that it can confuse us, but we should understand it and control it for it not to control us. Communication, dialogue, being there for each other, meeting halfway is important in any relationship. Let us continue with the discussions at different forums, in order to have fulfilled lives.

ARTICLE 38

DIY Should Not Be an Option
8 June 2011

Here are some comments and questions from some readers:

- *I read with interest your article in The Herald of the 1st of June. I have also seen one or two of your articles in The Herald, including the one on pulling ribbons that I also found to be very interesting. It appears that the issue of sex and sexuality and its discussion especially in vernacular languages still remains taboo in our culture. Judging from your extracts from the discussion, people will not probably be able to say some of these words"... unless you were editing the actual words in your article to make it suitable for a number of people given The Herald is a family paper".*

    Does this then not contribute to the reason why sex is not being discussed in detail in forums and between couples? I would presume dirty talk can be a good turn on and we deprive ourselves of this if we remain tight-lipped on sex and related subjects.

    I thought 'happy eating' (oral sex) was for the enjoyment of the person being 'eaten.' It appears some do enjoy the 'eating' even if the subject doesn't enjoy it. A comment I can make though on this subject – most people who like (this kind of style) prefer to have it after having a bath. You will probably not feel good having someone doing it on you after a sweaty day and would therefore avoid it which may be misconstrued as not wanting it. I also generally feel it is not a bad thing having a partner that doesn't want the happy eating method but possibly becomes a more of a problem if one wants it and the other partner doesn't want. Interesting subject though this one with no clear rules!

My Response:

I had to edit your letter as you have mentioned yourself that this is a family newspaper, and we have to protect those who might not know how to process the information and those who might fi d the taboo topics offensive. There is something about the whole thing remaining a mystery which has caused problems of not understanding what sex is. When people are talking about this subject they want to warm up, even as couples they have to take it slow and play; what they call romance. When talking about it, people tend to try to fi d their feet on how they are going to present it that is why even in the olden days, music or song helped to talk about it in a lighter way.

At the discussion that we had people were free to talk about anything but most of them came up with a language like '*happy eating*', I think it becomes more fun that way. The most important thing is to discuss about it and understanding what sex all is about and learning to control or deal with it in an informed manner and not the other way round. Depending on the topic and the environment, there is nothing wrong in naming things, but it has to be done in such a way that it does not become clumsy and distasteful. That now people can even talk about *'happy eating'* means that the issue is being discussed in detail at forums and when couples go home, they can build on that, and can be as wild as they want to be. I don't think I need to add anything on the way you have explained the happy eating method. – Thank you.

I have tried to answer some of the questions that you have asked below.

- *Where are these discussions that you refer in your article held? I would love to participate in these.*

  The discussions are held at *Motor Action Club*, we will resume soon, and we will let you know.

- *I find women don't generally want to have sex – is this maybe just linked to the women I have been involved in my life? Is it that there is not enough excitement that the man (myself and maybe a couple of other men out there) generates to make the women want to have sex?*

My Response:
Women sometimes fi d it difficult to express their feelings because of how their sexuality is controlled by society, it is important for men to help their wives, partners to be free. Women are also encouraged to be free and express their feelings to their partners and move out of that cocoon the society has confid d them for years.

- *What causes some women not to get turned on even after extended time on foreplay, am I touching or doing the right places or things during foreplay?*

My Response:
Where will you be touching, you need to ask where she wants to be touched, some women complain of men who during foreplay; it is as if they are wrestling. *'Unenge urikutswinywa - it is like as if you are being pinched* they say. Nowadays there is literature on that and can help you, buy the books and read together and you can tell what your partner wants. It has to be gradual and let it build up, you don't have to start in the *leisure room* but even while you are at work phone her and tell her one of those jokes, tell her you are coming home to cook and not only in the kitchen, tell her you are in the cooking mood, from the kitchen to the leisure room. Bring as many recipes as you can. She will laugh and continue to build the mood and it will reach a peak.

You need to be creative.
- *How many times of having sex in a week are considered normal? I would want most*

days in the week, whereas my partner would be happy with once or twice if not zero per week.

•

<u>My Response:</u>
You need to stimulate her. How? I can hear you say. Be creative. The problem is that we take playroom issues lightly that is why when we do not get results, we become angry and wonder what is wrong with our partner, but you need to strategise in order to get fulfilling results.

• *I generally see from comments by women, and in a way, this does come out in your articles as well, that women do want and love sex – is it that I have the wrong partner or that I am not turning her on well enough or my expectations on the number of times that we have sex is a bit on the high side?*

<u>My Response:</u>
Try to meet her halfway and also try to understand where she is coming from you will know why she does not want it as much as you do. Variety is also very important not just the missionary way. I would like to go back to some of the discussions and talks that I have had. A woman revealed that she was now tired of dating she dated about three men in two years. The first one she had her for two months and he disappeared, and she stayed for some time without a man and after some months she thought she had found Mr Right only to discover he was not the one, after six months it was over, then came another one whom she was with for almost a year, they broke up after learning that he was married. She said "I really got fed up and I felt that I was exposing my body to a lot of men, I then decided to buy friends who are not human beings who would not give me any problems. Whenever I want it, I do it myself. I am now into DIY; hassle free." She said to the amusement of those who were sitting on the same table. A brother could not conceal his disbelief he said: *"Unopenga, saka urikuzvi…So you do it yourself?"*

People laughed and she was not worried at all she answered: "What is the difference of having it with you?" She answered: "There is a difference." The man tried to reply. I enquired how many years she has been doing it and she said it had been two years. "Has it been working well for the past two years?"

I asked, she pondered and then she explained: "For the past two years yes it has been okay, but now I feel I miss something, I miss a human being who can hold me, I feel some emptiness and sometimes I want to cry, when these friends of mine will have made me travel to some other places, I miss the holding from a human being". There was some silence and then she suggested: "Why don't you and your team come up with a dating service and connect people."

The idea was seconded by a number of people who were around.

When partners take each other to an unknown world, they need to facilitate their landing or they come down crushing, they must assure each other, (It's okay they are now back into this world) and assure your partner that you are there for them and you have not gone anywhere. Th s makes the big thing more meaningful, and you both relax and sleep. Holding, talking, and touching after the big thing, it is very important as one does not feel used but loved.

Th s is what the sister who bought her friends who are taking her to another world but are not there when she is landing, misses. According to the research that I have done, women love the touching and holding part and if they don't have it after the big thing, they feel displaced and ungrounded. One woman has been into DIY for the past 20 years she has been married. When they have fin shed playing with her husband, it is said she starts on her DIY to quench her thirst. She is not the only one who is into this practice as a married woman, quite a number of married women have resorted to this practice to quench their thirst and to keep their marriages. I asked one a question, "When you are doing your DIY, what about your husband...?" Before I fin shed the question she knew what I wanted to ask, she said: "*Hapana zvaanombonzwa, kana angowana zvaanenge achida kwandiri, anobva atorara kutoridza ngonono, nhamo inenge yangosarira inini amai nhiya ndosaka ndakazoti ko kuita DIY - He does not even hear anything, when he gets what he wants, he just falls asleep and the problem will be mine, he will be enjoying his sleep, snoaring. That is why I resorted to DIY.*" Although like many women she misses that touch when landing. She crashes on landing!

While *DIY* might quench that thirst, it is important for women to know that it has to be done in the right position as most of women's ailments come from the way they do *DIY*, most women suffocate themselves during this process and blood does not circulate properly and it becomes detrimental to one's health. To those women who are doing *DIY* as a way of satisfying or quenching their thirst, talk to your partner and find a solution, it is not worth it.

Are you going to keep up appearances at the expense of your health? Do not be scared of your partner or husband, talk to them, and meet halfway. The *DIY* method was confi med by the leader of a young couple's retreat, where I had gone to give a talk. He said, "Some couples when playing have no emotions, feelings, nothing, it is just to quench their thirsts and it is not about love. Is it any different from *DIY*, only that this time it is two people doing it on each other."

"*Dzimba idzodzo dzine maproblems. Tinoda zvipere zvinhu zvakadaro ndosaka tati tizombokurukura, tigadzirisane, - those homes have problems, we need to put a stop to that by meeting and discussing how we can make our love life more fulfilling.*" I think most of us agree with him.

ARTICLE 40

Couples' Forums: Fountains of Wisdom
15 June 2011

The organisation of *Young Couples' Associations* is a welcome development as it helps the structures of our society to run in a balanced manner.

The formation of such associations is commendable, as it is easy to achieve results when the two parties involved in a union are present when issues affecting them are discussed.

Young Couples Associations are going for a holistic approach in solving marital and family problems in order to achieve fulfilling relationships.

While forums, which separate women and men serve their purpose in a given society, they are also important in their own way; forums like *initiation centres/schools* for boys and girls, *kitchen parties*, and *bachelors' parties*, are preparatory stages.

Kitchen parties and bachelors' parties serve as send offs for a bride or groom into marriage life and it is a way of having a farewell party with friends, and it is understandable for it to be exclusive to women or men.

However, I have not fully comprehended why baby showers are still being attended by women only yet nowadays men are present when their wives are giving birth and why are they excluded during baby showers when they are also supposed to be taught how to look after the baby.

Although kitchen parties and bachelors' parties are slowly being overtaken by associations like couples' associations or forums, which discuss marital and other family and social issues with all parties involved. However, kitchen parties and bachelors' parties can continue to act as platforms to send off the bride or the groom to the next level of being a married person, with the basic training provided for that day – as a *crash* course.

When people get married, they may incorporate what they have been taught through different stages of their lives, or they may decide to start all over with new ways of doing things.

Education received by women at kitchen parties and men at bachelors' parties might be difficult to introduce or convey to one's partner.

Several women who have tried to introduce what they have learnt at kitchen parties to their husbands have not been successful and also men from the bachelor's party.

I have heard stories of the two suspecting that one might have learnt it from someone else, a boyfriend or a girlfriend.

That is why the formation of couple's associations is a welcome progress, regarding marital and family issues.

Th s week, I was invited by a *couple's association* where they had a one-day workshop and were looking at various issues to do with the family, from how to raise children, issues of HIV/Aids and issues to do specifi ally with the leisure room.

How a child is raised has to be agreed upon by both parents as stories of one parent blaming the other on how a child is handled are common. That is why it is important for the two to agree on how they will raise their children. Some might think that raising of children is just out of instinct, yes but coupled with some education and proper information on parenting can be easier and enjoyable. Those who have more knowledge on the subject can help educate couples on how to raise their children from an informative point of view.

The facilitator who talked on how to raise children touched on several issues and one of the issues, which we tend to overlook as parents and society is how children are abused during funerals as the bereaved think everyone at the funeral has come to mourn with them and yet others have other motives.

It is common sight at funerals that children are left to wonder at night while those who have come to mourn with the bereaved are sitting comfortably in the house and one wonders why people come to a funeral if they cannot help looking after the vulnerable such as children of the bereaved.

Instead of looking after the bereaved children, some will be busy securing places to sleep, I think they should sleep at their houses if they are not going to help. She advised that whenever there is a funeral, children should be provided a place to sleep away from the funeral and elders should be assigned to look after them.

The way children are not looked after at funerals has changed my view on why we even gather at these funerals. Let us look after children wherever they are.

I also found the way she explained issues surrounding drug abuse informative and how as parents we always associate drug abuse by children as being influenced by peer pressure, yet it could be a way of a child crying out for help.

But what do we do as parents?

We beat up that child instead of talking and trying to understand where he/she is coming from or taking the child to a specialist who can help him or her.

One would think by now people understand what HIV/Aids is.

But it is surprising how people are still dying from the disease, and they are still getting infected with the virus. The transmission of the virus to the unborn child and how we are still ignorant on how it is spread still remain an issue.

How couples are afraid to go for testing and if they are infected how to live positively is one of the concerns raised at the workshop. People still need a lot of education regarding this topic.

Some couples only discover that they have this virus when expecting a child and it is important to protect the unborn child from having the virus.

While still on the HIV/Aids topic and how some people are not taking it seriously, I was shocked when we were discussing about the need to be open with each other regarding issues of the *leisure room*.

As usual, I encouraged couples to meet halfway in accommodating the needs of their spouses, or rather the new ways of doing things that they may be interested in.

A man told us of a story of his friend who had just died of Aids and on his death-bed, he said: "All this is a result of my wife who was refusing me my conjugal rights. I was left ith no choice but get it from those who would give it to me."

Before anyone in a relationship gets angry because she/he is not getting their conjugal rights, they must try and establish the problem. Why is the other party not interested in *playing*?

The blame game will not help the situation.

The mentality of separating *"Thombi/Ntombi"* from the whole body does not help. Thombi/*Ntombi* is a girl's name, and this is how some people sometimes talk about the vagina in a disguising way.

In one of my articles, I wrote about how a man said to his wife: "it does not matter how angry you are, and you are not in the mood to play but me and 'Thombi/Ntombi' we are friends, and we can go ahead and play".

Th s kind of playing is just mechanical, and it can have terrible effects in a relationship.

One of the participants gave an example of some of the causes of why a spouse might not be interested in playing.

"If a woman does not know how the husband has used money and the budget fails to balance because of that, that can put her off during *play time*, because her mind will not be settled.

"Did the man who told his friends on his deathbed that his wife was refusing him his conjugal rights ever try to fi d out why she was not in the mood of playing?" one participant asked.

Lack of communication has contributed to the breakdown of marriages and in this case, it contributed to the death of the husband who was too proud and macho to discuss with his wife and fi d a way forward.

But for some it is the advent of HIV/Aids, which has taught them to be more open with their partners and fi d ways to have a fulfilled life with one partner.

Couples Associations are facilitating that change of behaviour in couples.

Women should also learn to be open with their partners if they are not happy about something. Keeping quiet will not solve anything.

We have heard so many times how a woman is disadvantaged because of culture, but it is the women themselves who will free themselves from this bondage, because if they do not, they will remain in the worst prison under the sun for the rest of their lives. Is it really worth it? No, it's not!

The priest who blessed the occasion explained that the prison that one faces in an unhappy marriage is the worst one has ever seen. He explained: "You live under the same roof, you sleep under the same sheets, but you don't know what one is thinking, you are not happy. Is there any prison worse than that?"

I agree with the priest there is no prison worse than that.

I was proud of a woman who wrote to me and said: "I want to enjoy the *leisure room* while I am still here on earth as I don't think over there, they will be anything like it. I want to get maximum of it from my husband and I will make sure I do."

Here is another encouraging email: "I am a woman in her early 40s and really enjoy lovemaking with my partner. It is a fulfilling engagement and makes me look forward to a long life while thanking God for creating me in such a way that I enjoy this almost every time I get to do it."

My advice to my fellow sisters and brothers is that it requires an emotional connection with your partner, i.e., mutually appreciating and respecting each other.

Treating this kind of thing as an; we are both learning, I am doing it for you as much as I am doing it for me, and the life God has blessed us with.

Sex becomes the icing on the cake, but the connection is the well-baked cake itself.

Once there is lack of trust, appreciation and respect maybe resulting from cheating, comparing your partner to somebody else then the connection is dysfunctional and no turning on is accomplished."

ARTICLE 41

Communication – The Right Tonic
29 June 2011

It is embarrassing to note that behind closed doors couples are staying together yet they are total strangers. They are scared to express themselves to their partners. Some have been together for years, but they do not know what their partners want and who they are.

Disgruntled couples have resorted to *Do It Yourself* (DIY), as a way of replacing their partners, I was shocked by the e-mails I got of what is being used to replace partners.

One wrote: *"I have been married for 20 years. In most of these I've been frustrated because my husband was just too daft to just follow what I wanted. He took things too much for granted. I know his routine, from here he'll go there, and then do that, then kabam! It's over. So, playing became boring. I tried over the years to get it through, his thick skull kuti ita so . . . even guiding him do this. A little improvement came. If I am not creative, I never get to the other world, it only happens after a lot of effort. I have tried desperately but dofo chairo – he is a real daft person. I then decided to get myself a friend who would take me to that other world, I went shopping around and I got myself X-large. After using it I felt sick, I was peeing all the time until I could not control it, I had to use pads for about a week.*

One day I broke down, I could not believe I was even afraid to go to my doctor. What was I going to tell my doctor? My husband was getting worried why urine was just coming out like that, I broke down and I told him the truth. He realised how serious I was about my demands, he felt so bad, and he said he was going to change, which he did. It had to take this drastic measure for him to take my requests seriously. He sometimes jokes about it, but I would like to advice couples to take each other seriously. Thanks for your forum I feel so relived just sharing issues I have never shared with a soul before," she said

When toys are invited in one's life it is important to understand how they work. A woman was not so lucky after her husband discovered that she had bought herself a friend, he took her to an aunt, and she was given a divorce token. The husband said to the aunt: *"Ndauya nemwana wenyu, boyfriend yake irimu-plastic umu - I have come with your niece and her boyfriend is in this plastic bag."*

If couples can express their feelings to each other problems of this nature will not be experienced. When discussing this issue at the *Couples Association* a man had no kind words for men who want to victimise their wives in such circumstances.

He was very blunt and said *"Varume ava imbwende mumachira, kupamukadzi gupuro nokuti wamuwana anechitoyi, ko iwe waive wamboyendepi? -* These men are real cowards between the sheets. How can you give your wife a divorce token because you found her with a sex toy? What will you be doing in the fi st place? *Ndoda kukupayi rungano rwomumwe murume ayive asingabvire pavakadzi, mukadzi achingo gara achichema, arimatare woga, kwakazoti sekuru vake vanyatsomuvhunzisisa wanike Razaro wake haanyatsi kusevenza saka, anenge achiti akaenda paneuyu mukadzi oyendazve panemumwe achifunga kuti ndiko kuti agozoshanda zvakanaka. -*I want to tell you a story of a certain man who was such a womanizer, and the wife was always crying. They woud take each other to endless family courts. Then one of the uncles wanted to really understand what was going on and realised that Razaro (his penis) was not working well, so what he would be doing is that he goes onto this woman, then to the next, thinking that, that way his Razaro would work properly)." *Mukadzi akavhunzwa kuti ayizviziva here zvaRazaro ndokuwanikwa wayizviziva asi akanga adyayira zvakare chida murume wake. Sekuru vake vakanga vanerumwe ruzivo rwatisina vakaenda naye kwaakanotsvagirwa 'ring' inobatsira Razaro kuti asanete, ndipo pandakatanga kuzvizivira zvetu-toyi itwotu. - The wife was asked by the uncle whether she knew about this that the Razaro of her husband was not working well and she said yes, she knew it. The uncle knew some of the things that we did not know, and he bought him a ring that would help his Razaro not to get tired. That is when I started knowing about these sex toys."*

Th s man who was narrating the story at the *Couples Association* sent people into laughter, but he had sent a message to those men who did not know how to deal with their shortcomings and instead decide to play macho men or mystery men in order to cover up their ineffici cies and deficie cies in between the sheets.

A young man whose wife was expecting wanted to know when to stop playing and when to resume after the baby has arrived. He asked a question: "Is it true that breast milk is unpleasant in the blankets, because my brother left his wife after having a baby and he said *andidi zvekunhuhwirwa nemukaka' - I don't want the smell of breast milk."*

A much older man helped him out: "If you are a father and husband you want to be involved in whatever is happening to your child and your wife. If breast milking the baby, then how can it be unpleasant? Your brother was not a full-time father and husband.

"It is a joy to be part of this whole process to help your wife breastfeed, get to smell the scent of the milk even taste it, some of us tasted the milk. It is also during this time when your wife needs you most in terms of play and support," he said.

His advice was followed by women ululating, men clapping, and I could hear a woman say, *"Ndiko kunzi murume chaiye! - This is what we call real men!"*

As I mentioned in one of my articles; I am fi ding *Couples Associations* as the way to go, in fi ding solutions to couples' problems and building homes on strong foundations. Some *Couple's Associations* are even discussing issues of Wills and Inheritance and more other issues which spouses grapple with.

I was talking to a group of women and one woman said: "You know I have heard some say when they are in that room, *the leisure room*, things happen, but for me I have never had such an experience, it has always been dull," she gestured.

"What do you mean things really happen?" I wanted to understand what she really meant. She continued, "They are waves like going on in some other people's home, which do not happen in mine. I want those waves to happen in that room."

She was visibly unhappy of what was taking place during playtime, and she was very frustrated. "Have you ever asked your friends how these waves happen?" She kept quiet for a while and then she said, "I think it just happens."

It just does not happen; one needs to strategise to get the best in the *recreation room*. "How do you present yourself in that space" She was becoming a little bit nervous. "You mean to my husband?" she asked.

"Not really, but the *recreation room*, that space, the whole space. How do you present yourself?" I could see that I had put her in that room, she became uncomfortable, and she looked scared.

Some couples expect too much from each other, as they say it takes two to tango, one must not expect that things just happen, waves just happen, it begins with you.

While talking to women I have realised that they do not know themselves and yet they want their partner to know them.

They are scared of themselves and that is the energy they sometimes take to the *leisure room* and things do not happen. I asked the same group of women how many knew what defi es them, they looked down and did not know what to say - only a few mostly young women spoke. One woman whispered: *"Ah hee, ungasajamba kuti rumha yabva kupi? - oh no! Wouldn't you be surprised that where is this frightening thing coming from?"*

Women who were around her laughed.

"So rumha iyi ndiyo yaunoda kupa mumwe munhu kuti ayide - So this frightening thing is what you want to give to someone to love?"

How does it work?

Women, you should know your bodies so that when you go into that room you are confide t, it is the negative energies that some women carry in the *leisure room* that makes it impossible to have a fulfilling relationship.

They must love themselves and love what defi es them and say: "Wow! How did my creator come up with such a gem?" someone - your partner will also say, "Wow!

What did I do to deserve such a gem?"

You will have transported positive energies into the *recreation room*. Men take what your women in your life tell you seriously to build lasting and fulfilling relationships.

We continue to encourage communication, meeting halfway and most of all to support love between couples.

ARTICLE 42

True Beauty Is Deeply Rooted
24 August 2011

When we talk about beauty what do we mean? How do we understand beauty? How does our concept of beauty impact our lives? Beauty is explained in different ways.

The way we understand beauty from an early age has a lasting impact on our life and behaviour. We understand what beauty is and what it is all about through different agencies.

The media is the most dominant of all influences in shaping the way we see and appreciate beauty - from radio, television, magazines, etc.

One's peers can also shape the way you understand beauty. Our partners later in life can also influence the way we feel about beauty.

Thus, the way we understand beauty from an early age may shape our view throughout life.

When a child says to you: "You are beautiful", what is it that they would have seen?

One day I had just fin shed bathing with my granddaughter, she was four then, she is turning 11 sometime this year. We were applying our lotions, oils, and moisturisers, and we were singing, she said: "*Gogo, Grandma* you can be a cover girl."

I looked at her with a lot of questions and she said: "Yes gogo you can be a cover girl. You are beautiful."

I laughed and then I said, "As big as I am Mya. A cover girl?"

She said again confide tly: "Yes *gogo*, you can be a very good cover girl."

Mya what will I be wearing on the cover.

"A bikini and a bra *gogo*."

She was very sure of what she was saying.

"Oh, my angel! Who will buy the magazine?"

I asked: "But you can be a very good cover girl *gogo*, you can."

I looked at her and I did not believe she wanted me to wear a bikini and a bra and pause in front of a magazine cover.

She looked at me and laughed and again she said, "Yes *gogo* you can be a cover gril."

Mya did not want to be drawn into an argument 'as big as I am' and 'who was going to buy the magazine' talk, all she wanted was for *gogo* to be a cover girl because she is beautiful.

She did not want to commercialise *gogo* by answering who was going to buy the magazine that was not her problem.

Gogo was just supposed to wear a bikini and a bra and be a cover girl, full stop.

I was talking to my friend Sarudzayi Chifamba Barnes about what Mya had said to me years ago and how I responded, and she had this to say: "A child is influenced by parents, grandparents, and playgrounds etc. For your granddaughter to see a big sized African woman as beautiful, as compared to western beauty that sees thin and slim women as beautiful, it shows the influence of her environment on her. She was celebrating what was around her, what she sees every day, not what other people tell her. You were actually confusing her when you defi ed beauty in the western context to her. It should be a lesson to us all to celebrate what we have, and not to aspire to be foreign in the eyes of our own people and children. We should defi e our own beauty, after all "beauty is in the eyes of the beholder.""

She continued: "Although women on the cover of magazines portray western type of images, she did not relate to them. She does not know those people. It is you whom she knows, it is not just about your physical beauty but a lot to do with what you are to her, and it is a whole lot of other things about you and about her environment."

What Sarudzayi said is confi med in the *Bronfrebrenner Ecological Theory* (1979), which argues that children are influenced by the environment around them. Bronfenbrenner came up with environmental layers, which include the influence of family (macrosystem), playground, schools (microsystem), parents' jobs, government policy (exosystem) and influence of time/generations (chronosystems).

Our socialisation and the images we see when growing up have a lasting impact on us. When I was growing up, I had always wanted to look like my mother who was light in complexion and I asked her one day if she could buy me a skin lightening cream called Ambi, she asked me why I wanted to apply *Ambi* on my face.

I said to her I wanted to be as beautiful as she was and she said to me: "You are beautiful, being light in complexion does not mean beauty."

She introduced me to a mosturiser that I used since the 70's up until the 90's (The moisturiser tends not to work properly when one reaches a certain age).

My mother told me that this moisturiser would feed my skin and not peel it off as the skin lightening cream would do. Yes, for the years I used it, it did just that; fed nutrients to my skin.

I changed to another moisturiser, which fed my skin and did not peel it.

Since my mother told me that I was beautiful in my complexion, I never thought of bleaching my skin to be light in complexion like she was. There were quite a number of those who lived in my area who used skin lightening creams and they did not understand why I did not want to look 'more beautiful' by using lightening creams.

The media then encouraged the use of skin lightening creams and light skin was associated with being beautiful.

I feel so much pain when I see a sister who has peeled their brown/black beautiful skin, but some tell me they use skin lightening because of some skin problems, but some are very honest as they say that they cannot stand their dark skins.

They are also white people who tan their skin because they cannot stand the whiteness. There is nothing wrong about enhancing one's beauty as long as you do not look down upon yourself as it has detrimental effects to your inner self.

Outside beauty has to go hand in hand with inner beauty to bring out a whole person.

Since time immemorial women have gone all out to make themselves look more beautiful as it helps to raise confide ce levels. Long time ago women did all sorts of things to look beautiful.

They would have incisions on the face, done in a stylish way, some of the incisions would be on the thighs and these were to guide a man during play. The incisions are usually covered and if a man goes beyond the incisions, a woman would have allowed him to go into that very private space. The incisions are done in such a way that they are bumpy and when playing with them it's fun and ticklish, once the hand of the man goes past the incisions he would be heading towards a very sacred place, which he has to leave for a while and go to another decorated part of the waistline.

Women would decorate their waistline with beads, to enhance their beauty and for their sexuality, when the man play with the beads a woman feels something, and the beads also provided music in the *leisure room*.

The incisions and beads could also be played with simultaneously, which helped a woman to get ready for the big thing. We have also discussed about *ribbons* in past articles and how they enhance women's beauty and would be used during *playtime*.

When I discussed this issue, I was attacked by some readers as they saw it as being done to please men, this was/is also for the benefit of the woman to get maximum satisfaction during *playtime*.

Th s shows how African tribes were liberal as far as women were concerned, it is through women's sexuality that one can tell how a tribe or nation related to women.

Women could express their beauty and their sexuality. They were not oppressed. They had their space in their societies.

Men would also decorate themselves to appeal to women in the traditional African set up. Another way of enhancing beauty was the wearing of bangles and earrings. Girls would compete for bangles as this was a way of showing how enterprising one was.

Today's women are wearing earrings all over their bodies in different places.

Feeling good about yourselves helps to raise confide ce levels, but if one has to look good solely to please their spouse then they might reduce their confide ce levels and will not feel good about themselves inside.

A woman wrote a letter wanting to understand how to defi e beauty. When she married her husband, she was slim but now she has grown big. She was worried about the comments her husband made about her body and the issue of her weight brought unhappiness in their lives. She worked hard and lost weight, but this did not change the husband's attitude, there is so much unhappiness in the marriage that she does not know what to do.

I spoke to some big sized women who seem to be happy in their bodies and in their marriages and they felt the woman should lose weight because she wants to, and not because of her husband, it becomes a strain doing it for someone.

Whether you prefer to be a big size, or a small size make sure you exercise and stay fit. You can also be your own cover girl, put on that bikini and bra and look at yourself in the mirror and say, 'I am beautiful'. True beauty is inside, and the outside is just a mirror.

ARTICLE 43

Parental Issues on Sexual Guidance Vital
21 September 2011

I continue receiving mixed feelings from readers regarding topics on taboo issues. As I mentioned earlier, the whole idea is to demystify these issues. By not discussing them, we are pretending we do not have what makes us male or female.

Th s is where our problems begin by refusing to acknowledge who we are. People who understand these issues have fewer problems in life because they are whole beings.

Refusing to understand what defi es men and women and even pretending that those *ancestors - our private parts* do not exist is not going to help us. These *ancestors* are looked at as evil and some people use the ancestors to swear at others.

I suppose most of us have heard people telling each other off and in most cases, it is the female *ancestor* who is used to scold. There is an assumption that the mother's *ancestors* are more sacred than the male ones, so when they are used to scold, they raise real emotions. Males use their *ancestors* to pee even in public and they couldn't care less if anyone sees them. Denigrating one's mother's *ancestor* can raise emotions.

There is a story of a child who went to her mother crying because someone had used her *ancestor* to scold the minor. The mother asked: *"Iye aribe? Umfunse kuti iye aribe? - Ask her whether she does not have one herself?"*

The next day the child came back crying again. What was said to her was painful. She told her mother what had transpired. The scolding word in question she was crying about originated from Zulu/Ndebele.

The mother said: *"Chokapo! Mufunse kuti amai ake naathathe ake arikuita chiyani mubadarumu? - Go away! Ask her what her mother and father do in the main room?"*

What her mother had done is to demystify the way she thought about the words used to scold her.

Th s shows how these *ancestors* are regarded as evil. How these *ancestors* are stigmatised, instead of being objects of pleasure and not talked about in bad light.

Recently, I met someone I grew up with in Mbare who belongs to the tribe of the woman who demystifi d the *ancestors* to her daughter. He wondered why those things are such a big issue.

Wanting to distance ourselves from these *ancestors* is causing a lot of problems for us.

From a young age, people do not understand what they are carrying: the *ancestor* is such a mystery, just looking at it, one gets the fits. Th s is why in the olden days young people were educated about their sexuality. Sexuality was discussed to appreciate, love and respect it. It was explained to them that the time they would spend as young people was less than what they would in their adult life which is the time they would put their *ancestors* to use in a different kind than there were used to.

Th *ancestors* would be used for mating and recreation. The multi dimension purposes of the *ancestors* were explained in detail, in a no-holds barred environment during initiation ceremonies. There were schools which took care of youngsters to prepare them for adult life.

Today, young people make a lot of blunders regarding the use of their *ancestors,* because they know very little about them. They do not know how to deal with them. They remain a mystery on their bodies. These organs are important parts of one's body.

A friend told me of a story of her nephew who impregnated a girl. When he was asked whether he was responsible for the pregnancy, he refused and said he had intercourse with the girl once, so it could not be him. The aunt asked where this once-off encounter was, and he said it was at his parent's house.

How this could have happened and yet they are always people present at the house, the aunt wondered. He said that he sent the maid to the shops and had his friends manned the house to alert him if someone was coming. The aunt could not believe this. She asked him how long the sex took, and he said around two minutes. The auntie wanted to know what he derived from a sexual experience of less than two 2 minutes.

"I just wanted to taste what sex is all about. I never thought it would come to this."

"You tasted and ate at the same time. How could you? Tasting is when you taste, and eating is eating." The aunt charged.

"What do you mean auntie?"

"Imagine tasting food on the stove and you eat in two minutes, what happens to you?"

He was getting confused, and the aunt said she was waiting for an answer; she was not in a pleasant mood at all.

She repeated the question: "What happens when you taste food on the stove and eat the food in two minutes?"

"You get constipated aunt, and you get burnt," he answered.

"Very good! That is what happened to you."

He impregnated another girl, and the aunt asked him, "Were you tasting? For how long you are going to be tasting and eating at the same time?"

He will be eating and tasting for the rest of his life, because this is how he has introduced himself to sex, tasting and eating at the same time. Yes, there are men who are old *vachena imvi, with white beards,* and yet they are still tasting and eating in a short space of time.

They are always constipated and burnt. The problem with her nephew is that he was not in touch with his *ancestor*; he did not know how to deal with it. He did not also know how to deal with a female *ancestor*.

When he saw women's sexuality he got confused; he wanted to taste and eat at the same time. He did not have respect for what defined him as a human being, because it was not explained to him how it works how to appreciate, respect, and value it.

National Initiation Schools Critical
28 September 2011

While I was looking for answers to last week's responses, I realised how important it is for boys and girls to be initiated into men and women. This helps them to understand the world they will be going into as adults. It is important for boys and girls to be initiated into being men and women as they become well-informed of who they are sexually and emotionally. If they do not understand how their bodies work, they end up doing things they might later regret as they will not be well informed. They end up being caught up in not knowing whether they are boys or men, girls, or women, they struggle to understand in which world they are in.

The initiation process should provide the rite of passage for young adults to be full rounded adults. Today we seem to be concentrating on sex protection without explaining what sex itself is all about. A young adult wrote to me that he was using protection when having sex but after that he felt emptier than before engaging in the act, he felt the urge to have sex but he has always asked himself after that is this what it means, he does not understand it because it was not explained fully to him; What it is? The reasons for engaging in the act? How it affects one's emotions? How to deal with misdirected sexual feelings that may be caused by anxiety and any other stresses? Protection deals with the physical only and yet there is a lot to it.

Whilst circumcision is very important for boys as it protects them from sexual infections, it is also vital for young adults to know that it does not give them the license to go sleeping around. A friend of mine told me how her nephew who was circumcised would boast to girls that,

Ini ndiyekamenywa - I have a peeled one as if to attract them to his *ancestor.* His uncles had to sit him down and educate him that having a peeled one was not a license to go sleeping around. During initiation boys were also taught discipline in many ways. One of the ways some tribes taught discipline at initiations was to teach boys to hold on for an hour or more. Th s is one of the tests they were required to pass. It taught them discipline. If one passes this test then they would not taste and eat in 2 minutes time, because an hour is not a boy's play, it is a man's game. A serious game where body, mind and soul should be together. Th s taught young men to also be able to control their feelings.

A man who was initiated sometime in the 70's narrated how the old man, who led the initiation used humor to educate them, one day he said, "If your *ancestor* wants to leave your trousers ask whether it wants to pee and if it is so go and pee and put it back into your trousers, and if it keeps wanting to be a nuisance and protruding from the trousers, tell it to stop and go back in the trousers, put a leash on it like what is done to stray dogs." The education helped not to go about tasting and eating in 2 minutes.

Girls were also initiated to understand their bodies and also to have discipline. Tasting for those who are initiated or have been provided with sex education would mean looking at each other and admiring, holding hands, walking in the park, going out for lunch, and waiting for the right time which will not live body, mind and soul separated. When tasting food, you leave it to simmer and prepare the table, dish out food into plates, and create an atmosphere which is conducive. Th s way you will not get burnt and you will not be constipated, you will be relaxed and know and understand what you are doing.

We need initiation schools which are not just for a particular tribe but for the nation. Let us bring back the African pride of initiating boys and girls into adult life which was done by almost all African tribes in the continent, before the African belief systems were affected or destroyed. Some tribes continued and some stopped the practice, this wonderful way of doing things. It is important for the nation to provide schools which will help boys and girls with the rite of passage to womanhood and manhood. Th s will benefit the nation as men will be man and women will be women and not boys and girls in men's and women's bodies.

My childhood friends, a couple whom I last saw some years ago have been following this column, and when they read last week's article, they gave me a surprise call and they wanted us to meet and discuss the article. Their son had impregnated a girl, and the girl had been expelled from school. They were both in Upper Sixth Form. The *tete, aunt* of the girl accompanied her to the boy's parents, but the father of the boy refused to accept the girl and expressed concern that the two were just kids. The man sad: "I did not understand how the two could be husband and wife and yet there had both not even turned 20. I went to the parents and your friend (pointing to his wife) could not believe how I could go to meet the parents without a *munyai - a go between*. But I said this was crisis and it did not a need a *munyai*. We needed to talk as parents and fi d a solution to the crisis."

Together with his wife, their son, the girl and the *tete* drove to the girl's parents' house. The aunt of the girl and his wife had tried to plead with him, to do things in the right way but he disagreed with them as making this wrong right would be encouraging bad behavior.

When they got to the girl's parents' house the *tete* wanted to go and talk to girl's parents; her brother and sister-in-law to alert them that they had visitors, but the father of the boy thought that it was not necessary. He knocked on the door and when the father of the girl opened the door there was an exchange of words, but the father of the boy was not going to leave until he was let into the house to say his mind. Finally he won; the four parents, *tete* and the two children (the boy and the girl) sat and discussed the issue. The father of the son asked his son what he thought he was doing and he said that it was an accident, so when the father referred to the whole situation as a crisis he was right because there is a certain way of dealing with accidents! This accident was confirmed by the girl who when she was asked how it happened, she replied: *"zvakango itika - It just happened."* the two *ancestors* collided, and a child was created.

What an accident!

After deliberating for hours, they agreed that the boy's parents would pay damages and pay for the upkeep of their grandchild, but each parent would take care of their own child. They had to go back to school and complete secondary and tertiary education. The parent's wishes were fulfilled and there were sent to different universities, they completed their tertiary education, got jobs, saw the world, kept in touch but lived separately for years. There were to reconnect after 10 years, there were now man and woman and got back together.

I made the parents laugh when I said that if they had wedded this year, we would have sung them the song:

"Iwe neni tirvaviri togara zvedu zviri most bho, zviri most bhoo. -You my love and me, the two of us, we will live a good life."

Yes, now because there were man and woman, mature, finished school and working, they will certainly have a good life.

"Anyway." I said, "Let us sing them the song even if they are not here."

Iwe nani tirivaviri togara zvedu zviri most bho paghetto, iwe neni tirivaviri most bho, zviri most bhoooo...."

ARTICLE 45

Debunking Myths on Sex - Our Ancestor
28 November 2015

It has been long, since 2011 when I took a break from this column, I left abruptly because of the book that I was writing which was demanding a lot of time, it just took over my life, the book: *Women Musicians of Zimbabwe 1930's- 2013; A Celebration of Women's Struggle for Voice and Artistic Expression.* When I fin shed the book, I rested for a while and started on another one *Women in the Arts in Zimbabwe.*

I have been receiving emails from the readers who followed my articles asking me why I stopped, and urging me to resume the column, I was also yearning to come back to this column for the past four years. Writing for this column was such a joy, an enriching experience but unfortunately, I left without notifying the readers because of other pressing issues that I did not have control over as I have mentioned. The column started as *Women's Histories*, and then it changed to Inside Out because of the issues that I ended up discussing which were sex, sexuality, and taboo issues. It all started when I was discussing how women used music to air their grievances through music, even grievances to do with how their husbands performed in the main room. Little did I know that I had triggered something in my brain which just went into discussing sex, sexuality, and taboo issues? I even surprised myself until I realised that that's how I am wired. Th s wiring has been influenced by a number of factors, my genes, and the way I was socialised.

Because of the interest that the articles generated I was invited to give talks to organisations, women's groups, youth groups and conferences. I even won an inaugural award for the new category, *Triple T (Tackling Taboo Topics)* at the fourth *Gender and Media Summit Awards* convened by *Gender Links, Gender, and Media Southern Africa* (GEMSA) and the *Media Institute of Southern Africa* (MISA) in Johannesburg.

I have always seen the need to demystify sex and sexuality. The mystifi ation of sex has caused us serious problems which I cannot even start to recount. The ignorance which is brought about by not wanting to understand our *ancestor* called sex contributes to unhappiness and the confusion that we sometimes fi d ourselves in. From youths to adults this has been a serious problem, that of not embracing our *ancestor* whom we are identifi d with, we don't want to acknowledge this *ancestor.* For people to say: "*kozibani kuzelwe umtwana oyintombi kumbe umfana/kwanhingi kwazvarwa mukomana kana musikana - so and so's family has been blessed with a son or a daughter.*" it is because of the *ancestor* that one carries but now why don't we want to understand what defi es us. Th s has been the demise of human beings of suffering some amnesia and pretending that we are not sexual human beings, but then our *ancestor* always reminds us that: 'I am the one that defi es you and you will have to acknowledge and embrace me.' As long as we do not lay bare issues of sex and sexuality from a young age, we will not be able to live full lives and we will forever be mystifi d by this *ancestor* and fail to handle her/him and fi d ourselves in serious problems. A story of a guy who used to peep at girls when he was at school just to see how their ancestor looked like seem to have not stopped the practice. Although now he does not peep at them, it is said he has changed woman after woman, for him that excitement that he had when he peeped at them and the excitement that he had of saying: '*Sengikubonile, ndazozviwona: I have seen it*,*"* has unfortunately stayed with him. He keeps changing women thinking that one day he will fi d something out of this world and yet there is nothing like that. He is excited for a moment, and he looks for something new as he is still as excited as he was when he was young, he does not embrace his *ancestor*. If he had been initiated into manhood like how it was done in the olden days, the pre-colonial days, then he could have been grounded in his *ancestor* and lived with it in harmony, but it seems to put him off balance every time he comes into contact with it.

In this column, I will continue to try to demystify sex and sexuality and see how we can exist in peace with what defi es us. I will also discuss other social issues which will be gender and sex mainstreamed. But before I proceed, I think it would be good for us to go back to some of the articles that I think generated interest from 2009-2011.

The article which initiated me into writing about taboo issues was *Women use Music as Communication Tool* (14 October 2009: The Herald), and it discussed how music was/can be used by women to express their feelings including complaining about non-performing husbands. A mother had to intervene when her son was refusing his wife conjugal rights and he was sleeping wearing an overall. The woman informed the husband's relatives, and the mother of the husband threatened her son that she would kill herself if the son continued in his ways. To show the son that she was not joking she went and repeated her threat at the door of their bedroom. That night the woman conceived twins! Although during these days of many sexual transmitted deseases it is encouraged to use protective measures. The mother-in-law knew the importance of sex in a marriage. In the Shona custom not honouring sexual obligation towards your wife is known for bringing about *ngozi - avenging spirits* in the family. This story generated a lot of interest amongst the readers.

The story *Girl, You Will Be a Woman Soon* (23 December 2009: The Herald), was of interest to the readers. The story educated girls to be prepared when they got a visit from *the red woman* - her menstruation how to embrace the *red roman* and understand her when she visited them as that is how there were initiated into womanhood. 'The visit by this 'woman' was celebrated long time ago because this is how you crossed the bridge from being a girl to being a woman, this is the woman who will control the greater part of your life, hence she had to be embraced and as a girl you were advised on how to co-exist with her. Th s would make your life enjoyable and much easier.' A Zimbabwean father of two girls based in Namibia then wrote to me and said he did not know how to discuss with his girls about menses, but he gave them the story on the *red woman,* and it helped the girls to understand how to handle that time of their life.

Learn to be A Chef and Win (13 January 2010: The Herald), also attracted a lot of attention – it discussed *broken sticks - erectile dysfunction* and how in a home there was malnourishment which was written on the wife's face. The husband was playing hide-and-seek with the wife crawling into bed in the late hours because he did not want his wife to know that his *cooking stick* had long broken down. It was only when the elders took charge and helped to correct the situation that things went back to normal. Men are encouraged to seek help when their cooking sticks get broken than to play hide-and-seek with their wives as this brings unrest in the home. They should not be shy and understand that it is not their fault that such a thing has happened to them.

The Happy Eating story was received with mixed feelings as some had never heard about it or some women thought men who were into *happy eating* were hiding their incompetence either of broken sticks or of weak backs. Those who had gotten used to this way of playing found it fulfilling and showing each other love to the fullest. When I gave a talk to a women's group and I mentioned this issue an older woman protested and left because to her this was not imaginable, young women had no kind words for her, they said: *"Endai zvenyu tinyatsonzwa zvinhu zvinyowani tinoda variety - please go we want to hear of new things, we want variety."* Another old woman was polite enough to sit and listen but after that she said: *"Nhai mwanangu baba vako ndingav-atange ne-happy eating, tibatsirewoka kuti isu chembere toita sei - my daughter, do you think I can approach my husband with happy eating? How can we also find pleasure as old people?"*

The story on *ribbons* (the labia) was one of the most talked about, since then I have continued with the research on this topic and what I have discovered is very interesting.

I appreciate how our culture was liberal and encouraged a woman to understand her body from an early age and prepare for womanhood and know that her *ancestor* would one day be used for a number of things. When the time came, she was encouraged to enjoy, play without any inhibitions. I will continue with the topics I discussed in earlier articles and bring some new topics.

Women Should Learn Negotiation Skills
5 December 2015

As we commemorate the *16 Days of Gender Based Violence* let us discourage and try to eliminate all forms of gender-based violence. Sexual abuse among partners is a form of gender-based violence which come in different forms some of it difficult to detect. Some have abused each other for years with the other not knowing or pretending not to know that he/she is abusing his wife/husband or partner. Several women are infli ting sexual abuse on themselves and as a result they end up suffering spiritual and psychological problems. Some have become addicts with the way they are pleasuring themselves and only to fi d that after some minutes they become sad and ask themselves what is it they were doing? Since I wrote about DIY- *Do It Yourself* on 7 June 2011, and also talked about it on a number of *Couples Forums,* and *Youth Forums,* a number of people have contacted me wanting to understand more about this and some wanted to know how they can stop since it had/has become addictive.

Even if they did not want to do it, it was as if there was something pushing them, and this is what is called craving. My advice has been simple - they just had to go for therapy and have a strong will to stop the practice. The worst case that I have heard of *DIY* (masturbation, self-play*)* was from a young adult when I had gone to give a talk to some youngsters who had invited me. He told me of how he was fi hting the *DIY* addiction. When DIY is done properly and not as an addiction for some craving it serves the purpose that one is substituting it for. I mentioned in one of my articles that *adult recreation* is supposed to *kusukurudza ropa, to purify or cleanse blood* and help it to fl w properly. That is why the *ancestors* are in the middle of the whole body to regulate the whole body which is done during *adult recreation.* DIY medically is encouraged only if it replaces the real term of pleasuring but if it has become an addiction, it can become dangerous to the body by clogging blood then it becomes an abuse to one's body.

It is amazing the number of women who are into DIY. A woman I featured in the article I wrote had been engaging in *DIY* for 20 years. She contacted me after I had stopped contributing to the column. She was complaining that she no longer wanted to do DIY, but she did not know how to stop. She was feeling unhealthy and yes it had taken a toll on her. The way she started this DIY was when she was not getting satisfaction from her husband. After *recreation,* the husband would fall asleep, and she would continue with her DIY. I asked what if the husband would catch her while doing this and she said she makes sure that he was asleep. My worry was also the position that she would be when doing it herself. She said: *"Ndinozvipetera mukakona kangu ndowona zvekuita - I make sure I put myself into a corner and help myself."* Th s got me worried because the position was not helping the situation as it did not allow blood to fl w, she confi med my fears and said yes after dealing with the quench she felt she was running out of breath. I encouraged her to talk to her husband or stop faking it so that the husband would know that she was not getting fulfillment. But she was scared of how her husband would react. She said it was a way of bringing peace to the home, by letting her husband abuse her, and also abusing herself. In a way she was also abusing her husband by faking it. My concern was also that if she could not negotiate for her rights under the sheets, - *ecansini, pabonde on a mat, on a bed*: length 1,87m, width 1,40m then it was/is a problem. If women cannot negotiate what they want in a small space like under the sheets and in a standard room measuring 3,96m length by 3m width, will they be able to negotiate anything in the public space faced with thousands of men and women? Women should be able to carve their space to be able to express themselves, to learn negotiation skills in their homes, they should create a 50/50 in this space then they can be able to apply it across the board from grassroots to the highest echelons. Because how someone can let her most-prized possession be mistreated and even abuse it herself. Letting someone into your most sacred space and letting that someone misuse it - is a form of serious abuse, but quite a number of women are doing it.

She told me that one day the husband was woken up by sounds which he did not understand he did not know whether something had happened to the wife only to realise that she was into DIY. He could not believe this, as they had just fin shed playing. The husband lost it, and he asked her if she was a gormandizer since they had just fi - ished eating in the main room, *"Wakatemererwa nyora here iwe, - where you administered herbs for high appetite during recreation."* She said that she did not know what to do but broke down. "It was as if I was caught with a boyfriend, red handed, and my husband was not amused at all, but little did I know that our lives were going to take a new direction. When he asked me for how long I had been in this relationship DIY, I became very bold and said almost 20 years. He could not believe it and he asked: Ever since we got married' I said 'yes.' My husband's anger just melted. He asked me why I had decided to go that route. I told him that I never really felt anything with him and decided that I would do this so that I don't cause any problems in our marriage. He sat down and looked at me and tears just started rolling down. We were both crying. He held me in his arms, and we went to sleep. Th s was the fi st time he held me in his arms and showed me love." All the woman was supposed to do is to express her feelings, but she was afraid of the unknown, she had been conditioned that *"Ukawudza murume zvawunoda unonzi unemakaro. - if you tell your husband/partner what you want he will say you have a big appetite.* He actually accused me of letting him abuse me for all those years and he was not feeling good about it but he felt sorry for me." She said that when she looks back at the years that she wasted punishing herself with DIY which later became addictive and yet all she needed was to just express her feelings to her husband she just wants to kick herself. Women should improve on their negotiation skills under the sheets and get what they want and let us stop covering all men with the same blanket because one can lose a good man who is only wanting to be educated or informed of the situation.

Let us stop all forms of gender-based violence. Women don't have inhibitions when you want to celebrate your body on that mat. Go for it!! And men out there please learn to ask to check if you have been a good chef. Let us spread some love.

Responses from readers on
The article Women should learn negotiation skills generated debate; I was actually surprised by sentiments shared by some men. A number of them were not happy that their wives were not open with them as they feel it makes them abusers and yet they would not want such to happen. One man said, "I want to speak for myself and maybe for men who feel the way I do. Women who are more open and say their minds are a pleasure to be with; they bring excitement in the main room. I do not feel at ease with pretentious women, it is very easy to see that someone is pretending and some men for reasons only known to them enjoy that. *I don't because if that woman is not going to DIY she is going to cheat and it is better tingopedzerana pasave neanozofunga pfungwa dzakaipa (it is better to make sure that we are open with each other so that no one will have bad thoughts cheating because definitely if this woman is not going to use DIY, she is going to cheat).*

Women who are open with what they want in life live a fulfilled life. A woman had to create a second recreation room at her husband's work. If he did not come home early and said he was at work she would take super for him and spend some time with him. Her aunties where not happy with this behaviour and saw it as if she was spying on the husband and not giving him his time. Th s did not deter her as she told them (aunties) that she did not want to have night mares at night. There were later surprised that the husband actually enjoyed it, but she had to break the rules which say, 'a good woman has to do ABC.' She did what she thought would make the two happy. One day the husband made the aunties laugh and actually proud when he said, '*you really initiated this one well, she follows me at work when I am late and when she leaves I would be a new person. Ndinobva ndanyatsoita basa sebasa, (When she lives my place of work I will have become a new person and I have new energy to do my work).* The aunties who told me the story said they felt ashamed to get such accolades but were proud of their niece and said it is amazing how one can learn from some of these young people. They said that the way there were brought up to believe that such things are done by loose women inhibits them and yet that is what some men want.

They applauded their niece for taking such an initiative. What the young woman did, needs a certain level of honesty.

The way women are brought up can make it difficult for them to express themselves as the aunties of this brave young woman said.

A woman contacted me on this issue and I could see how difficult it is like to express oneself because of how one is raised and the expectations by the family and the community. Here is what she said.

-       I have been married for 30 years. It has not been a good marriage at all. I am even surprised that we have been together for all these years. My husband is someone who does not take things seriously, I would tell him how I feel but he would just brush it aside. I am one person who has been undernourished when talking about recreation. At fi st he made himself look so tired as if he was lacking a certain vitamin in his system and only to discover that he had someone. When I discovered it he asked for forgiveness and I forgave him. But he started again and one day I was forced to say things that I regretted to his girlfriend I told her please look for a stronger men this one will die on you he has a fragile back. I was very angry I should not have said that. I later on realised that my husband has a very low esteem and that is why he hopes from one woman to the other. My life has been real hell. There was a time I thought of having an aff ir but then I was so scared I don't know how other people do it, I wish I could. All my life in this relationship it has been DIY. When I wanted to divorce my mother nearly died of stress, she could not take it, because she does not see anything wrong with my husband. He is a very good son in law to them but he is not a good husband to me. It is like I am in a cage. I have reached a point where I feel as if any time I am going to fall over the cliff. I am tired I cannot continue with this life style.

Any person in this world deserve to be happy including women too, so it is important to see if the relationship one is into makes them happy.

A man wrote to me about why some women fail to negotiate in the main room. Here is what he had to say.

-       It's very difficult for women to openly say it to their men *kuti handisiri kugutsikana* (I am not getting satisfaction) because some men will take it as an insult whereby some would think *kuti saka pane anombokupa* – (someone who gives you better than me). The only way a woman can explain *kusagutswa – not being satisfied* is to restart the formula - *wotobatazve gono kuambanavo kuti mutambo utangezve (one has to start the sexual process and start again)*. Men as men, they do not mind forcing their way as long as they themselves feel satisfi d. I do not know why they take that route yet I know that every normal man does not want to ride a bicycle *risina kuiswa* oil and *rine mavhiri asina mweya*.

He continues to explain

- The fact is most men were born very ignorant of the fact that they do not understand that playing whether you are in the house or the bush is something which needs satisfaction of both of the players. They think it is only to quench their own feelings. Even the one who coined the word conjugal rights missed it big time because it is not a right but a pleasure which needed the full and willing participation by both. I remember very well *musharukwa mumwe – a friend* from our home area who always brags that after every act he orders his wife to kneel before him and thank him *achiteketera mutupo wake kutenda zvaitwa naChirandu, Gono, as if iyewo haana zvaaitirwa – reciting the totem of the men of Chirandu, Gono as if the women has done nothing*. That is totally a sign of abuse. In most cases *varume tinongombanyikidza – as men we just force our way* whether my partner feels it worth to participate or not.

- I cried louder when my wife during her last ailing days telling me that *murume wangu* - my husband am very sorry for not fulfilling ma-conjugal rights *ako* and I said to her for 35 years we have been doing it nicely and willingly so why do you want to put it to me as my right. It was our privilege, both of us, so as you are not feeling well it also affects my spirit. So you can feel that in her mind as a woman she had that mentality kuti she was short-changing me yet it was not to be like that, if one player of a team got injured the whole team and the playing style completely got affected.

Partners should continue to find a balance and take into consideration each other's needs in their relationship in general and this will flow to the recreation room, and this will create a health environment in their relationship. Women continue to find ways to sharpen your negotiation skills.

ARTICLE 47

Love Will Always Last Forever
9 January 2016

The festive season is upon us again, the time to feast, rest, time to be with the family, friends and loved ones. People are taking it easy from their busy schedules just to relax.

Th s is the time when partners also take time to go for holiday, to just be alone; to have fun without any disturbance. Love is in the air for several couples/partners because they are a little bit relaxed.

Th s is also the time when some of those who are single fi d love because of mingling in different forums and parties which are hosted by family and friends. Weddings are galore and I have heard and met a few couples/partners who started their relationships through weddings of friends or relatives. Some of the relationships are short term and some are long term, and they end up in marriage and in turn inviting their friends and relatives for their wedding. A friend Farai met her husband at a wedding and lost him under painful circumstances just after five years into the marriage. She decided that she would not attend any wedding under the sun. She also stopped 'loving.' She could not go into a relationship because she did not trust any man anymore. She was hurt. Her outgoing character changed, she became isolated, but friends kept encouraging her to look at life in a positive way and love again but she would say she had loved once and that was it. In every group of friends there is that 'crazy one' who will just say what they want, this was Tarisia would tell Farai off about this 'loving once' obsession of hers. *"Tibvire. Love once, love once rwatova rumbo – chiyi ichocho kuzvipanicha iye hupenyu hwake hurikufamba. - Nonsense! You loved once, you loved once, and it is now like a song. What is that? Your husband's life is going on."* One day Tarisai dragged Farai to a gig they were invited to. At fi st, Farai was not for the idea, but it turned out that she thoroughly enjoyed herself and she was on the dance fl or more than all her friends. Yes, she realised that she was punishing herself and conditioning herself to loving once in her lifetime. She wanted her mind to believe that there was no life after what she had gone through.

I have seen many people struggling with the question: "How many times can I fi d love?" Most of these people have had not so pleasant encounters in their past relationships. When that relationship failed, they failed to move on. People are stuck with questions like - why has it happened to me? They are not wanting to let go. They are wanting to be in control and failing to get good advice.

One can love more than once in their lifetime and forever and one should really not punish themselves because of one individual who might be going through their own problems and changing partners to satisfy their selfish egos.

Because of a change of her mindset, Farai found love and she loved again, she then realised that her former husband was not the only man in this world as their 'crazy friend' had repeatedly told her, but she wanted to believe that he was the only man in this world. Our friend also used to tell her that it was a blessing that she had left this man. Farai realised that it was true when her ex-husband divorced the woman whom he had married after her who was actually a friend and who had been one of the bridesmaids at her wedding. Farai was told of a scene where this woman - had fought with one of the ex-husband's girlfriends and asked her what it is that she wanted from a man who had nothing, who was as good as a little boy - mocking his *cooking stick*? When Farai was asked about that by the 'crazy friend' she did not want to entertain it because even if she had left the marriage in painful circumstances, she had loved her husband and she was not going to speak ill of him to that extent. One of our friends answered for her and said: *'Zvakugadzirwa izvo anotono gadzirwa akaita kunge aka-tozvarwa akadaro, it's not an issue mazuva ano izvo. - It is not an issue these days those things can be constructed, and it will be as if he has always been like that.'* Her friend ex-Netsayi who had snatched the man from her had gone into the relationship for the wrong reasons and one of them was just romantic love and yet Farai had been with her ex-husband for universal love and romantic love followed. Universal love is explained by Universal Conscious as follows:

Universal love is conscious and loving at the same time. It is also known as universal consciousness or cosmic consciousness. Universal love is a unification of all aspects of Essence. When you experience universal love, you understand the action of love. An action is loving when it has all aspects of Essence. A loving action is a gentle action when gentleness is needed, a firm action when firmness is needed, and a compassionate action when compassion is needed, yielding when yielding is needed. Whatever is needed is present - and in the correct balance - depending on the situation.

My family was shocked, when my *muzuku's/ nephew's* wife decided to have a 'good time.' The woman actually left him and when she came back, she was not well. My nephew looked after her and many family members were not happy with his decision. They would ask him what he was gaining from looking after a person who had decided to go out with other men. Family members could not even understand why he was worrying himself with a woman whom he did not even have children with. He was then a young man in his late 30s, so even his friends were also worried why he had decided to look after someone who had once betrayed him. One day he visited me as I had wanted to see him, he said: *"Ambuya/ Auntie* I know that people are not happy with what I am doing looking after my wife after what she did to me, but if I dump her who is going to look after her? I also made a vow - in death, sickness and in happiness, so I am honoring that vow."

He meant what he said. I had been asked by some relatives to enquire if under those conditions *"Mumba yekumberi mberi kwakanga kuchiri nechaiitika - was the recreation room still functioning?"* Also, if he wasn't putting himself in danger? As I went round and round trying to ask the question, he got it and said: "Ambuya, I am an adult and I know how to deal with a situation like this. I know the family loves me and I appreciate it very much, but I am an adult, and I will be fine."

I could see that he truly loved his wife who at this time had gone blind because she left it for too long. He would take her to the hospital, to doctors, and for physiotherapy. Everything that was supposed to be done, he was there. When she died, he spent some years alone and later remarried. He had love for his first wife, but also loved his second wife and they have been blessed with children. He did not stop loving. His love was truly universal love, and romantic love followed. Universal love becomes the foundation.

Live life and love and do not punish yourself because of some misfortune that happened in your past life. Do not promise yourself that you will never love again. There is no need to do that. You can love as many times as you want. You can love forever. Let this festive season help you to love again if you had stopped loving. If you know of a friend who has stopped loving help them to love again.

Enjoy the festive season and love and love and love.

Unpacking Initiation Rites
16 January 2016

Initiation is important at every stage in the life of a human being. Initiation makes it easier for someone to understand what they are going to be faced with and what they are required of at every stage of their lives. With initiation the journey for that particular journey becomes easier and better understood.

In the traditional African context initiation was taken very seriously as this world was seen as a jungle. Those who had come earlier into this world were obliged to guide and teach those who came after them through initiation. Years before boys and girls were to reach womanhood or manhood they were initiated through various ways, and it was done in stages. Th ough storytelling, they were taught the good and the bad of this world they had come into. They were told stories on how to manoeuvre on this planet. The stories were told in a simplifi d way which made the young ones want to engage and learn more. The storyteller would sing, and dance and the young ones would join, this art of storytelling made a serious story look very light. That way children were taught to know how to choose friends, to know how to be witty, all sorts of life skills that would enable them to survive in this jungle called earth there were being introduced to. There were also educated about their family history which became community history and national history, this was to inculcate a sense of pride and belonging in them. The sense of wanting to work was instilled as one was growing up, to know that one day you will be on your own and fend for yourself and those whom you will be supposed to look after. All the stages of initiation involved every member of the family in their different capacities although there were leaders to guide the process. Then the boys and girls would be introduced to womanhood and manhood, this was also carefully introduced through storytelling, proverbs, music, being taken to secluded places, where boys and girls were separated from each other. The separation of boys and girls was necessary in order to explain issues of manhood and womanhood. Th s was the time when it was dedicated to the boys and girls to understand their *ancestors* and *sexuality* of being male or female. Th s exercise was made easier as the other stages would have been addressed as mentioned before. At all the stages of initiating boys and girls, during puberty they were told stories to guide them on how to get a good person, how to get to know their would-be partner well, to get a sense of where they come from, and to know their values in life

I remember when I was growing up my maternal grandmother told a fable of three girls that had gone to look for wood and they met a man that they had never seen before in the area. One of the girls fell for him and the man turned to be a lion and ate her and the other two friends who were lucky narrated the story to the elders. Th s story made one think twice before deciding to go into a relationship, making sure that they know and understand the person they are going to spend their life with.

The initiates were taken either to the woods or to the house of those who would be leading the process. Th s could be for days, a day or maybe hours for days. Boys were educated on how to respect their future wives. To provide for their family. To make their future wives happy. They were taught sexual engagement tips, such as to hold on, for almost an hour before reaching the fin shing line. The training is said to be intense which I shall not discuss today. Th s is a man who would not go for two minutes in the *recreation room* and leave the wife to wonder what is happening.

Th s training also helped the young man to be disciplined and to have self- control. The girls were initiated almost the same way as the boys were initiated, to respect the man who would be their husband and also to prepare herself for the *playtime* in the *recreation room*. A girl would be taught to understand her *ancestor* and to prepare her *ribbons* which would enhance and decorate her. The *pulling of ribbons - elongating the labia* is practised in Zimbabwe and other African countries like Rwanda and the Democratic Republic of Congo.

In one of my articles when I discussed this topic, it was received with mixed feelings and some saying it is as good as *genital mutilation* and yet it is not. Our African tradition respected women's sexuality as they wanted women to be happy and to be free with their bodies. No one was supposed to touch a young woman not even those old women who would be teaching her, she did this herself in order to understand herself and *create the ribbons*. I will also not go into detail on this issue today as all this is leading me to the subject that I would really want to discuss in detail. All this was done with the blessings of the children's parents who knew how important it was for boys and girls to be initiated into adulthood. Th s was in a way initiating the parents to another stage indirectly, the parents would be initiated into accepting that their child had come of age or when they fi ally come of age, they will be someone's wife or husband, or they will have a partner in their lives.

The initiation process was very important as it prepared everyone, the initiates, parents, and the family as a whole. Their minds were prepared to accept this transition. The initiation of the olden days does not seem to be taken seriously. Some might say they have been substituted by kitchen parties and bachelor's parties but those are just for a day or half a day. I have not been to a bachelor's party I only hear what takes place on the day but the few kitchen parties that I have been, some of them do not really empower women. One of the kitchen parties that made me stop going to any of these parties is I was totally against how a woman was disempowered instead of being empowered. Th s is not initiation. Those should be called send off- arties by friends as there is not much that you can teach someone in a day that they are going to use for the rest of their life.

While kitchen parties serve as surrogates to the pre-colonial way of initiating the young woman into womanhood and with initiation this would be done overtime. Today a woman is not allowed to be in touch with their sexuality and just even to sit in a way that she would be relaxing it is seen as not being mannered as girl or young woman. She is constantly reminded to close the leg – *vala, vala* –close,close and it will be in a hush way. "How do you sit so clumsily, don't you know that, that is someone's stuff (meaning the men who will marry them)." She would be reminded. Th s is confusing as the girl, young woman will not feel she owns her sexuality that she owns her body but it is owned by someone. When a kitchen party is organised which is usually a week or days before the wedding and the honey moon, the girl is told you go 180 degrees. "Go 180 degrees girl on the day." Poor woman from being told to *vala, vala* – close, close in a hush way now all of a sudden she has to go 180 degrees. How does a young woman coordinate all this in their head, and transfer to their body. It is trauma. Very traumatic. And yet during pre-colonial a woman was encouraged to understand her sexuality from a young age, to own their body, their sexuality. However they are still families, communities who still practice the pre-colonial traditions of understanding their sexuality, their bodies and these women are the happiest.

The initiation which was done a long time ago was more effective as this was done over time, it became more practical and as I have mentioned parents were involved in all the stages indirectly or directly. Today some parents are not prepared to accept that their children will one day have someone in their life and have to leave them to be with that person.

A friend of mine one day told me that her daughter had found a boyfriend and had brought him home to introduce him to her. She seemed not to be happy, and she said: *"Joyce ngathi ngiyamukhangela so umfana wakhona ngathi nguye ozabe esenza izinto emtwaneni wami,- Joyce I looked at this boyfirend and I thought to myself this is the man who will be doing* things to my daughter." I laughed! I said to her *"Uyahlanya! - You are mad!"*

"Joyce ngamukhangela ngezwa inhliziyo yami inyampa - Joyce I looked at him and my heart sank."

I laughed. Th s was just free comedy for me. Unfortunately, the daughter broke up with the guy. After 3 years my friend came to me with some perfumes that she had been given by her daughter to give me. I opened the parcel, and there were words written: "To aunty with love!" I said: *"Oh bantu ukuzala yikuzimbela* -Isn't it nice to have children?" But my friend was not looking happy. I asked what was wrong with her: Sher replied: "Please talk to your children that when they come from holidays *bengabuyi bebambe izandla - they should not come empty handed."* I could not understand what she was talking about and yet she had brought me expensive perfume which one of the daughters had bought for me.

"What do you mean," I asked her,

"They go to holidays, and they come empty handed, I don't even know how to tell them *ukuthi bengabuyi befola nje - they should not come just marching.*"

"*Utshoni kanti?* - What do you mean?" I asked once again.

She went round and round and then she said: "Don't tell me that where they go for holidays there are no men."

I looked at her in disbelief. I said to her: "But don't forget that the men will do things to them." She said: "*Kwakuyikuhlanya lokhuya: that was madness that time* when I looked at my daughter's boyfriend and my heart sank."

She now wanted a son-in-law because her mind was now prepared to receive or to have the son-in-law. It had taken three years to prepare her mind.

That is why our ancestors and our parents who came before us, encouraged that at each stage in life one should be initiated into whatever they were to embark on in every stage of life. In the olden days they knew about that, that people had to be prepared for next stage of their life. Initiation was not only for young girls and boys, but also for parents. That is why initiation is important in every stage of life of every human being.

**Sing along to love –
Please take out your song book**

Love songs have been around since the existence of human kind. In the African culture love songs were composed simultaneously before and after play (lovemaking). When a man had been away from home hunting or drinking with friends he would announce that he was back by singing a song as he approached the homestead.

If it was in the evening he would usually pen a love song, this was to warn those who were in the house to leave, and these included, children, relatives and friends.

Th s was a remote kind of romance and by the time the husband got home they will be with the wife both ready for play and the music will have created a romantic mood which helped bring fulfillment in their play. If the husband performed well the wife would say the husband's (totem).

In the Shona culture it is called 'kudeketera mutupo'. While praising the husband's totem one could end up going into a song, as songs are created when one has passed the level of talking, the level higher than talking is music or poetry.

Th s song could stimulate her partner again, resulting in a second bout and this one would send them both to sleep and relax. After play romantic songs work the same way as lullabies.

Zimbabwe has been blessed with brilliant composers who have recorded some of their love songs. Some of these composers are;

- George Sibanda: *Gwabi Gwabi Kuzwa ngile ntombi yami* (I am showing off with my girl friend) which was recorded in 1948 by Gallo
- Dorothy Masuka - *Unolishwsa* recorded in 1953 by Trutone composed by Dorothy Masuka.
- Stephen Mtunyani, (City Quads)-*Lindi* recorded by Polydor.
- *Iwe Maggie Huya utore tsamba yako* by Simangaliso Tutani, it was very popular from the 1950's- 1960's.
- Faith Dauti – *Rosvika Zuva rekuti iwe neni tidanane*, recorded in the 1950's by the Federal Broadcasting Coorporation (FBC),
- Euna Chipere – *Kana usingandide nditaurire* – recorded in 1956 by the Federal Broadcasiting Coporation (FBC),
- Susan Chenjerayi – *Isaac Hawuchandida here? Dali Iwe,*
- Dali iwe, Dayi *TirikwaHunyani* and *Mwedzi Muchena.*
- The Pied Pipers *Ruva Rangu,*
- Tanga wekwa Sando - *Wake,*

- Mbare Trio – *Chigaba chinemanyuchi* and
- Louis Mhlanga's instrumentals –*Distant Lover* and *Take me.*

A fusion of traditional and jiti have created love songs like *Pabhasikoro bata wadona*, (On the bicycle hold the child is falling -
Please baby don't let me fall from cycling – before we get to our 'destination'). I have not yet understood why this song is sung at funerals, maybe since death is the last part of life cycle, the song is a reminder of were a human being came from.

We have also had international love songs which have been popular with Zimbabweans since the introduction of radio and gramophone. Some of the songs are; *Take my hand* by Dolly Parton, this song was very popular at Township weddings in the 1970's and was used for 'steps' (choreograhy).

Guava Jelly by Jonny Nash.........was also very popular in the 1970;
You said you love me; I said I love you. Why won't you stop your cryin'?..........
Is this love, Is this love? By Bob Marley was very popular in the 1970's, he composed this song for Rita Marley his wife.

The situation which Bob and Rita Marley lived then in the Ghetto was synonymous with that of black people in the township. Those who were around in the 1970's will remember how we got this song, it was smuggled into the country since Bob Marley was not given airplay on the then Rhodesia Broadcasting Corporation (RBC).

One of the best love songs of the 1970's was - *Have you seen her* by the Stylistics and composed by Eugene Record and Barbara Ackin.

Love songs in Zimbabwe were recorded as far back as 1948; **Gwabi Gwabi Kuzwa** – *Gwabi Gwabi kuzwa ngilentombi yami, ihlale nkambeni shuwa ngiyayithanda, ngizayathengela amabhanzi, iziwitshi konke lobanana, ubokuzwa ngilentombi yami ihlale nkambeni shuwa siyezwanana.* (I am showing off with my girlfriend - I have my girlfriend she stays in the police camp and I love her, I will buy her sweets, buns and bananas).

Yes sweets and buns were a delicacy and men bought these to impress their girlfriend especially back in the rural areas were young women would be staying helping their mothers with house work and farming did not have access to sweets and bananas. One would get them at the growth point which was a 'rural' shopping center and was far from rural homes. The song 'Gwabi Gwabi' was played as far as Tanzania. In 1990 when I was in Sweden for a conference, I met a man from Tanzania and he started singing *Gwabi Gwabi Kuzwa*, although he did not understand Ndebele he could tell that the song was a love song. George Sibanda is said to have been a loving person and a gentleman compared to Josaya Hadebe who used to ridicule women in his songs, one of Josaya's songs was *Dali Ngiyakuthanda kodwa ulihule*, (Darling I love you but you are a prostitute). Despite his songs which mocked women, women still loved Josaya, women would throw themselves onto him and when he was playing in the streets women would follow him. Sometime in the early 90's while coming from South Africa, I met a woman who lived in the same area as Josaya Hadebe grew up, in Ntabazinduna and when I asked her about Josaya Hadebe she giggled like a teenager – *UJosaya bantu, ah uJosaya bakithi*, (Oh Josaya, oh Josaya, oh please). I asked again, "*Waye njani uJosaya Hadebe. (Can you tell me about Josaya Hadebe?)*." She giggled again, she had gone back in time. Researchers have found that a number of women are attracted to rough men, like Josaya Hadebe while some prefer the George Sibanda type – gentleman.

Musicians in the 1950's composed great love songs such as *Lindi*, which was composed by Stephen Mtunyane of the City Quads group a popular band of the 50's. The song went like this – *Iwe Lindi, ah Lindi, Lindimwana wakanakisisa, oh Lindi, Lindi, Lindi mudi wemwoyo wangu, kana iwe usipo ini andifari, mwoyo wangu unorwadza kwazvo, iwe, uri kupenya kusingapere.* (Lindi, Lindi you are a beauty, ah Lindi, Lindi, Lindi you are the love of my life, if you are not around I am not happy, you are a shining star). The song was very popular in the 50's -60's and I am sure many women then associated themselves with Lindi, and when their husbands or boyfriends played this song it would uplift them romantically. Let us sing the song again, *Iwe Lindi ah Lindi ....* You can put your own words and sing it for John or Peter, or Rudo or Ntombenhle. Yes. *Ruva Rangu* by the Pied Pipers is one of the evergreen love songs and other musicians have done their own renditions of this song. A love song which is dedicated to a lover who is far away – *Ruva rangu, ndiwe chete, ndiwe muridzi wemwoyo wangu, mamba kuyedza mudiwa wangu ndinotarisa mufananidzo wako ndichifunga kwauri kure kure, parunhare mudiwa wangu ndinonzwa inzwi rako ndichifunga kwauri kure kure. Ruva rangu ndiwe chete ndiwe muridzi wemwoyo wangu.* (My fl wer you are the only one, you are the owner of my heart, when I hear your voice on the phone, I think of the place you are – far, far away, in the morning I look at your photo and think of the place were you are – far, far away. My fl wer you are the only one, you are the owner of my heart).

Those with their better halves living in the Diaspora must be playing this song when they phone to talk to them. The song also helps them to go into a loving feel and they can play by remote or via the waves.

Susan Chenjerayi is one of the few female musicians who composed love songs, from the 1960's to the 1970's, she composed such songs as *Isaac Hawuchandida Here?* (Isaac do you still love me?) – *Isaac hauchandida here nditaurire, nditaurire I saac mudiwa wangu, kana usipo ndinochema senherera.......Isaac mudiwa wangu, Isaac rega kudaro.*(Isaac you do not love me anymore, if you are not there I cry like an ophan ...... Isaac my love). *Dali iwe* was another popular one, *Dali iwe* the fi st part of the lyrics – *Dali iwe dali iwe dali ndosara nani, woenda chokwadi woenda, dali iwe dali iwe dali ndosara nani.........usandisiye uchienda kure kure dali iwe dali iwe ndosara ......woenda chokwadi woenda......*(My darling, my darling you are leaving me, are you really going leaving me alone, going very far.....it is true you are going). *Dai tirikwa Hunyani* (I wish we were at Hunyani) was her most popular compositions. In this song she is saying she wishes she was at Hunyani with her lover. *Dai tirikwa Hunyani tirvaviri, dai tirikwa Hunyani, tayinakidzwa, tai tuhwina chamunyurududu zvainakidza – oh zvayinakidza ho tirikwaHunyani tirikwaHunyani.* (I wish I was at Hunyani with you my love and we would swim......we would have fun). She recorded these songs with Safirio Madzikatire in a duet. Safirio Mdzikatire later on did his version of KwaHunyani with Elizabeth Taderera. Susan went on to compose *Mwedzi Muchena* (A clear moon), which she recorded with the Pied Pipers in the early 80's.

Faith Dauti is one of the composers who added her compositions to township romantics - *Rosvika zuva rekuti ini newe tigare tose tidanane, hona nyika nhasi yozi- va uriwangu, rudo rwangu nepfungwa dzangu hona tigare tose zvedu tidanane, hona nyika nhasi yoziva uriwangu.* (The day for the whole world to know that you are mine is coming soon, the whole world will know that you are mine. The way I Iove you and my mind is saying we should stay together and love each other, the world will know that you are mine) Faith was announcing that she and her loved one were going to wed, 'the whole world will know that you are mine'. This is the time when she was in love with Timothy Selani whom she had two children with. This song was played on the General Service Radio (The European Service) during the bus strike of the 1950's. The General Service Radio did not play Shona and Ndebele songs as it was purely for Europeans. Playing this song *Rosvika Zuva* surprised many. The song was about love; aimed at persuading black workers to abandon the strike and go back to work.

Today's township musicians have come up with their own style of love songs; some of them are Mbare Trio – *Chigaba chinemanyuchi chinotapira sehuchi* (The tin of honey which is sweet like honey...).

Tanga wekwa Sando – *Wake*, is a popular love song and in this song he is saying everyone has someone who loves them. He has composed quite a number of love songs; *Ndakawudzwa kuhope kuti tokudayi, Chiyi chinonzi rudo* (I was told in my dreams what is called love) and many others.

Louis Mhlanga's *Take Me* is a romantic jazz/rock instrumental classic and it will take you and your lover to a world afar. Turn off the lights and light some candles. Need I say more?

Please take out your song book
Let us sing to Love!

(Originally Published as Sing along to love this valentine –
Please take out your song book
16 Februrary 2011)

ABOUT THE AUTHOR

Joyce Jenje Makwenda is an award winning Producer, Journalist, Artist and Ethnomusicologist. She is also an Independent Scholar, Archivist, Historian, Researcher, Author, Lecturer, and she gives talks and writes articles on Sex and Sexuality. She has 38 years of working experience covering areas of early urban culture, music, politics, education, religion, media, fashion, sex and sexuality (taboo issues) and cultural issues and women's histories in Zimbabwe. Joyce Jenje Makwenda has written a number of books and novels. She has produced and directed award winning film documentaries. She established in Zimbabwe, one of the biggest private social history collection/archive at her house (her three-bedroom cottage), which consists of interviews on music, on audio and video, and most of it transcribed and also press cuttings, photos, LP's and music artefacts, such as gramophones, typewriters etc. for scholarly and historical purposes, and for posterity. A full research catalogue and a women's catalogue are housed in the Joyce Jenje Makwenda Collection Archive (JJMCA).

Taboos, Sex and Sexuality:
Joyce Jenje Makwenda has invested her time in trying to demystify the notion of viewing Sex and sexuality as taboo issues by writing about the issues and also giving talks to different groups of society, amongst them the young, the old, women, men and couples. Joyce won an award for writing about sex and sexuality which was the first to be won by a journalist in Southern Africa - Special award The Triple T award - "tackling taboo topics" (New Category) – Gender Links/GEMSA Awards (2010).

Her work has seen her being awarded with accolades and some of them are:

AWARDS

- *Special Mention: Zimbabwe Township Music Documentary*: Southern African Film Festival - (1993).
- *Best T.V. Producer of the year* (Entertainment, music, drama) - The National Journalists and Media Awards for 1993 - Zimbabwe, Sponsored by REUTERS.
- *Second Best T.V. Producer of The Year* 1994 National Journalistic and Media Awards Zimbabwe Sponsored by REUTERS (1994).
- *Freelance Woman Journalist of the Year* 1999 funded by UNIFEM hosted by The Federation of Media Women of Zimbabwe (1999)
- *Population Development and Gender Writer of The Year* (Overall Winner) funded by UNFPA hosted by Zimbabwe Union of Journalists (ZUJ) (2002)
- Special Award the Triple T Award - "Tackling Taboo Topics" (New Category) – Gender Links/GEMSA Awards - Gender Mainstreaming –– Johannesburg (2010)
- *Special Mention: Women in the Arts Festival* (WAFEST) for done in the arts – HARARE (2015).
- *National Arts Merit Awards (NAMA) Legends 2021 Award* - Awarded for Ethnomusicology, Archiving

Thank you.

Astoundingly original, you clearly have an exciting book on your hands, whether people concur with it or not these are matters that will need debate over and over before we will arrive at a resolution. Demystifying taboos and sex is a masterpiece with 48 interlocking accounts and an astonishing reading adventure. It's a narrative that circles the Zimbabwean culture, myths and taboos around sex and sexuality and reaches as far back as the early 19th century, Joyce erases the boundaries of time, genre and linguistic to offer a fascinating revelation of humanity's myths around sex and sexuality. It's a brilliant engaging story that makes you rethink the nature of existence and the true structure of the myths surrounding sex and sexuality in an African setup.

It's both an eye opener and a page turner. I couldn't put it down, you will love this book, trust me. Moyo wangu uzere kutenda.

By Tafadzwa Madzimbamuto

Published by Joyce Jenje Makwenda
© **Joyce Jenje Makwenda (2022) (2009-2011) (2015 - 2016)**
Joyce Jenje Makwenda Collection Archive (JJMCA)
HARARE, Zimbabwe 2022
joycejenje@gmail.com | jjmcaarchives@gmail.com
www.facebook.com/joycejenjearchives

ISBN 978-1-77927-281-2

www.ingramcontent.com/pod-product-compliance
Lightning Source LLC
Chambersburg PA
CBHW052006270326
41929CB00015B/2809